8953369 BOWYER. C. (ED)   The fall of an
 Ø/UDE | SHOVEN   eagle

-0 NOV. 1983   HERTFORDSHIRE LIBRARY SERVICE

Please return this book on or before the date shown below or ask for
it to be renewed

Please renew/return this item by the last date shown.

So that your telephone call is charged at local rate,
please call the numbers as set out below:

	From Area codes 01923 or 0208:	From the rest of Herts:
Renewals:	01923 471373	01438 737373
Enquiries:	01923 471333	01438 737333
Minicom:	01923 471599	01438 737599

L32b

THE FALL OF AN EAGLE

When I was a young boy my father used to tell me about a legendary German pilot who could pick up a handkerchief with the wing of his aircraft. I dedicate this book to the memory of my father.

Armand van Ishoven

The Fall of
an Eagle

The Life of Fighter Ace Ernst Udet

Armand van Ishoven

English version
by
CHAZ BOWYER

WILLIAM KIMBER · LONDON

First published in Britain in 1979 by
WILLIAM KIMBER & CO. LIMITED
Godolphin House, 22a Queen Anne's Gate,
London, SWIH 9AE

© Copyright 1977 by·Armand van Ishoven
ISBN 0 7183 0067 X

Photoset by Input Typesetting Ltd
and printed in Great Britain by
Redwood Burn Limited, Trowbridge & Esher

Contents

		Page
	Preface to the English edition	9
	Author's Preface	11
	State Funeral	13
I	Sunday's Child	16
II	Apprenticeship at the Front	22
III	Leader of Jasta 37	39
IV	Pour le Mérite	54
V	Just a pilot	73
VI	Udet-Aviation begins	81
VII	Displays	100
VIII	Stunts and Safaris	118
IX	Hell-divers and Glaciers	132
X	In uniform again	149
XI	Paperwork and records	159
XII	Bluff, counter-bluff and war	172
XIII	The 'Happy Time' – 1940	186
XIV	Destiny	197
	Appendix: Udet's Combat Record, WW1	209
	Bibliography and Sources	212
	Index	216

List of Illustrations

facing page

Udet as a child. *Author's archive*   32
Benzin-Hussar. Udet as an army motor-cyclist, 1914.
                                              Author's archive   32
Udet with Weingärtner at Habsheim. *Author's archive*   32
Udet with his Observer, Leutnant Justinus.   32
Udet in the cockpit of his Fokker D. 111 biplane.   33
Udet with Oberleutnant Grashoff at Douai, 1917.   33
Udet with his Albatros D. 111 at Habsheim, 1917.
                                                      H. Thiele   33
Udet wearing his 'Blue Max', 1918. *A. Buck*   64
Jastaführer. Udet as commander of Jagdstaffel 37, 1918.   64
Informal moment in the Richthofen Jagdgeschwader.
                                              Author's archive   64

between pages

Testing new fighter designs, Berlin, 1918.
                                  Imperial War Museum   64–65
Udet with his Fokker D. V11, Summer 1918.
                                  Imperial War Museum
German fighter aces at the Adlon Hotel, Berlin 1918.
                                  Imperial War Museum
Udet with Bruno Lörzer at Coblenz, 1919.
                                          U.S. Signal Corps
Franz Hailer; Udet; Lothar Freiherr von Richthofen.
Fighter aces at Adlershof, Berlin 1918.

facing page

Udet in the cockpit of the Fokker V. 35, 1919.
                                  P. M. Bowers Collection   65
Udet with his first wife, Lola Zink in 1919. *K. Schnittke*   65
Udet demonstrates the Udet U-2 near Buenos Aires, 1923.
                              Archivo General de la Nacion   65
About to set out in Rumpler C.I,D-138, 1919.
                                          Archiv Schliephake   96

The Udet U-2 converted for ski-undercarriage.
                              Author's archive   96
Udet with Walter Angermund, Innsbrück 1926.
                              Author's archive   96
Udet and Milch in the cockpit of the U-11. Lufthansa   96

'Scintilla' – Udet's Flamingo D-822 on the Eibsee.
                              Erich Baier   97
Marga von Etzdorff, Udet and Gerhard Fieseler.   97
Udet with René Fonck, Paris 1928. Musée de l'Air   97
A group of pilots at the Cleveland Air Races, 1931.
                         World Wide Photos   128
Udet meets Eddie Rickenbacker. USAF   128
Walter B. Wanamaker is given a souvenir.
                              Author's archive   128

Udet's De Havilland DH60 Moth in Greenland, 1934.
                              K. Schnittke   129
Udet in Greenland, 1932. K. Schnittke   129
Udet and his mechanic, Baier. E. Baier   129
Udet with young model-makers A. P. Photos   129
Udet with Erich Baier. E. Baier   160
Udet with Hans Grade. K. Schnittke   160
Udet, Bruno Lörzer and Arthur Laumann, 1933.   160

                              between pages
Udet with Thea Rasche and Gerhard Fieseler.
                         Lufthansa-Archiv 160–61
Udet's Curtiss F-11C Hawk in German markings.
                              O. Rumler
Udet with his Rhönbussard, 1936. K. Schnittke
Udet's skill at altitude and zero height. Author's archive
Udet and Leni Riefenstahl, 1936.
A Focke Wulf 'Stieglitz'.
                              facing page
Udet demonstrating a wing-tip 'skid'. A. P. Photos   161
A meeting of Nazi leaders, June 1938. Author's archive   161
Udet with Flugkapitän Hanna Reitsch, 1937.
                              Author's archive   161
Siebel Fh 104s. Author's archive   161
Milch and Udet at Dubendorf, July 1937. Photopress   192
Udet with Friedrich Christiansen, 1940. Bona Schaller   192
Göring receiving Udet at Karinhall, 1940. A. P. Photos   192

Udet and the Luftwaffe Chief of Staff, 1940.
　　　　　　　　　　Archiv Schliephake　　192
Udet and aces at the Channel Front, 1940.
　　　　　　　　　　Archiv Schliephake　　193
Udet with Inge Bleyle.　*K. Schnittke*　　　　193
A selection of Udet's mementoes.　*K. Schnittke*　　193
Udet's funeral procession.　*A. P. Photos*　　　193

Editor's Preface to the English Edition

Ernst Udet emerged from the slaughter of the 1914–18 war as Germany's highest-scoring, living fighter pilot; second only to the legendary Rittmeister Manfred von Richthofen – the 'Red Baron' – as the Fatherland's most revered and honoured war pilot. A man of uncomplicated tastes and passions, Udet's greatest love throughout his life was for flying, be it in the cockpit of a high- or low-powered aeroplane or the fragile plywood cocoon of a glider's cabin. Politically naive, with no trace of deviousness in his soul, Udet was gradually led to involvement in the grandiose ambitions of cruel and self-seeking 'comrades' as the Nazi hierarchy rebuilt a shattered Germany and aimed for eventual world domination. Given high rank, status, and awesome responsibilities in the emergent Luftwaffe, Udet became trapped in a world of intrigues, jealousies, naked ambitions and crude status-seeking by those who surrounded him. Too honest by nature to believe that 'friends' could act so grossly, Udet grew disillusioned, dismayed and finally desperate; taking his own life rather than bear such calumny.

Retaining a traditional code of personal honour in his dealings with his fellow-men when most such men merely used his naivety to further their own ambitions, Udet was a man born out of his true era. He truly belonged to the age of chivalry, decency, pure patriotism and simple honesty; an age which sank without trace in post-1918 Germany with the arrival of Hitler and his henchmen. In that black nightmare of cruelty and devilish 'ideals', Udet was an anachronism; a true patriot with no greater ambition than to be able to continue flying until sheer age or swift death snatched the control column from his gentle grip. Indeed, in many respects Udet was the 'Peter Pan' of those golden years of aviation; retaining always that first rapture of youth when it first explores the heavens in a man-made craft.

This new biography traces the story of Udet from that early fascination with flying, through the heady years of using the sky as his playground, into the gathering stormclouds of the Nazi rise to

9

unfettered power, and on to the ultimate, lonely moment of his life. It illustrates vividly the gradual destruction of an honest man, perhaps too honest, by the power and greed of evil men. No one, after reading this account, can question Udet's courage or honesty of purpose; tragically such qualities are patently not always sufficient in themselves to ensure a future for mankind free of dictatorial cruelties.

Whatever his nationality by accident of birth, any truly courageous man deserves his niche in history, and Udet, with all his 'failings', was just such a man. I regard it as a personal privilege to be invited to help in the preparation of this account of Ernst Udet's life and death, and commend it to all students of aviation history. I would also like to record my gratitude to D. Allan, A. Pulverness and the students of the Bell School of Languages for their expert assistance in certain aspects of translation from the original German edition.

CHAZ BOWYER
Norwich, 1979

Author's Preface

The glider has almost reached cloud-base. I set course again towards the south. Slowly the French town of Verdun comes into sight. I think of Udet in 1913. To the right the Argonne hills are barely discernible. Even further off the starboard wing-tip I can visualise the town of Rheims – near Rheims Udet shot down two opponents. I am flying a glider above the bitterly contested front lines of the First World War, where the 'Knights of the Air' fought gallantly – Guynemer, Ball, von Richthofen, Udet and so many others. I am exploring their skies, their battlefields, in a plywood cockleshell of a glider, a glider on a free-ranging flight, gloriously unnecessary, yet so deeply rewarding, in our computerised world. In this rather unconventional way I am 'researching' for my Udet biography, a thousand metres above the earth; alone, where my only engine is the atmosphere's energy.

Other forms of the research may have been less fun, but not less interesting and rewarding. For example:

Hans Waldhausen, Udet's World War One friend, who took me on a forced march through Cologne on a bitterly cold day. It lasted for two hours, but the 80-years old WW1 fighter pilot called it 'just a stroll'.

Erich Baier, Udet's mechanic for many years, who shared his joys and sorrows in Africa, Greenland and the USA, and who spoke to me about 'Herr Udet' for three days at a stretch.

Kurt Schnittke, who flew with Udet on his very last flights.

Frau Bleyle, who sat silently weeping when I questioned her about Udet, who spent his last years with her.

Walter Angermund, who knew Udet best of all people on earth, and with whom I sat for many hours in a '*Lokal*' near Munich's *Hauptbahnhof* before he departed for a vacation in the Black Forest . . . his last vacation ever.

The engineer of the Reichsluftfahrtministerium, trying to find for me that photograph showing him with Udet.

Werner Junck, telling me 'Yes, I knew Udet very well', then

supplying me – the last historian he ever spoke to – with a score of Udet anecdotes.

There were hundreds of interviews with people who knew Udet well – or thought they knew him well. And also many thousands of letters, seeking the sometimes elusive trail of Ernst Udet – 'Ernie', 'Kneckes', 'Udlinger' – a man who so passionately liked to fly.

To all these people, my grateful thanks, which also go to Mr Chaz Bowyer, who has edited my book for British readers, from the original German edition, thereby saving me from the agony of reducing the original manuscript by half to a book of manageable proportions.

Armand van Ishoven

The State Funeral

While testing a new weapon on Monday, 17th November 1941, Generaloberst Ernst Udet had such a serious accident that he died of his injuries during transportation. For the officer who so tragically left us while performing his duty, the Führer has ordered a State funeral. In recognition of his excellent achievements as a fighter pilot who was victorious in 62 air combats, and to honour his great part in the building of the Luftwaffe, the Führer has given his name to Jagdgeschwader 3.

German News Service, 17 November 1941.

Berlin, 21st November 1941:

In the hall of the Reichs Air Ministry lie hundreds of wreaths. On the staircase and the gallery also lie countless farewell gifts. In the Honour Room, bedecked with the national flag, and the dagger and helmet of the deceased, rests the casket holding the remains of the Generalluftzeugmeister. From four high, black-velveted pylons, adorned with the Iron Cross, the sacrificial flames burn.

Officers of the Luftwaffe form the guard of honour. Next to them stand the adjutants of the Generalluftzeugmeister, carrying the medal cushions. Eight proud flags of the victorious Luftwaffe form the background.

The mother of Generaloberst Udet, his next of kin, and Frau Göring take their places in front of the bier.

At exactly 11 o'clock the commands of the mourning parade ring in the silent room.

The Reichsmarschall and officer in command of the Luftwaffe enters through the Honour Porch of the Wilhelmstrasse and is received by the Chief of the Central Office, General der Flieger von Witzendorf. Then the Führer enters, accompanied by Generalfeldmarschall Milch. The Reichsmarschall announces him and Generalmajor von Heyking orders the presentation (of arms). Together with the Reichsmarschall and Generalfeldmarschall Milch, Hitler inspects the mourning parade. When the Führer enters the Honour Hall those present raise their arm in salute.

13

The Führer and the Reichsmarschall salute the dead hero who lived and died for Germany. Then the Führer turns to the mourners. At length, and with sincere sympathy, he shakes hands with the mother of the Generaloberst, he greets the next-of-kin and Frau Göring. Meanwhile the State band starts the mourning march from *Götterdämmerung*. When the heroic notes have ebbed away the Reichsmarschall steps in front of the catafalque with raised Marschall's baton and speaks:

'Now the moment has come to say goodbye. Unbelievable is the thought that you, my dear Udet, are no longer amongst us. We cannot yet understand it because your ways were so forceful, so alive, so happy, and you were such a good comrade for us that any one of us felt deeply united with you. I think back twenty-six years. We were both young then, and fighter pilots, and you were the most joyful of us all. And yet how strong was your will and how clear your eyes when the enemy had to be destroyed. And how often we said that we longed for the day that our air force would rise, new and stronger. And that day did come. . . .

'Where could one find a Chief of the Technical Office who tried every new machine himself? Now you too have died for us, still wanting to do everything yourself. . . .

'We do not yet know how we will fill the void you have left. The Almighty has called you, and now you can join the others who have fallen before you. . . .

'Now the last thing I can say – my best comrade, Farewell!'

Now the Führer rises, Luftwaffe officers bring in front of the casket the wreath which the Führer lays down. Next to it, also carried by Luftwaffe officers, the Reichsmarschall's wreath is laid. The Führer and the Reichsmarschall salute the deceased for the last time. At the same moment the strains of the *Gute Kameraden* sound, flags are lowered, the arms of all those present are raised. The Führer turns to the next of kin. He shakes hands with the mother of Generaloberst Udet. In that moment Frau Udet receives from the hand of the Führer the compassion of the whole German people. After the Reichsmarschall has also expressed his sympathy, the Führer leaves the mourning service. Lofty sounds of the variations upon the *Deutschlandlied* of Josef Haydn fill the room while the wreaths are carried away by non-commissioned officers of the Luftwaffe. Last are those of the Führer and the Reichsmarschall.

Those carrying the medal cushions and flags leave the room. Then the casket is taken from the catalfalque and Ernst Udet finally leaves the place where he worked. When the bier leaves the portal of the Reichs Air Ministry, the mourning parade presents arms. To the sombre sounds of the band of the 'General Göring' regiment the casket is placed upon the gun carriage. The Reichsmarschall steps behind the carriage and all male participants form an almost endless procession. Commands sound, the mourning parade slowly marches past the carriage with the casket. A Luftwaffe heavy battery follows. Then comes the carriage and the long procession of mourners. Passing thousand upon thousand, across the Wilhelmstrasse, the Wilhelmplatz, the Luisenstrasse, the mourning procession makes its way. Ernst Udet finds his last resting place in the old soldiers' churchyard of Berlin, the Invalidenfriedhof.

German Press, Saturday, 22nd November 1941.

CHAPTER ONE

Sunday's Child

His forebears had fled from France more than two hundred years before, as Protestants, unwanted, persecuted under the reign of Louis XIV, *Le Roi Soleil* – the Sun King. Now he stood before the civil servant who slowly, meticulously filled in the text on Page 188 of the large official town register. He declared that three days before, on 26 April 1896, his wife Paula, née Krüger, had given birth to his first son. He was to be called Ernst. After waiting patiently until the clerk had finished writing he took his pen and elegantly wrote his name under the section 'Read, found correct and signed'; Adolf Udet. Ernst Udet's introduction to the world was now officially recorded in the stately town hall of Frankfurt-am-Main.

Paula Udet was very fond of her son. He had been born on a Sunday, so he was a *Sonntagskind* – a 'Sunday's Child'. And legend had it that children born on a Sunday were very lucky or as the old rhyme has it, 'bonny and blithe and good and gay.' Soon after the birth of his son, engineer Adolf Udet moved with his wife and child to Munich, capital of Bavaria, where on a clear day one could see the mighty chain of the Alps. Munich, with its familiar domes and towers, the oldest of which was the *Löwenturm* – the Lion's Tower. Its origins went back to the times of Henry the Lion when Munich was merely a small settlement. They took up residence in one of the uniform three-storeyed apartment houses on the Kazmairstrasse which ends at the vast expanse of grass of the Theresienwiese, where the traditional October Festival is held annually.

As he grew up little Ernst proved to be very fond of animals and soon Flott, his Airedale terrier, became his inseparable companion, accompanying him every day to and from the school in the Stielerstrasse where Ernst had been enrolled in 1902. Flott was always an active participant in the many fights between the boys of the Stielerschule and those of the Schwanthaler Höhe on the other side of the Theresienwiese. On one occasion Udet and his friends captured the Schwanthaler gang's flag, and Flott, proudly carrying it, gaily galloped clear across the huge Theresienwiese – that vast expanse which saw many a battle between the rival youngsters, fought under the gaze of the huge bronze statue of Bavaria shrouded in her ancient Greek costume. A real *Lausbub*, young Ernst 'compensated' for his bad school reports by becoming an expert marksman with his *Zwille* (catapult), but when not playing with his many friends he mainly occupied himself at home, where he was particularly fond of drawing, illustrating some story or other. Another early hobby was making paper aeroplanes, later to be replaced by proper models.

From his earliest years Ernst adored his mother and his love for her lasted until his death. She hailed from Pomerania and many of her relatives were civil servants with the Prussian State. Not without a little pride she used to point out that her father looked somewhat like Bismarck. In 1906 Ernie – as he was now usually called – transferred to Class 1C of the Theresien grammar school amidst the stately homes of the Kaiser Ludwig Platz. In the summer of the following year, the end of his first year at the grammar school, his teacher's confidential report read:

Physically normal, mentally well endowed. He understands quickly, but forgets just as rapidly. Interested in everything but only superficially, chatters easily and pleasantly about many things; in short, displays the characteristic qualities of a sanguine temperament. Profundity and meticulousness do not appeal to him. His oral exams were good, his conduct faultless.

During the next few years, part-inspired by the contemporary activities of the ageing Count Zeppelin, a flood of enthusiasm for airships and flying machines swept through Germany; and these became the favourite subject of discussion. Many a youthful imagination was fired at the thought of flying – including Ernie's. And in 1909, when preparations for the first International Aviation Exhibition in Germany to be held in Frankfurt from July to October were made public, Ernie and some friends, aged between ten and thirteen, founded the 'Aero-Club München, 1909'. Each Wednesday afternoon, their day off school, they met in their 'club-house' – the attic of the Udet home – where they built models. On Saturday afternoons they trekked to the banks of the river Isar or its tributary, the Stadtbach, where they tried to achieve flight with their models. Every noteworthy flight earned the model's builder a certificate carefully written by the 'secretary', Otto Bergen, duly signed by the 'President', Willy Götz.

Occasionally the small group organised an outing beyond Munich's main railway station, across the Nymphenburger Canal to the Oberwiesenfeld, an army training ground where the barracks of the army balloonists – the *Luftschiffer* – were situated. Until then only an occasional cable balloon could be seen being raised by the *Luftschiffer* but gradually the early Bavarian pilots began making flights at the Oberwiesenfeld, to the great dismay of the local cavalry whose horses were frightened by the crackling engines. Then, when Gustav Otto, son of Dr Nicolaus Otto, creator of the four-stroke petrol engine, started building aircraft in his wooden sheds at Milbertshofen; outings to the 'Gustav Otto Flugmaschinenwerke' became events never to be missed. For hours at a stretch the boys stood outside the wooden fence, gazing at the mechanics struggling with the temperamental Anzani engines which powered the Otto biplanes and Blériot monoplanes. The boys were soon able to identify some of those Bavarian pioneers, like Dr Lindpaintner and Baierlein; and when there was no flying to see there was plenty of space in which to indulge in every form of play – or skulduggery. . . .

Apart from his drawing, Ernie had also become very interested in photography, but it was aviation which captured his imagination the most. Soon building models was not enough; he wanted to fly. He would build himself a glider! He was not alone in his wish to construct a man-carrying glider at that time. Other young men had similar ambitions. Such as a certain Willy Messerschmitt and his friend Friedrich Harth, who were experimenting at Bamberg; or Erwin Rommel who at Easter 1908 built his first glider at his hometown of Aalen with the help of his friend Hans Keitel. This duo even performed what was probably the first-ever flight in a two-seat glider. Messerschmitt was later to form his own aircraft company; Keitel became a leading engineer with the Dornier company; while Rommel earned international fame during both world wars before – like Udet – taking his own life.

Ernie's desire to build his own glider reached its fruition during the annual holiday of 1910 when, with his mother, he went to the little village of Aschau, some 70 kilometres from Munich and nestling against the Alps. There, with his friend Berndthäusl he assembled his machine – a very primitive hang-glider built from bamboo rods and linen-covered. Built on just four trestles, borrowed from some villagers, the finished glider weighed just 35 kilogrammes and had a wing surface of 17 square metres. Its wings had no camber; they were simply flat surfaces, and the only method of flight 'control' was by shifting the pilot's body. As soon as his brainchild was complete Ernie took the contraption to the Lehmbichl, a hill near the hamlet of Fellerer, where the local inhabitants gathered excitedly to witness their first 'flying meeting'. By running down the hill Ernie managed a few short 'hops' – then disaster struck during one 'landing' and the 'flying machine' was wrecked. There and then young Udet decided to stick to model-building for the immediate future. At least his excuse for not flying again immediately satisfied the host of spectators, not to mention illustrating Udet's fertile imagination, when he explained to the villagers, quite seriously; 'Here in your part of the country the earth's magnetism is too strong to permit flying'. . . .

Further efforts with his models included attempts to fly across the green waters of the river Isar*, and his perseverance was finally rewarded when a model earned him the 'Aero-Club München's' official brevet' by flying a prescribed distance – all of three metres! – on 9 January 1911. Udet's obsession with aviation did little to help his scholastic career, however, where he was regarded as 'somewhat slow' with a 'superficial but volatile mind'. Ernie's interests now widened to include the various activities in his father's workshop. Here he became an apprentice and was taught welding by another young workman, Carl Moser, who occasionally accompanied Udet and the other members of the 'Aero-Club' on their outings to Oberwiesenfeld. The flying field suffered its first fatality on 27 July 1912 when Joseph Fischer and Georg Kugler crashed to their death from 1,000 feet in an Otto biplane; yet even this did not deter the would-be aviators in their ultimate ambitions.

To broaden his horizon and to improve his schoolboy French, Udet spent one of his summer holidays at Luc-sur-Mer in Calvados, not far from Arromanches. He also spent a period at Verdun, being accepted as an au pair with the Corre family at the Collège Charles Buvignier. Here he passed two hours each day conversing with the French students in their native tongue, and at the same time attempting to teach elements of German to them. One of his favourite outings here was to Belleville-sur-Meuse, some two kilometres north of Verdun, where a military airship, the 'Adjutant Reau' (Type Astra No 11) was based. In 1913, back again in Munich, Udet finally succeeded in passing his First Year Examination and

---

* The same river on which, some 35 years later, the ashes of Hermann Göring were to be scattered.

was rewarded by his father with a truly 'regal' present; a motor bicycle. This examination gave successful candidates the right to serve one year in the army as a volunteer.

In the autumn of the same year Herr Leo Roth was engaged for eight weeks as a 'test pilot' with the Gustav Otto Werke, and he quickly noticed the well-dressed eager youngster hanging around the airfield. When Udet finally plucked up the courage to speak to Roth it was to plead for an actual flight. Roth was quite willing but insisted first that Udet obtain his father's written permission. The following day an ecstatic Udet ran to the airfield, waving the all-important piece of paper, and Roth prepared his Etrich Taube for a 'spin'. At last he opened the engine to full power with a mighty roar. With every wire vibrating wildly, the Taube waddled forward over the uneven ground, increasing speed, until its wire-wheels left the earth.

For the first time in his life Ernst Udet was really flying. The boy could hardly believe it; he was actually sitting here, in the open, leather-rimmed cockpit, looking down on the vast expanse of Munich. He could see it all; the baroque gardens of Schloss Nymphenburg, resplendent in their autumnal colours and shades; the twin bulb-topped towers of the cathedral, the railway tracks running like a black arrow to the city's heart, the bright green Theresienwiese where he used to play, the Isar with its many bridges and tiny islands, the hazy horizon. . . . Udet's ambitions had at last been realised.

Udet's childhood had been a happy one in which he had been loved and protected by modern-thinking parents, and in 1908 they presented Ernie with a young sister, Irene. He made many friends among the boys who regularly visited Oberwiesenfeld; among them a young law student Walter Angermund. This friendship was to last all of Udet's life. The early months of 1914 promised to be equally happy for Ernie while waiting to be called for his national service in the army. Witty, affable, popular with all, Udet loved riding his motor bicycle, and now began taking an interest in going dancing with the young Fräuleins. One in particular captured his interest. Vivacious 'Lo' – Eleonore Zink, the daughter of a wealthy merchant from Nuremburg. Life was sweet. Then, on 28 June, a dangerous spark was struck. A Serbian 'nationalist', Gavrilo Princip, shot to death the heir to the Austrian throne and his wife when they visited Sarajevo. . . .

Fire had been set to the accumulated political tensions in the

Balkans; international reactions across Europe were unforeseeable, like a proverbial gunpowder barrel. With nationalism running rampant most European countries mobilised in quick succession. Before the close of the year no less than 19 declarations of war were to be formally handed over by politely bowing diplomats. At 6 pm on 3 August Germany declared war on France, to be followed next day by England who declared war on the 'Prussians'. Europe was at war. . . . All over the Continent soldiers, many accompanied by their wives for the last time, cheered on by huge crowds, flowers in their rifle muzzles, marched gaily to railway stations. Within a few weeks victory would be theirs. . . .

CHAPTER TWO

Apprenticeship at the Front

'I felt stirring in me an urge to serve the Fatherland,' Udet later recalled. The urge soon vanished. 'No unit's going to take you on, you're not even five feet three inches tall,' he was told on 2 August at the recruiting centre for volunteers. Nevertheless, two weeks later he was on his way to the front. The Allgemeine Deutsche Automobil Klub had made a public appeal for volunteer motorcyclists who were prepared to go into action with their own machines. Udet immediately applied and was accepted. As far as the club was concerned, it was not his age or his size that mattered, but the fact that he owned a motorcycle.

On the evening of 18 August Udet's train left Munich's central station. He had had to provide his own 'uniform' – a heavy leather suit – but was given a cap by the military. Two days later he arrived in Strasbourg, along with four friends, and was posted to the 26 Württembergischen Reserve division as a messenger-rider. The same day all five men were motorcycling the 50 kilometres back to Schirmeck, where the division's operational headquarters were situated. On the road west they met for the first time the grim reality of war; supply columns moving forward, French prisoners and German wounded going in the opposite direction, and as they neared their destination they could hear the distant thunder of the guns.

In Schirmeck they were given pistols, though the 'war volunteer drivers', as they were officially called, were not taken particularly seriously; being mockingly nicknamed 'Gentleman drivers' or 'Motorised Hussars'. As the division slowly fought its way in a south-westerly direction, through Saal to St Dié, Udet was principally assigned to the delivery of mail between Strasbourg and the divisional headquarters. Yet the work of the volunteer drivers was not without danger. One of Udet's friends was killed while riding to the front-lines, another suffered a nervous breakdown and shot himself. Nor did Udet escape danger. Coming into St Dié one evening with the mail, he suddenly realised that the German forces had evacuated the town and that the first wave of French troops might appear at any moment. He withdrew under artillery fire, being delayed by the dead and wounded, bodies of horses, rubble and wreckage. It was a crazy journey. Too late he saw a shell hole which stretched across the road, and before he could brake or swerve there was a crash and everything went black.

A stabbing pain in his shoulder brought him back to consciousness. Painfully, he dragged the motorcycle out of the crater, but there was no question of going any further on it. The cycle, which his father had given him the year before when he passed his one-year examination, was seriously damaged. His first impulse was to leave it there, but then he thought how often his father had criticised him for being frivolous and 'cowardly'. So, gritting his teeth, and despite the pain and pouring rain which had set in, he began to push his motorcycle along the dark road. After a few kilometres a horse and cart picked him up, and next morning they arrived in Strasbourg, where Udet went to the military hospital and his cycle was put into the workshop for repair.

By 15 September Udet and his bike were again ready for action, but meantime the 26th Division had moved to Belgium. Udet followed it, partly by train and partly on his recently repaired cycle, though when he arrived in Namur no one could tell him the actual location of his division. It was then suggested that he should serve in the vehicle depot in Namur instead. Udet agreed and was officially transferred with effect from 25 September, and took lodging in the Hôtel de Dinant. Life in Namur was not without its charms, and his knowledge of French stood him in good stead, especially in his relationships with the young girls of the town. More important to Udet was the opportunity to meet officers of the active flying section stationed at Chauny, thirty kilometres west of Laon, who stayed in the Hôtel de Dinant while passing through Namur. Udet told the flying officers he met in Namur of his own early attempts to fly, and of his wish to become a pilot. So they took him with them on a flight, and then advised him to get himself transferred to Chauny to serve with them as an observer. Udet succeeded in setting up such a transfer, but on the day that he was due to get his orders for Chauny the army dispensed with all volunteer motor-cyclists, and on 20 October 1914 Udet was sent back for the disposal of the recruiting authorities. On his return to Munich Udet's personal records included entries indicating his participation in the battle of the Central Vosges from 20–22 August, and in the battle of Nancy-Epinal from 23 August to 10 September.

As soon as he got home Udet did everything in his power to get back to the fighting again. The war office had made a public appeal for volunteers to be trained as pilots and aircraft mechanics, and – though Udet was unaware of the huge response – some 15,000 applications were received. Full of hope, Udet applied to Major Friedrich Stempel, head of the Schleissheim Flieger Ersatz Abteilung (lit. Flying Reserve Section) and creator of the Bayerischen Luftstreitkräfte (air force). Stempel explained to him: 'A very large number of active officers have already applied for this training and they have preference. It'll be months before your turn comes. It would be a different matter if you were a trained pilot, then you would be taken on immediately.'

There was only one possible course of action – he had to learn to fly. Why not with his family's friend Gustav Otto, who owned an aircraft factory in Oberwiesenfeld and possessed one of the first flying licences, No 34? At first Udet's father was against it but his mother proved to be a successful advocate and Udet was taken on at the flying school for a sum of 2,000 marks – and some new bathroom equipment from the workshop of his father's firm. The training was unconventional. Otto's factory built LVG machines for the Luft–Verkehrs–Gesellschaft in Berlin. Every completed aircraft had to undergo an acceptance test-flight, and Udet was taken up as a passenger to familiarise himself. In February 1915 he was allowed to begin by taxying across the field in an aircraft at 800 revs. This soon became boring, so he put his foot right down, took off, and landed again after a short hop. Nobody objected, and next day he was allowed to make his first solo flight. From then on he trained regularly, using a sandbag as ballast at first, and later an occasional passenger.

When he came to his flying tests his mechanic warned him, 'Don't fly any longer than eight minutes; your engine won't hold out any longer.' The man was too optimistic – the engine actually cut out after five. . . . It was not until Udet made a second attempt in a better machine that he passed his flying tests, and was given a civilian pilot's licence at the end of April 1915. He immediately went to the Schleissheim Flieger Ersatz Abteilung, now commanded by Oberst Edmund Weber. The latter took one look at Udet's licence, then asked, 'How old are you?'. 'Nineteen, *Herr Oberst*.' 'You'll have to wait,' said Weber, 'You're too young.' It was enough to make Udet despair – first he'd been too small, now he was too young – at least, for the Bavarian air service. Perhaps people elsewhere would think differently? Udet went to the nearest post office and sent telegrams to the Flieger Ersatz Abteilungen at Warnemünde, Döberitz and Darmstadt, describing himself as an aerobatics and high-altitude pilot, and asking to enrol.

All three flying units answered in the affirmative; his call-up papers from Darmstadt coming first, including a ticket to travel there. Before leaving Udet said to his mother, 'You must promise me not to be too anxious, or I won't be able to do my job without worrying. If you'll promise me that it'll help me.' He then left and on 15 June joined Flieger Ersatz Abteilung 9 at the Darmstadt-Griesheim airfield as a pilot. His dream had become a reality.

Nevertheless the long saga of disappointments along the path to becoming a military pilot was by no means at an end. After getting his uniform at Darmstadt he was posted not to a flying school but a ground company. All his suggestions that as a trained pilot he belonged in the flying school fell on deaf ears. The company sergeant didn't think much of 'gentleman pilots' with their 150 marks' supplementary allowance. When even friendly bribes in the form of beer for the sergeant's evening meal didn't work, Udet then avoided the official 'channels' and applied direct to Kapitän Bruno Steffen, head of the flying school. His interview with Steffen proved successful; the same day Udet was transferred to the flying school and immediately went up in an LVG two-seat trainer. His instructor was 22-year-old Hermann Weller who came from Württemberg; despite his youth, he had the nickname 'Papa'. The training programme was hard but Udet was an excellent pilot.

As a soldier, however, Udet was not so excellent. He had little understanding of the niceties of military 'etiquette', and even less respect for authority – characteristics which he was to have throughout his life, and which led to his first punishment. Each free afternoon the pilots would go into Darmstadt by train. On one of these trips Udet was stopped by Kapitän Steffen and sent back to camp – for wearing 'fancy trousers', which Udet had had made to his personal taste when he was a volunteer motor-cyclist. The penalty was two hours' drill. This took place under the supervision of a junior officer who had a kind heart – as they marched to the exercise yard Udet's pack was full of stones, but when they arrived at the yard it was empty. Udet's 'fanciful' ideas were not restricted to trousers; during his active pilot's test he flew off course and had to make a forced landing in a woodland clearing, running into a tree stump and bursting one of the undercarriage wheel tyres. Having ascertained the correct direction for Darmstadt from somè farmers, Udet then removed the other tyre, took off on the rims of his wheels and flew back to his airfield.

Following this test – after which he began to instruct trainees in piloting – Udet had to undergo the advanced pilot's test, for which it was necessary to accomplish an overland flight of 250 kilometres. He flew with Leutnant Gerlich, following the Rhine as far as Bonn-Hangelar, where both men went into the town to eat. When they returned to their aircraft they found that one tyre wheel had burst – probably from the heat of the sun – but Udet merely took off on the metal rims, flew to Cologne, where they stayed overnight, then flew back to Darmstadt non-stop.

Once he had been awarded his advanced pilot's licence, Udet pressed for service at the Front. By then, as a result of the experience of the first months of the war, a number of changes had been made in the organisation of the army flying service. Major Hermann von der Lieth-Thomsen had been appointed chief of the Feld Flugwesen at High Command on 11 March 1915, and one of his first actions had been to supplement existing flying sections with 14 artillery flying sections whose job was to co-ordinate the fire of the artillery batteries. One of these, Flieger-Abteilung (A) 206, had been posted to Heiligenkreuz, south of Colmar, and one of the unit's observer-officers, Bruno Justinus, came to Darmstadt looking for good pilots. Born in Bayreuth on 22 August 1892, Justinus had joined the army in October 1911 and had been promoted to *Leutnant* on 25 October 1913. At Darmstadt his choice was Udet who, when asked, 'Do you want to be my pilot?', answered rather brazenly, 'Certainly Leutnant Franz'.*

Justinus took Udet's cheeky reply in good part, and they celebrated their flying 'union' with a party which went on until the early hours, and on their return to the airfield Justinus wrapped his officer's cape around his future pilot so that he could get past the sentry unchallenged. On 4 September 1915 Udet commenced his service as a pilot with Flieger-Abteilung (A) 206, which at that date was attached to the Gaede army division. The airfield lay west of the Vosges, some five kilometres south-east of Colmar on the road

---

* In the German Air Service then all observers were nicknamed 'Franz', and all pilots 'Emil'. 'Franz' reputedly derived from the Kaiser's army manoeuvres of 1912, when Wilhelm II asked a Leutnant Bluthgen the name of his observer, and received the reply, 'I don't know, your Majesty, they change every day, so I always call him Franz'.

to Mülhausen. At the same time, in Flieger-Abteilung (A) 204, based between Metz and Verdun, was a young Wilhelmshaven-born observer *Leutnant* named Erhard Milch. Flieger-Abteilung 206 had just four pilots at its disposal, and these flew Aviatik B II's, a biplane with a 120hp Daimler engine, produced in the Freiburg factory of the Leipzig Automobil Aviatik company. Udet's aircraft was doped white; Walter Behrend, always known as 'Fatty', was appointed his mechanic and was to remain Udet's mechanic until the end of the war.

The airfield was in reality nothing more than a large meadow, but it served adequately, given the low take-off and landing speeds of contemporary aircraft. Round the edge of the field were big grey tents, each holding two aircraft, manufactured by the Kassel firm of Baumann & Lederer. Udet had a civilian billet and was regarded by his landlady as a good tenant – he did not deduct the cost of insect powder from the rent. In general the people of Alsace were well disposed towards the German soldiers, and Udet had to thank them for a new nickname 'Kneckes' ('Titch') which all his friends now called him.*

The first operational sortie with Justinus passed off without incident; above the dark forests of the Vosges they saw a few flak bursts, and in the distance a Farman biplane testing range for the French batteries. Of necessity – in the main artillery aircraft were unarmed – they left each other unmolested. The second sortie, on 14 September, proved more eventful; it was almost Udet's last. All flying sections in the sector had been concentrated for a major attack on Belfort, sixty kilometres south-west of Colmar and only twenty kilometres from the Swiss border. The route was over Thann in Alsace, the only German town to have been taken by the French up to that date. Udet and Justinus joined the attack with their aircraft, the white Aviatik loaded with six 10 kg carbonite bombs, while Justinus took along a Mauser automatic rifle for defence. The sky was grey and to the west lay thick cloud cover through which they broke at 3,500 metres.

About fifteen minutes after they had flown over the front, they realised that it was impossible to attack Belfort due to the dense cloud, and decided to turn back. Udet put the Aviatik into a left

* Udet, in his memoirs, called himself 'Knägges', but his close friend Hans Waldhausen, who knew Alsace well, confirmed that it should be written 'Kneckes'. (Author).

turn and at that moment there came a metallic, lashing sound, 'as if a piano string had snapped', as Udet described it. Immediately the aircraft began a left spin, dropping 2,000 metres before Udet, with great difficulty, managed to restore it to a normal flying attitude by turning both aileron and rudder hard over to the left. The bracing joint for the main wire connecting the upper right wing with the fuselage had broken. The loose wire whipped in the slipstream, the wings arched dangerously up and down each time Udet attempted to increase speed, and the aircraft looked certain to crash. Looking around they realised they were almost over Montbéliard, south of Belfort – over enemy territory. Justinus pointed in the direction of Delle, near the Swiss border. They were managing to maintain height at 1,800 metres and had a chance of reaching neutral Switzerland in a glide.

Keeping very carefully on course, Udet then saw Justinus haul himself out of the front cockpit and crawl out along the lower right wing to preserve their equilibrium. With neither parachute or safety belt, he then sat down, his legs hanging in the slipstream. His courage was to little avail. Udet had to strain every nerve and muscle manipulating the controls to keep the Aviatik in a flying attitude, but gradually his strength was weakening. As Justinus realised this he crawled back, smashed the wood partition between the two cockpits and with bloodied hands grabbed the control column.

Through their joint efforts they succeeded in keeping the Aviatik airborne and reached the Swiss border five kilometres south of Delle at an altitude of just 600 metres, but German territory was still 16 kilometres away. Gliding on, getting lower and lower, Udet did everything possible to hold his height. Several villages slipped by below – Courtemaiche, Coeve, Vendlicourt – still two kilometres to the border – then at last the border, and Udet touched down in a potato field. Exhausted but happy to be down, both men jumped out of the Aviatik. They had come down near a village, from where they were able to telephone to Heiligenkreuz. The village blacksmith made them a new bracing joint and they were invited by officers from a nearby airfield to join them for lunch.

After the meal, with their machine repaired, they were about to take off when a staff officer appeared. First congratulating them both on their feat, he then launched into a fierce tirade for having disposed of the broken bracing joint. While they had been fighting for their lives on the flight from Belfort another Aviatik from their section had crashed on the peak of the Hartmannsweiler. Its crew, Leutnant Winter and Vizefeldwebel Preiss, were both killed; the cause of the crash was a broken bracing joint. Udet and Justinus ferreted the defective joint out of the smithy's manure heap, handed it to the staff officer, and this was eventually sent for testing; it resulted in all Aviatik Type B aircraft being withdrawn.

A quieter period of operations followed. Udet and Justinus flew along the main ridge of the Vosges, testing and co-ordinating German artillery fire, and occasionally pushed forward as far as St Dié where Udet had his first experience of war as a 'motor hussar' a year earlier. On 21 September Udet was promoted to the permanent rank of Private 1st Class and was decorated with the Iron Cross, 2nd Class for '. . . saving an aircraft', while Justinus received the Iron Cross, 1st Class. Udet's joy in receiving his award was shared with his friend Walter Angermund, at that period company commander of the 6th Bavarian Infantry Regiment, who visited him at Heiligenkreuz. Three days after his promotion and decoration Udet took off with Justinus to fly a routine artillery 'spotting' sortie. The aircraft was carrying two machine guns – recently other German 'spotters' had been attacked by armed French aircraft – and in Justinus's cockpit was a wireless set. As if these additional loads weren't enough, Justinus had also decided to load some bombs aboard for use against likely French field targets. The grossly overloaded machine took off slowly and eventually struggled to a height of 100 metres.

Making a very wide steady turn, Udet flew back towards the airfield; he wanted to gain height over the Rhine plain before setting out for the Vosges. Over the airfield he began another turn – and fell away in a spin; the overburdened aircraft's stalling speed was higher than normal with its increased load. Udet tried frantically to pull the machine out of the spin, but there was insufficient height in hand. At the last moment Justinus crawled out of his cockpit and hoisted himself up onto the bracing struts to avoid being crushed by the engine – then the aeroplane crashed. When Udet regained consciousness he felt a severe pain in his knee. His next thought was for Justinus, but the observer had been thrown clear on impact and had only suffered bruises. By a stroke of sheer luck the bombs aboard had not detonated.

Both men were admitted to a reserve military hospital in Colmar where they were separated due to their respective ranks. Two weeks later Udet was discharged from hospital. To his personal surprise no one from his unit had visited him in the hospital, nor had he received any mail. At Heiligenkreuz, on his return to duty, he was greeted with icy glares. His mechanic Behrend explained, 'Immediately after the crash the divisional commander telephoned the aviation staff officer at Mülhausen, demanding strict punishment for Udet's "insane turning manoeuvres." ' Indeed, an order posting Udet back to Gaede airfield in Neubreisach was awaiting him, his replacement had already been designated and Udet barely had time to say goodbye to Justinus before leaving the airfield. The two men never saw each other again; Justinus was killed in action as a fighter pilot in 1918.

Udet arrived at Neubreisach in the evening of 2 October, and next morning the commander of the airfield held a parade of the student pilots. In front of the assembly he then read out Udet's punishment. 'Seven days' light field punishment for endangering the life of his observer, and destroying a valuable machine by making extremely careless turns. It is only in consideration of his previously good performance in the field that he is not drawing a heavier sentence.'

Udet was then taken by an NCO to Diesheim military prison, an old fortress two kilometres north of Neubreisach, where his pocket-knife and trouser-braces were taken away from him, and he was put into a bug-infested cell. For the next week Udet remained in his solitary cell, and twice daily, during 'rounds' by the prison authorities, he was required to stand to attention and repeat aloud the entire official sentence passed upon him: 'Seven days' light field punishment. . . .' To add to his misery Udet was woken each morning by the sounds of the aircraft engines starting up and then flying from the nearby airfield.

The seven days passed slowly and then Udet returned to Neubreisach. He arrived to find the airfield in some confusion; orders had just been received for a bombing raid on Belfort with 'all available machines'. Udet heard a shout behind him, 'Hey, you, Private! Are you a pilot?' 'Yes, sir!' 'Let's go then, we mustn't miss the show!' It was a new observer officer, Leutnant Hartmann, a stranger to Udet.

The two men ran to the hangars where an old LVG was being fuelled and loaded with hand bombs. A few minutes later Udet took off. The machine was a 'tired old crow', probably a training school reject, and could barely reach 1,800 metres altitude, but Udet was overjoyed – he was flying again; something he had only dared to hope after his recent punishment. As he approached Belfort he saw two French Farmans and a Morane monoplane coming towards him. The ancient LVG was unarmed, and its soggy performance made it useless for any air combat, so Udet avoided these opponents and headed southwards.

Over Montreux, twelve kilometres east of Belfort, they saw some barracks and military depots, so Hartmann indicated that he'd bomb these. He opened a small trap-door in the floor of his cockpit, and as Udet manoeuvred onto target, proceeded to hand-drop the bombs singly through the trap. The first bombs landed on target – then Hartmann turned to Udet with a horrified expression on his face; one of the bombs had lodged in the LVG's undercarriage! Udet tried gentle turns to loosen the bomb, while the observer stuck his leg through the trap-door attempting to reach the bomb. His effort was to no avail; his leg became stuck and remained so until Udet eventually landed. Udet tightened his turns – with the ironic thought that he was doing precisely what he'd just been imprisoned for – until a final, near-perpendicular banking turn finally dislodged the bomb which fell in an open field and exploded. Landing back at Neubreisach, Udet promptly reported to the airfield commander – the same commander who had originally paraded him and sentenced him a week before. He studied Udet for several minutes, then spoke curtly: 'You are transferred to Kampfeinsitzer Kommando Habsheim.* Your aircraft will arrive in two days' time, then you can leave. Dismiss!'

Udet left the captain's office in utter confusion – him, a fighter pilot? This was the dream of all pilots – how could it have happened to him? An orderly room clerk soon enlightened him. That morning the *Stabsoffizier der Flieger* at Mülhausen had telephoned to ask if Udet had yet returned from his arrest. After a search of the airfield, a mechanic reported that Udet had taken off with an officer to join the raid on Belfort. 'Directly from arrest?' asked the astonished staff officer. 'Yes,' replied the airfield commander. Mülhausen rang off. Two hours later Udet's orders for transfer to Habsheim arrived; apparently the staff officer at Mülhausen recognised Udet's qualities as a fighting pilot.

Udet's transfer to a *Kommando* was in part indicative of the

---

* Literally, Fighting Single-Seater Detachment at Habsheim. These Kommandos – groups of three or four single-seat fighting aircraft – were the precursors of the later *Jagdstaffeln*, or pure fighting units.

latest developments in the aerial war. The time when unarmed aircraft could venture over the fighting front was over. On 18 April 1915 a German reservist guarding the railway line near Courtrai, with a well-aimed rifle-shot, brought down a Morane Saulnier Type L monoplane, piloted by the well-known pre-war French flier Roland Garros. When the Morane was examined it was found to be armed with a Hotchkiss machine gun which fired forward through the propeller arc. The gun was not synchronised in any manner to the engine, but metal deflector wedges had been bolted to the propeller in the line of fire. Engineers at the works of the Dutch-born aircraft designer Anthony Fokker, on being shown this primitive device, rejected it as a sound basis for development. Instead they produced a simple but effective gun interrupter gear synchronised by mechanical means to the engine of a small, shoulder-wing monoplane, the Fokker M5K – later redesignated E.I*

Before the close of 1915 improved variants, the E II, III and IV, were in operation along the Western Front; it was the start of the so-termed 'Fokker Scourge', when the nimble Fokker *Eindecker* pilots created havoc among the poorly armed and highly vulnerable Allied two-seater aircraft.

At Neubreisach Udet received a Fokker E III with which he was ordered to join his new unit at Habsheim. In front of a large crowd of student pilots he started the rotary engine and began his take-off run. The new Fokker began to veer to the right, so Udet pulled the control column to the left to correct this swing – but nothing happened; the column was jammed. Seconds later the Fokker hit a hangar and fell apart, leaving Udet, unhurt, amid a heap of tangled wreckage. Subsequent examination showed that the machine gun's Bowden cable firing release had jammed the controls; Udet was exonerated from any blame for the crash, and another, older model Fokker *Eindecker* was sent for him to fly to Habsheim. On 29 November 1915 Udet's official transfer to Flieger-Abteilung 68 was effected, and on the previous day he was promoted to *Unteroffizier.*

Habsheim airfield lay some five kilometres east of Mülhausen, in the middle of the Harthwald. It had been inaugurated in the pre-1914 years and had been the venue for a large aviation meeting in 1910; the year in which the Automobil und Aviatik AG firm was founded, with its flying school at Habsheim. When Udet arrived there the airfield housed Flieger-Abteilungen 48 and 68; the former

E – *Eindecker* (monoplane).

Future Ace. Udet as a child

BENZIN-HUSSAR. Udet in his first 'uniform' as a motor-cyclist for the army, 1914.

Fighter pilot. Udet (l) with Weingärtner at Habsheim. In background a Fokker E III.

Udet (rt) with his Observer, Leutnant Bruno Justinus in Fl-Abt (A) 206 Heiligenkreuz, 1915.

Udet seated in the cockp
of his Fokker D III biplan
(364/16) wearing the
contemporary style crash
helmet and eye-goggles.
Note leather padding on
of his machine gun;
necessary to diminish fac
injuries in the event of a
crash-landing.

Udet (rt) with Oberleutna
Kurt Grashoff, commande
Jagdstaffel 37, at Douai,
1917. In background a
Nieuport Scout of 40
Squadron, RFC. Udet wa
succeed Grashoff as
commander of Jasta 37 i
November 1917.

Ernst Udet with his
Albatros D III (1941/16)
Habsheim on 1 January
1917. His mechanics,
Gunkelmann and Behren
are working on the aircra
engine.

equipped with twin-engined AEG bombers, and the latter with single-seat fighters. In command of the field was Hauptmann Walter Mackenthun. With him, Udet brought his permanent mechanic 'Fatty' Behrend, but for the first few weeks the pair found little to do. They were based on a relatively quiet front; indeed, the Heeringer army, to which they were attached, was known as the 'sleeping army in the Vosges'. Udet and his fellow Fokker pilots flew many purely defensive patrols, usually singly as it was considered a 'luxury' to despatch two or more single-seaters on any individual sortie or patrol. Leader of the tiny *Kommando* was Leutnant Pfälzer, whose three pilots were Vizefeldwebel Weingärtner and Unteroffizieren Glinkermann and Udet. The four lived in a villa just outside Mülhausen which had been inhabited pre-war by a rich American but had by now acquired the title 'Fokker Villa'. Udet also became very friendly with Leutnant Kurt Grashoff, while much of his free time was spent in Mülhausen – a town with a turbulent history, having been Swiss until 1798, then French until 1810, and now German. In the bookshop of the widow Seiffert in Mülhausen Udet bought a black, bound exercise book, which he later filled with sketches, portraits and caricatures, and even an occasional rhyme. Thus one rigger who had been injured while cranking up an engine was immortalised in verse:

If you're cranking the engine up
Keep well away from your kneecap.

Shortly before Christmas 1915 Udet had his first taste of aerial combat as a Fokker pilot. A French Caudron twin-engined aircraft was reported approaching Mülhausen, and Udet took off to intercept. At 2,000 metres he spotted the Caudron and flew towards it, his finger on the Fokker's machine gun trigger-button.

'He is now so close I can make out the head of the observer. With his square goggles he looks like a giant, malevolent insect coming towards me to kill. The moment has come when I must fire. But I can't! It is as though horror has frozen the blood in my veins, paralysed my arms, and torn all thought from my brain. . . . I sit there, flying on, continuing to stare as though mesmerised at the Caudron, now to my left. . . .' Udet's reverie was rudely shattered as the Caudron's observer manned his machine gun and put an unhealthily accurate burst through Udet's Fokker. One bullet whipped away Udet's eye goggles, shattering the glass and sprinkling his face and eyelids with tiny splinters. Instinctively, Udet pushed his control column forward and dived into the nearby clouds. Landing at Habsheim, he had his facial wounds treated, then went to his own room, where self-doubt about his courage and ability crept through his bemused brain, giving him a sleepless night; he thought over and over again, 'I've failed, I'm a coward. . . .'

Next morning Udet decided how best he could regain his self-respect; he must become an expert shot and a superb pilot, and thereby prove himself worthy. With Behrend he constructed a wooden mock-up of a Nieuport Scout, and then spent hours in the air, practising his shooting against the grounded 'Nieuport'. For the next few weeks Udet and his comrades were mainly engaged in ground-strafing the French trench system along their front, but Udet's second air combat – a fruitless, long-range exchange of fire with a French Voisin – restored Udet's confidence a little. A few days later he attacked a Caudron, but after firing only three rounds his machine gun jammed, and he broke off the combat.

Early in 1916 Udet took charge of a new aircraft, a Fokker D III biplane, 364/16, and – typical of Udet's ingenuity – he had Behrend make a silhouette of a helmeted 'observer' from tin metal, then painted it in lifelike colours and mounted it just behind his single cockpit. The idea was to prevent surprise attacks from the rear, though no evidence is available to confirm the 'observer's' usefulness as a 'defender'.

In early March 1916 Udet was promoted to *Vizefeldwebel*, and on 18 March he finally gained his first aerial combat victory. He had returned the previous evening from an attack on some French machine gun nests near Thann, and while making a night landing by the aid of the light of torches had damaged his Fokker's undercarriage. On 18 March Udet was awake before dawn and working with Behrend to repair the undercarriage damage. About mid-day the repair was completed; then at 3.30 pm a report came through to Habsheim of 'two French aircraft' approaching, some 20 kilometres south-west of Mülhausen. Udet promptly took off and climbed to 2,800 metres. Over Altkirch he spotted the enemy aircraft – and got a shock. Instead of the 'two French aircraft' he was expecting to see, he counted a total of 22 Allied bombers, Caudrons, Farmans and Voisins – a veritable armada!

Udet scanned the clear blue sky around him – he was alone, there were no other German aircraft in sight. The French formations – there were three main gaggles – continued to head towards their target, Mülhausen; while Udet circled cautiously above them, undecided where to start on this huge bunch of opponents. He decided on a large Farman in the middle of the bunch and dived at full throttle. Deliberately reserving his fire until he was only at 30 metres' range, Udet pressed his gun button and sank a burst into the Farman's engine. The bomber staggered, a blue flame ejected from its exhaust pipes, and it began to heel over. At the same moment fire from some nearby Caudrons slashed around Udet's head and he pushed his control column hard forward and dived clean through the formation until pulling out at 300 metres' altitude.

As Udet began to climb again the Farman he had attacked hurtled past him, a flaming torch, trailing a black plume of smoke and bright flames. Its observer also fell past Udet – arms and legs spread wide, turning and falling to inevitable death. The wreckage finally crashed in the centre of Mülhausen.

Rejoining battle, Udet was now no longer alone; the other Habsheim pilots were there, with other German pilots from nearby units. The sky was a maelstrom of individual combats, and Udet noticed a Caudron attempting to fly westwards to safety. He set off in pursuit at full throttle, opened fire briefly at 150 metres' range, then closed to 80 metres for his second attack. This time he hit the Caudron's starboard engine which ground to a halt. A further burst and Udet saw the French pilot collapse in a huddle – then his gun jammed. Udet hammered the gun with his gloved fists, but to no avail. Reluctantly, he withdrew from combat, landing back at Habsheim at 5.25 pm.

As the other Fokkers returned he learned that each had also registered a victory; all four celebrated their successes that evening with high spirits – they were young, and victory was sweet. Two days later Udet was notified of his award of the Iron Cross, 1st Class, and on 17 April he received his *Ehrenbecher* – the silver cup sponsored by German industrialists for presentation to all German fliers officially credited with a victory in aerial combat.*

In the summer of 1916 the first German *Jagdstaffeln* were formed – units wholly equipped with single-seat fighting aircraft for pure combat duties. The first of these, Jagdstaffel 1, was formed on 23 August by retitling the Kampfeinsitzer *Kommando* Nord at Bertin-

*Inscribed *Dem Sieger im Luftkampf* – 'For Victory in Air Fighting' – these were awarded later in the war for any aircrew member achieving at least eight victories; by which time the cup was made, not of silver, but of iron. . . .

court, commanded by Hauptmann Martin Zander. Five days later
Jasta* 2, also at Bertincourt, came into being under the command
of Germany's contemporary leading 'ace', Hauptmann Oswald
Boelcke. Five more *Jastas* had been formed by 1 October 1916. In
the Vosges area, however, where the fighting was relatively 'quiet',
the former units remained unchanged for the time being. Udet
continued to fly routine patrols, though without achieving any further combat successes, and on return from a dusk sortie over Ensisheim – some 15 kilometres from Habsheim – had his Fokker's engine
suddenly cut out. Attempting to make a forced landing in a field,
he crashed into a dyke hidden by tall corn. For about fifteen minutes
Udet was pinned under the wreckage, which fortunately did not
catch fire, until he was freed by Leutnant Sigwart from the nearby
Einsitzer Kommando. The Fokker had lost both wings and its tail
section, while the engine and machine gun had been hurled yards
away on impact. Amazingly, Udet received no injuries, apart from
bruising and mild shock.

In the autumn of 1916 the Habsheim *Kommando* was finally
converted to become Jagdstaffel 15, with Oberleutnant Reinhold
appointed as its new commander. Udet was officially 'transferred'
to Jasta 15 with effect from 8 October. Four days later he achieved
his second confirmed aerial victory. In most respects it was in
circumstances reminiscent of his first combat success. A report
reached the unit of Allied aircraft crossing the front during the
afternoon, and Jasta 15 took off in strength to intercept. Unbeknown
then to Udet and his fellow fliers, they were about to encounter the
first mass combined strategic aerial attack by the British and French
air services. The target was intended to be the Mauser factory at
Obendorf, sixty kilometres north of Freiburg.

A virtual armada of Allied aircraft had set out from Luxeuil-les-
Bains; 20 Farman XLII's and Breguet-Michelin IV's of the French
4th Groupe de Bombardement, and 26 Sopwith 1½ Strutters from
3 Wing, RNAS. Flying alongside as escort were 12 Nieuport Scouts,
some of these from Escadrille N 124, the legendary 'Lafayette' unit
comprised mainly of American volunteers. Jagdstaffel 15 met this
massive formation – already diminished by ten aircraft – over Neubreisach, and Udet saw below him seven Breguet-Michelins, protected by two Nieuports. Udet dived past the Nieuports and opened
fire on the leading bomber, pouring almost 350 shots into it. The

*The popular abbreviation for *Jagdstaffel*.

French pilot fell away and eventually made a forced landing, still intact. Udet immediately tried to land alongside his victim, hoping to prevent the bomber's crew destroying their machine, but his Fokker had suffered combat damage and a wheel tyre burst as he touched down, resulting in the Fokker tipping over onto its back.

Udet, uninjured, was helped from the Fokker by the French pilot, Maréchal de Logis Barlet, who was unwounded. His observer Luneau had been wounded in his left arm. The Bréguet-Michelin belonged to Escadrille BM 120, and was decorated with a checkerboard *insigne* each side of its nacelle nose, with an inscription '*Le voilà le foudroyant* – ('Here comes the thunderbolt'). On its racks still hung thirty small bombs, while the airframe showed evidence of some eighty bullet strikes.* Udet shook hands with his latest victims, conversed politely for some minutes, and expressed his regret at having wounded Luneau. He later visited the Frenchmen in Mülhausen, each time taking along cigarettes for them.

On 17 October Udet was promoted to *Reserveoffiziersanwärter*, was awarded the Württemberg Cross of Merit with Crown and Swords on 4 November, and the following day promoted to *Offizierstellvertreter*. He had achieved two confirmed combat victories to date, but was still a long way from becoming an 'ace' – the appellation applied by the French to their most successful pilots around whom a special cult of hero-worship was growing in each combatant nation. On 16 November in France was published the first issue of a new weekly magazine, *La Guerre Aérienne* devoted exclusively to the war in the air. This first edition published a table of German 'aces' as at 1 November. First it listed the most successful pilots who had already died in combat; Hauptmann Oswald Boelcke (40 victories), Kurt Wintgens (18), Max Immelmann (15), Max Mulzer (10), and Otto Parschau (8). Then followed a list of surviving 'aces'; Wilhelm Frankl (14), Walter Höhndorf (12), Hans Joachim Buddecke (10), Ernst von Althaus (9), Rudolf Berthold (8), Gustav Leffers (7), and Albert Dossenbach (7). Manfred von Richthofen and Ernst Udet – eventually to become Germany's two most successful fighter pilots – had yet to be included in any 'aces' listing.

Before the close of 1916 Udet scored his third victory. At about 11 am on Christmas Eve, over Niederaspach, he met two Caudron

---

*Some of these from an Ago C II crew who also fired at the bomber during its descent.

G IV's on an artillery-ranging sortie, escorted by a Nieuport scout. Coming out of the wintry sun, he approached one Caudron unnoticed and at a range of 200 metres opened fire. The Caudron's starboard engine burst into flames, its pilot manoeuvred frantically, and then, enveloped in flames, the Caudron crashed to earth. The second Caudron and its Nieuport 'escort' promptly fled westwards, accompanied by long-range and ineffective firing by Udet. For half an hour after its crash the burning Caudron sent up a column of black smoke – a sight which was to become increasingly familiar to Udet during the following two years.

On 12 December the four Central Powers, via neutral countries, had made an offer of peace to the Allies. '. . . animated by the desire to prevent further bloodshed and to bring to an end the horrors of war. . . .' Before the end of the month came the response that the ostensible offer appeared to be less an offer of peace than a manoeuvre of war. The bloodshed continued. . . .

CHAPTER THREE

Leader of Jasta 37

On 22 January 1917 Ernst Udet was commissioned as a *Leutnant der Reserve*, and inclusive of his 150 marks 'flying pay', now drew a sum of 460 marks monthly. At this time too the *Staffel* was re-equipped with new Albatros D scouts. The Albatros illustrated the extent to which the aerial war had become a race for technical superiority. In the previous year German aircraft designers had noted the excellent combat qualities of the French Nieuport Scouts, and had adopted certain features in their latest products. The Albatros D I and D II fighters brought into operational service in the autumn of 1916 had set a new pattern for the future; armed with twin synchronised machine guns, with a strong, ply-covered semi-monocoque fuselage and a relatively powerful engine. Thelen, an Albatros engineer in the firm's Johannisthal factory, had now designed new, more graceful wings for the D II fuselage, resulting in the D III variant, an exceptional design by any standards.

Udet was allotted D III, 1941/16, and promptly had the name 'Lo', his bride-to-be, painted on the fuselage. Opposing the Albatros by now was a new Nieuport design, the Type 17. Although the Albatros had a 160 hp Mercedes engine and the Nieuport only a 100 hp Le Rhone, both designs had roughly the same maximum speed in the region of 175 km/hr. Both had a ceiling of some 5,500 metres, and both could remain airborne for approximately two hours. Of the two the Albatros was heavier, better armed, but less manoeuvrable in combat than the Nieuport.

On 20 February the two types clashed. About noon three Nieuports flew over the front at almost peak altitude and reached Mülhausen. Udet and Glinkermann, who were flying an interception sortie, climbed to more than 5,000 metres to bar the Nieuports' way home.

As the opponents got within fighting range, two of the Nieuports turned tail and dived away westwards; the third was made of sterner stuff and joined battle with Udet. As the pair circled in combat, firing whenever the opportunity arose, they inevitably lost height, and at 3,000 metres Udet's fire shattered the Nieuport's engine and its propeller juddered to a stop. Even then the fighting spirit of the Frenchman was not diminished, and as Udet flew past him he shook a gloved fist at the Albatros pilot. Udet could do little about it; his guns were jammed.

Their combat had taken them some 10 kilometres west of Mülhausen and by now they were down to 400 kilometres height, and the Frenchman was attempting to glide to safety in Allied lines. Udet tried flying across the Nieuport's nose to dissuade the French-man, but the Nieuport finally touched down near Aspach, in no-man's-land, whereupon the doughty Frenchman evacuated his machine and dived into the nearest 'friendly' trench. German artil-lery promptly laid a barrage of shells around the downed Nieuport and destroyed it, but this was no consolation to Udet. He had fired some 500 rounds at the Nieuport before his guns jammed, yet had still failed to destroy it 'properly'. Nevertheless, he could claim his fourth confirmed victory.

At the end of February Jagdstaffel 15 received orders to move base northwards to a more active front. Pleased at leaving the 'forgotten front' in the Vosges, the *Staffel* made up a long convoy departing from Mülhausen station. Led by Reinhold, the pilots now were Leutnant Udet, Hänisch – known to all as 'Puz' or 'Putz' ('Elegant'), Esser – Udet's closest friend, and Vizefeldwebeln Müller, Eichenhauer and Glinkermann – 'Glinkerle', the Wendel brothers and a few recent replacement pilots. In addition the air-craft, mechanics, armourers and other ground staff and, of course, all the technical equipment and workshops had to be moved. The journey north lasted three days and nights, repeatedly delayed by stops to allow troop and ammunition trains to overtake them, or casualty trains to pass to the south. When the *Staffel* finally disem-barked in Champagne, some thirty kilometres east of Laon, it was pouring with rain and the prospect of this new zone, compared with the Alsace scenery, was bleak and dreary. Four aircraft were made ready immediately, to be flown next morning to an airfield six kilometres away at La Selve. During the night these became covered in a blanket of snow, and underneath it a layer of ice which had to be laboriously scraped away before they were able to take off.

The remaining aircraft were convoyed to the new base by trucks and the pilots took up their quarters in some small, single-storey, clay-built houses in La Selve's main street. Udet and Esser, together with their batmen, took four days to furnish their particular 'hole', and with the help of sheets, blankets, carpets and a red lamp created what Udet termed a 'sultry cosiness'. On 3 March Jagdstaffel 15 was ready for action. The main front lay 25 kilometres further south, where the German higher command had, at the beginning of the year, led their troops back to well-consolidated positions which they then prepared to defend against an expected large-scale Spring offensive by the Allies in the area between Lille and Rheims. The French on their side were busy preparing for such an attack, and on 25 March French Groupes de Chasse were gathered some 37 kilometres south-west of La Selve at an airfield near the town of La Bonne Maison. Slightly further south was based Groupe de Chasse 11. Thus Jagdstaffel 15 was directly opposing the élite of the French fighter units, among them the famous '*Les Cicognes*' ('Storks') *escadrilles*, in whose ranks fought Georges Guynemer, 'Père' Dorme, Herteaux and other top-scoring French aces. In the main the French fighter-pilots flew the Spad S VII biplane, which with its 150 hp Hispano-Suiza 8Aa engine was almost 20 km/hr faster than the Albatros DIII and nearly 30 km/hr faster than the Halberstadt D scouts also flown by Jasta 15.

On 7 April, the day following the declaration of war against Germany by the USA, the French artillery commenced a bombardment which was to last for ten days, of an intensity never before experienced; the long-expected offensive was about to commence. The awesome bombardment turned whole stretches of land into a morass of mud and craters, while the noise of the unceasing guns drowned the noise of aeroplane engines. The continuous barrage of shells rent the skies above the front, shaking any aircraft flying nearby, and on one sortie Udet actually watched a black object rise to his height, pause, and then curve to the ground – a mortar shell in full flight.

Yet for the moment there was almost no aerial combat activity, and it was not until 16 April – the day prior to the infantry attacks – that Jasta 15 pilots met any aerial opponents. On that date Esser shot down a Nieuport, while Glinkermann accounted for a Caudron two-seater. Esser then pursued another French machine, but failed to return to La Selve. The news of his death arrived on the *Staffel* at noon – Esser had crashed in his own lines.

It was the first occasion on which Udet was personally affected by a death; never before had he had a friend '. . . with whom I was bound up in such a deep and harmonious friendship'. A personal letter to Esser's parents was the last good turn he could do for his dead friend. For the next few days Udet lived alone in his clay cottage; then Leutnant 'Putz' Hänisch volunteered to share the accommodation.

As the French offensive started, their first target was the Chemin des Dames, leading over the hills of Soissons and Craonne – the 'Ladies' Path' originally constructed to make the journey between Compiègne and Château de la Bove more comfortable for the daughter of Louis XV. In the evening of that first day of assault German General Headquarters announced:

'On the Aisne one of the greatest battles of this mighty war, and thus in world history, is going on. Early in the morning of 17 April the well-organised French opening offensive moved into action from Soupir on the Aisne to Bétheny, north of Rheims. The attack was along a 40-kilometre front with a massive weight of infantry followed by reserve divisions coming through in support.'

Instead of the confidently expected breakthrough, however, the fighting on the Aisne and Champagne fronts dissolved into a drawn-out, bloody war of attrition on the Chemin des Dames, with only minor territorial gains. Wave after wave of French infantry was shattered by the German defences, until the French troops finally refused to continue the battle. In all 54 French divisions were involved in a general mutiny, and 55 'ring-leaders' were summarily executed before Général Pétain, in command of the sector, gained control of the troops again.

The German command knew nothing of these incidents – had they done so, they might have exploited the situation and broken through on a thoroughly weakened front. The battle of attrition was not confined to the land battles. In the air the German pilots faced opponents whose equipment was superior, whose skills were outstanding, and whose tactics were highly successful. Jagdstaffel 15 was decimated during this fighting, and when the French offensive petered out the unit had only four aircraft intact.

On 24 April, during this offensive, Udet registered his fifth victory; catching a Nieuport 17 at 7.30 pm which, after a brief dogfight, erupted in flames and crashed in a shell-torn field at Chavignon, twelve kilometres south-west of Laon, near the road to Soissons. Two days later Udet invited his friends to celebrate his birthday and this first victory on the Aisne front. He was now twenty-one years old, a *Leutnant der Reserve*, holder of the Iron Cross, 1st and 2nd Class, and victor in five air combats.

As the group sat down to coffee and cakes, however, the general bonhomie was marred. Oberleutnant Reinhold, their commander, had not returned from a sortie. Near 5 pm they received a message from a German unit at Lierval, eight kilometres south of Laon. A German fighter had come down, virtually intact, nearby – were they missing any pilot? Further conversation left no doubts – it was Reinhold. Piling into a car the *Staffel* pilots raced to Lierval. In the middle of an open field stood Reinhold's aircraft, almost undamaged. Nearby infantrymen told the pilots that they had found Reinhold still in the cockpit; sat behind his control column, his right thumb on his machine gun button, his face frozen in the tension of his ultimate fight with the left eye squinting, the right wide open, sighting for a shot. A single bullet had passed through Reinhold's head from the rear. Glinkermann turned to Udet and said quietly, 'This is the way I would like to die'. . .

Reinhold's successor in command arrived on 30 April; Oberleutnant Heinrich Gontermann, just twenty-one years old and lately of Jagdstaffel 5, where his green-painted aeroplane was well-known. By 11 May Gontermann was to bring his personal victory tally up to 21 and soon after be awarded the coveted 'Blue Max' – the Ordre Pour le Mérite. His particular penchant was for destroying Allied observation kite-balloons; highly dangerous targets usually well protected by anti-aircraft guns and fighter aircraft. Shortly after Gontermann's arrival Jagdstaffel 15 was moved again, this time to Boncourt; a welcome change for the pilots who were now billeted in an old castle instead of their former earth-floor cottages.

Inspired by Gontermann's successes, Udet tried his hand at destroying a 'sausage' (balloon). Gliding steadily towards one kite balloon, he was about four kilometres away when a Spad loomed up behind him. A turning, twisting fight ensued, during which Udet's flying suit was ripped by a bullet and his aircraft was hit in several places. Deciding he was outclassed, Udet spun down to 500 metres and flew home to Boncourt; the Spad had carried a black death's-head *insigne* – possibly the personal marking of the great French ace Charles Nungesser.

Only days later Udet discovered that enemy fighters were not the only expert shots – enemy anti-aircraft gunners were equally excellent marksmen. Along with Hänisch, Udet attacked a pair of French Farmans over Brimont, north of Rheims, but Hänisch's aircraft stalled and his intended victim was able to escape to safer skies. The other, attacked by Udet, plumed black smoke and spun down.

Udet was now alone, at a height of 1,400 metres, and turned for home into an unusually strong headwind which made progress slow.

Suddenly he was surrounded by a host of small black flak-bursts; then, as if struck by a huge fist, his aircraft was blown onto its back; a shell had hit the upper wing. Finally levelling out, and flying with great care, Udet returned to Boncourt. His luck held on 7 May; his sixth officially confirmed victory was a Spad S VII which crashed in a wood at 7.30 pm, north of Villers-Cotterets.

On 17 May Gontermann was awarded his Blue Max and granted four weeks' leave in recognition of the honour, and Udet was appointed as temporary *Staffel*-commander during his absence. It proved to be a tragic period for Udet. On the 25th Udet led a five-man patrol over the front – the Wendel brothers, Hänisch and Glinkermann. High in the clear blue air death came swiftly out of the sun as a lone Spad, piloted by Georges Guynemer, dived and put one concentrated, accurate burst into Hänisch's Albatros.

Still unaware of the Spad's proximity, Udet had a sudden pre-monition of danger, looked to one side, and saw Hänisch's Albatros in flames. Then, as he watched in horror, he saw Hänisch's right hand go up to his helmet – a last salute from a doomed comrade – before the flaming machine fell to oblivion. Below him Udet spotted the lone Spad, and with hatred surging within him, dived as fast as possible to avenge his friend 'Puz'. As his Albatros reached its highest diving speed its wings began to shudder alarmingly – Udet was forced to abandon the dive before his aircraft shook itself to pieces.

A few days later Vizefeldwebel Müller crashed to his death at Mortiers; while that same evening Glinkermann failed to return from a sortie. His burned remains were later identified in the ashes of an Albatros which had crashed near Orguevalles; only that day Glinkermann's promotion to commissioned rank had been officially notified to the *Staffel*, though Glinkermann knew nothing of this when he died. On 4 June Vizefeldwebel Eichenhauer was also killed in combat. To Udet fell the task of composing suitable letters of condolence to each man's nearest relatives. On the day he wrote to Eichenauer's family, Udet also wrote to his former friend Kurt Grashoff of the Habsheim days, who was now commander of Jagd-staffel 37:

I'm the last of Jagdstaffel 15, the last of those who used to be together at Habsheim. I should like to move to another front, to come to you.

Bad though the situation was, it was not quite as desperate as Udet had written. Four pilots still survived in Jasta 15, and these continued to fly in action daily. Early one morning Udet set off alone with the intention of bagging a 'sausage'. At 5,000 metres in the clear, icy sky he noticed an old French artillery-spotting machine below, but then saw a smaller biplane approaching fast at his own height. He prepared for the inevitable fight. The light-brown-coloured Spad flashed by him, tight-turned, and the combat was on. For nearly ten minutes the two men fought, each circling hard to get on the other's tail.

As he passed the Spad very closely in one move Udet could just make out a French name in large letters on the Spad's fuselage – '*Vieux* – it must be 'Vieux Charles', the personal Spad of Georges Guynemer! He was fighting the best French ace. For a fleeting moment Udet found Guynemer's Spad in his sights and immediately pressed his gun button. Nothing happened – both guns were jammed. Udet was now trapped; to dive away would bring instant death, he could only continue circling and try to get his recalcitrant guns going again. As the Spad passed over him Udet hammered with his fist on the gun, and it seemed that Guynemer must have seen Udet's action, because the Frenchman waved briefly to Udet and then cleared westwards allowing Udet to live. Subsequent accounts of this combat have suggested that Guynemer's guns were also inoperative, or that he feared an attempt to ram him by the defenceless Udet; but Udet himself always maintained that Guynemer had displayed an age-old chivalry in not attacking a helpless foe.

On 19 June Gontermann returned from leave and resumed command of Jasta 15. That evening Udet mentioned to him his wish to transfer to another unit, but it was to be two months before Udet finally left the *Staffel*. In the interim he continued his almost daily routine of patrols and sorties, though without gaining any further combat victories. On 24 June a new air formation was inaugurated when four *Jagdstaffeln*, Nos 4, 6, 10 and 11, were grouped under the title of Jagdgeschwader Nr 1, with Rittmeister Manfred von Richthofen in overall command. Its terms of reference, drawn up by the Chief of Staff, Lieth-Thomsen, stated: 'The *Geschwader* is a complete unit. It is designed to fight for and secure control in the air of particular sectors.' As its first operational area he allotted Jagdgeschwader 1 to the Courtrai sector of Flanders.

That same summer, in the same part of Flanders, three men – none of whom even knew of the others' existence – were on active service; and each one would cross Udet's path in the future and have significant parts to play in his eventual fate. On 12 July the List Regiment was sent into Flanders, and in its ranks was a certain Adolf Hitler. A few kilometres away from the regiment's front, near Iseghem, Jagdstaffel 27 was based, commanded by Oberleutnant Hermann Göring; while a few kilometres south, near Lille, Flieger-Abteilung 5 was stationed, with its deputy commander Erhard Milch.

When Udet's request for transfer finally received approval, he moved on 6 August to Moncheaux, a small village ten kilométres north of the industrial town of Douai, where his new unit, Jagdstaffel 37, was based. From the start Udet felt at home in his new surroundings. His quarters were in the small, dilapidated Château Bellincamp, situated near the airfield and generally referred to as the 'Flight Castle'. In Douai, which could be reached in a few minutes in a squadron car, there was an extremely good restaurant, Weinhaus Palmier, where the cognac was good, cheap and plentiful. Udet was given a warm welcome by his old friend Oberleutnant Kurt Grashoff, the *Staffel*-commander, and soon made new friends, in particular Hans Waldhausen. The latter had served with the Bavarian Flieger-Abteilung 9b, and had come to Jasta 37 from the training school at Valenciennes.

Life with Jasta 37 was full of incident, both with his fellow pilots and, of course, with the young girls in the neighbourhood. On one occasion in Moncheaux, after a night's heavy drinking, Udet evaded an officer-patrol by way of an ash-dump, in which he sank up to his knees. And in one abandoned house he had one room fitted with a bed, the size of which led Grashoff to remark, 'With a "landing area" of such size, you can set yourself down as you wish, whichever way the wind is blowing!'

Based some twenty kilometres east of the front lines, Jasta 37 had, to date, made little contact with the aerial enemy, and Udet used some of the spare time to train the other fighter pilots, with Waldhausen's assistance. In 1935, Waldhausen described these training 'exercises' in the magazine *Luftwelt*;

I was involved with Udet in the daily training of our fighter pilots. There were times when we couldn't bring it to a close, so involved were we with each other. From it I gained a knowledge of the maximum potential of my machine in respect of manoeuvrability, tight turning, spinning and nose-diving. It was equally instructive when I played 'tag' in the air with Udet, especially when the disposition of the clouds made it possible to suddenly disappear behind one of 'Mrs Holle's feather cushions'* and emerge unexpectedly somewhere else. . . . For a long time I'd imagined that I could do without precision aiming during an air battle if I was as close as possible to an enemy. From Udet I learnt that it was always a great mistake to shoot without first aligning sights and beads precisely, however close the enemy may be. Udet also warned me never to attack two-seaters from above.

Grashoff, who watched these exercises from his canvas chair on the edge of the airfield, commented: 'No more of my men are going to do this kind of thing!' – stunt-flying was not yet part of a fighter pilot's training. . . .

Udet put practice to good use within a week of arriving on Jasta 37, when, on 13 August, he came up against British opponents for the first time. He tackled a formation of five Nieuport scouts, one of which he forced to land in German lines. Landing near the downed Nieuport, Udet was surprised to find that the French aircraft was piloted by an RFC officer. Shaking hands with his adversary, Udet accepted an English cigarette and relished its aromatic flavour, compared 'with the 'straw' German equivalents.†

Next day he was again successful. At nearly 8 pm while on a routine interception patrol he spotted five Bristol F2b two-seaters flying deep into German territory. He patiently waited for them to return, then attacked the leading F2b which immediately began to smoke. Despite this (or possibly because of it?), the Bristol's pilot retaliated, and when Udet dived the smoking Bristol dove after him. Going into a further dive Udet saw the Bristol attempt to follow

---

* A German popular name for clouds.
† There is apparent confusion with regard to this victory. The official German records make no mention of any victory by Udet on this date; indeed his official 8th victory is annotated as a 'Martinsyde' on 14 August, while his 7th official credit is for a 'Sopwith' on 15 August. 'Martinsyde' was an understandable error in identification for the Bristol F2b, which was only recently introduced to operations in France. In his *Mein Fliegerleben* autobiography, Udet did not include this Nieuport in his victory list tabulation.

him – then it exploded in mid-air, hurling its two-man crew to earth
in a hail of burning debris.

Udet's run of success continued next day, 15 August. It was a
rainy afternoon, with the cloud ceiling down to 300 metres, and
Udet had just returned from an uneventful sortie, when a low-flying
Sopwith 1½ Strutter strafed the airfield. Udet jumped into a
freshly-fuelled Albatros, its engine still cold, and was joined by two
more pilots in pursuit of the daring Sopwith. In Udet's own words,
'it was a wild hunt, just right for the cinema. . .' Flying very low,
contour-chasing across woods, railway embankments, church towers, they reached a long, poplar-bordered avenue. Udet flew along
the right edge of the avenue while the Sopwith flew along the left
side, its observer keeping up a rather wild barrage of gun fire in
Udet's direction. In the vicinity of Pont-à-Vendin, some fifteen
kilometres from Moncheaux, and almost within its own lines the
Sopwith broke up in flames. Its pilot started to land, but the aircraft
then exploded in the air.

On the 21st he pursued a formation of six De Havilland 4 RFC
bombers – aircraft fitted with 250 hp Rolls-Royce Eagle engines,
giving them a speed almost as fast as any Albatros. The further the
DH4's flew east, the harder it became for Udet to keep them in
sight, as there was little flak to give any indication in the rear areas.
Just beyond Valenciennes six more aircraft joined with the bombers
and the whole formation then swung north towards Doornik in
Belgium. Finally Udet caught up with his prey and he attacked the
nearest DH4, mortally wounding its gunner who collapsed into his
cockpit. The bomber began to trail smoke and gradually lose height.
Near Ascq the DH4 tried to land, but turned over, throwing out
the body of its gunner. After returning to Moncheaux Udet drove
out to the wreck and talked with the DH's pilot, an Australian
lieutenant. Udet took an instant dislike to the man: 'He told cock-
and-bull stories about fights with single-seaters and thought himself
frightfully brave – an Australian show-off'. . .

Udet claimed only two more victories on this particular fighting
sector – a DH5 scout on 17 September, and an unidentified RFC
two-seater on 24 September, near Loos* – then came an order for
Jagdstaffel 37 to move to a new base, at Wynghene, sixteen kilometres south of the beautiful city of Bruges. Here, the sea was only

---

* Described in his combat claim report as a 'truss-fuselage' type – almost certainly
an FE2b or FE2d two-seater 'pusher'.

some forty kilometres away, and this could be seen each time the pilots gained height. The fighting front followed the Iser, where Belgian troops were defending, about thirty kilometres west of Wynghene. The heavy concentration of air units around Wynghene reflected the intensity of fighting in this area. Apart from Jasta 37, there were Schutzstaffeln 4 and 12, and Fliegerabteilung 40 – these being direct tactical support units for the infantry, which flew morning and evening reconnaissance sorties, and gave direct support in the form of low-level strafing sorties against enemy infantry positions with bombs and machine gun fire.

Udet was billeted with the Brouwers family of lace manufacturers in Brugge Street – the son of the house, at that time, was serving with the Belgian Flying Corps – and life in Wynghene was characterised by Udet's description of Flanders as, '. . . the land where there was still milk, honey and butter'. The local population bore the German occupation with dignity but without hatred and, generally, German servicemen respected this. Quite of their own accord flocks of schoolchildren would come and spend every free minute around the airfield, asking the pilots for sweets or a cigarette.

The high concentration of squadrons in the area led to some interesting visitors, most prominent of whom was Rittmeister Manfred von Richthofen, leader of Jagdgeschwader 1, who talked with Udet and Waldhausen for a long time.

Waldhausen, with six victories credited, was on his way to becoming an ace, and his Albatros D Va, D 2284/17 was marked with a half-moon and star *insigne*. On 27 September however, following an attack on an Allied observation kite balloon, he was shot down· intact by Allied fighters from 40 Squadron RFC and 8 Squadron, RNAS, and remained a prisoner of war until 1919.

Not every visitor was welcome at Wynghene. On one occasion Udet carelessly addressed a pompous officer from the general staff in the *Staffel*'s officers' mess as '*Sie* instead of using the third-person mode of address '*Herr Hauptmann*. When the guest indignantly asked him if he hadn't noticed the officer's insignia on his shoulder epaulettes, Udet replied, 'Good Lord! I'm afraid I've only just seen them, otherwise I'd have said *Du* to you from the start.'

At Wynghene Udet usually flew sorties alone, hoping to achieve the element of surprise in attack thereby. In the evening of 28 September he took off to intercept a reported Allied artillery-spotter but as he patrolled five British Sopwith Camels in tight formation crossed his path. Manoeuvring behind the arrow-head quintet, Udet cautiously crept up to the rear of the Camels. The British pilots flew on unsuspectingly. Eventually Udet was literally in formation with them, at the rear of the Vee, with the tail Camels only 30 metres away on each side of him. Taking a deep breath, Udet slammed a short burst into the Camel to his left, which immediately erupted in flames. Switching quickly to the leading Camel, Udet fired again, sending it down to a forced landing near Wingles, 22 kilometres north-east of Arras. The remaining trio finally woke to their danger and scattered wildly. The whole episode had lasted just 20 seconds.

On his return from this sortie Grashoff took Udet to one side and told him, 'When I leave here, Kneckes, you'll inherit the *Staffel*.' Grashoff, unable to achieve any victories for some time, had applied for transfer to the Macedonian front, in the hope of easier 'hunting'.*

On 1 October Udet was out again, hunting alone, when he noticed below him two German LVG two-seaters being attacked by a pair of Sopwith Camels. Diving hard he tackled the Camels, one of which immediately fled westwards. The second Camel was clearly piloted by a novice and Udet quickly got within 40 metres of him, sank a burst into the Camel's left wings and watched it go down near Deulemont, 14 kilometres south of Ypres at 10.35 am. As he returned to base he saw another combat below, ending in the British aircraft breaking up in mid-air.

Udet decided to follow the German pilot back to his base at Ghistelles, south of Ostend, in order to congratulate him and to confirm his victory. The pilot was Offizierstellvertreter Julius Buckler of Jasta 17, an 'ace' with 16 credited victories already. After talking, Udet invited Buckler to breakfast with him at his own base and both men flew to Wynghene. After their meal the two 'aces' took off again; Buckler turning south to go hunting again on his way back to base, while Udet set off northwards towards the flooded region around Nieuport and Dixmuiden. Here flak bursts drew his attention to a British RE8 ranging artillery batteries below.

Diving onto the tail of the RE8 Udet was about to open fire when the two-seater made a sharp bank and its observer-gunner opened fire with his ring-mounted Lewis gun. Udet felt a violent blow to his knee, a sizeable jet of petrol poured from his holed petrol tank, and seconds later his propeller ground to a halt. The Albatros was then at a height of 1500 metres and about four kilometres over

---

* Oberleutnant Kurt Grashoff was killed in action on 12 June 1918 while serving with Jasta 38 in Macedonia.

enemy lines, leaving him plenty of space in which to regain German territory – always providing his aircraft didn't catch fire.

At that moment a formation of Sopwith Camels appeared overhead, and three of these peeled off to attack the crippled Albatros. Udet had no choice; the thin plume of escaping petrol left an obvious trail and any combat was out of the question. Fortunately for Udet the Camels stayed at some 300 metres range as they chased him, firing ineffectually.

Once within German lines Udet set the Albatros down, rolled along the ground for a few metres, then crashed nose-first into a water-logged trench. Pulling himself out of the cockpit and along the top of the fuselage, he joined the commander of a local anti-aircraft battery in his dug-out as the first Allied shells began to fall around the Albatros. In the dug-out the two men emptied a bottle of schnapps, then Udet set off for Wynghene about 3 pm. At first he walked, then 'borrowed' a horse and cart – only to have the horse refuse to budge. He next hitched a ride from a passing lorry, but a few kilometres on the lorry's axle broke. All this time it poured with rain, and Udet finally reached an operational airfield from where he telephoned Wynghene and had a *Staffel* car sent to fetch him; arriving back at base eventually at 8 o'clock the next morning.

Grashoff's transfer to Macedonia came through, and on 7 November 1917, by Order 411a 38662/4, Ernst Udet was officially appointed commander of Jagdstaffel 37. He was twenty-one years old, and it was only three years since he had been told that he was too short and too young for active service. With this appointment Udet's lone hunting sorties had to cease; his duty now was to lead the *Staffel* into battle. He immediately concentrated on training for his pilots, insisting that they become absolute masters of their aircraft first. 'How can I ask anybody to shoot down the enemy if he cannot control every aspect of his machine?' He had little time for such showy manoeuvres as looping, but had his men practise endlessly spinning and side-slipping in order that they might '. . .effortlessly get out of even the most difficult situations.' On 13 November he received the Knight's Cross of the Order of Hohenzollern.

To celebrate this award, and his promotion, Udet decided to have yet another try at destroying an enemy kite balloon. That evening, west of the Houthulst Forest and still a couple of kilometres from his selected 'sausage', he was jumped by five SE5a's, one of the RFC's latest fighter designs. Twisting and turning Udet managed to evade their assault and escaped into some nearby clouds. Here his compass failed and on emerging from the clouds he found himself over unfamiliar territory, with no sign of the front anywhere. He was completely lost, possibly over enemy-held territory which made the prospect of becoming a prisoner of war an unpleasant possibility.

Frustrated and angry with himself, Udet continued flying aimlessly, anxiously searching the ground below for some sign of identity until, with relief, he spotted some white chalk cliffs; he was close to the front at Lens, almost 75 kilometres from Wynghene. Crossing the lines he fired a signal flare and received an answering flare from the ground. He landed on the airfield of a Bavarian *Fliegerabteilung* in whose mess he was served with beer to the ringing of a house-bell. Though ending happily, his latest attempt to destroy a 'sausage' had been as unsuccessful as all previous such sorties.

Udet's next combat victory came after a night of heavy celebrating in the *Staffel* mess. Arranging to be called at 5 am, in order to 'get some fresh air into my head and through my hair', he took off and climbed quickly to reach the cold, clear heights, then headed towards the lines. Spotting three Allied single-seaters, he thought at first that these were Sopwith Camels flying upside-down! Shaking his head, he looked again and realised that they were the peculiarly back-staggered wings of De Havilland 5 scouts. One DH5 flew straight towards him, then broke away at 30 metres' range; only to fly right through Udet's sight-line and to break apart as Udet fired one brief burst. His next opponent, and his last victim of 1917, was an SE5a which went down a week later between Poelcappelle and Westerboeke.

Jasta 37 had by now been re-equipped with the new Albatros D Va. The one Udet usually flew had a black fuselage, fin and rudder. On its fuselage sides it carried the usual letters LO and on the fuselage nose, a white chevron. Even more unusual was the large white letter U on the underside of the lower wing. This made it easier to find eye-witnesses for his victories, amongst military personnel on the ground.

The year 1917 had been one of success and personal grief for Udet. He had been commissioned, promoted to *Staffel*-commander, decorated, and credited with 14 combat victories. Yet he had also learned the full bitterness and grief of war. Reinhold, Gontermann, Esser, Hänisch – all had been killed, as had his friend of younger days Otto Bergen, who at the beginning of the year had written saying he hoped to obtain a transfer to Jasta 15. Bergen failed to return from a combat over Hendicourt on 26 September. In contrast

Udet was truly 'Sunday's child'. He had not even been wounded, only grazed three times, twice in the sleeve and once through a boot.

As he flew over the wintry front, a devastated landscape lay below him; Passchendaele, Langemarck, once flourishing villages, had been razed to the earth by the pitiless trench warfare in which ground gained was measured by the metre rather than the kilometre. And yet there was still every reason to look forward to 1918, the fifth year of the war, with confidence. The 'October' Revolution had shaken up Russia, and on 15 December the armistice treaty of Brest-Litovsk was signed. Now Germany could withdraw its many troops from the eastern front and throw them against the French and British in the west. It was in the west, in 1918, where the war would now be decided. . .

CHAPTER FOUR

Pour le Mérite

Udet began the new year by shooting down three more victims; on 6 January he brought down a Nieuport Scout over Bixschoote as his 17th victory, a Sopwith Camel nine kilometres north of Ypres on the 18th, and a Bristol F2b on the 19th. He then took a short leave of absence from the front to go to Berlin, where a series of evaluation test-flights to compare the qualities of the latest German fighter designs began on 21 January. The series, ostensibly to guarantee that the fighting *Staffeln* at the front were given the best available machines, was arranged in three stages. First, the various machines were rigged, weighed and tested under the surveillance of officers. They were then flown and demonstrated by works' pilots; and finally tested by operational pilots from the front. The latter's judgment on speed, climbing power, manoeuvrability and other vital matters was the decisive factor in the placing of production orders.

At Berlin's Adlershof there was a collection of 28 aircraft on display, though not all took part in the trials. Five firms were represented by just one design each; an AEG DI, an Aviatik D III, Kondor D II, Schütte-Lanz D III, and a Siemens-Schuckert D III. Rumpler displayed two D I's, with differing strutting, while Albatros showed four D Va's with different engines; Pfalz offered two D IIIa's, a D VI and a D VII; and Roland had brought two D VI's, a D VII and a D IX. The strongest contingent came from the Fokker works; a V9, V11, V 13-1, V 13-2, V17, V18, V20 and two improved Dr 1 triplanes.

The cream of Germany's fighter pilots came together at Berlin for these evaluation tests; there were days when one could have bumped into half a dozen holders of the Pour le Mérite at Aldershof. They were national heroes and led an exceptional life. Whereas the vast majority of the fighting services were housed in trenches and earthen dug-outs, and were in constant danger from shell bombardment and the vagaries of trench warfare; fighter pilots, after being tested to their limits in the battlegrounds of the sky, would usually return to comfortable quarters which might be a Nissen hut one day or a castle the next. Wherever they were based they could expect food, drinks, cigarettes and a car or aeroplane at hand to help them forget the war for a few hours.

Nevertheless, all the conveniences available at the front were modest when compared with the luxuries offered to them in Berlin. The aviation industry ensured that they contributed much more to the evaluation trials than merely the latest aircraft designs. Whole floors of the best hotels in Berlin were taken over by firms for the operational pilots, and in their rooms they found plenty to eat, drink and smoke, as well as 'presents' such as fur coats, watches and cigarette lighters – and, later each evening, young ladies, pretty and ever-willing. Anthony Fokker received his guests at the Hotel Bristol, while the Everbusch brothers from Pfalz entertained theirs at the Hotel Adlon. One rumour which reached the frontline was that the Berlin dancing-girl Kieselhausen had accepted a great deal of money to dance naked on a table. . .

If all this luxury smacked of bribery and corruption, there was a lot at stake for each aviation company. Fokker's V 11 – subsequently retitled D VII – won the evaluation trials, prompting a production order for 400 machines, each worth 25,000 marks; a round figure of ten million marks. Next to such a fortune the modest relative expense of a few hotel rooms sumptuously furnished with cold meat and warm flesh was quite insignificant. The winning Fokker was a worthy triumph for its designers, an outstanding fighter in service. Simple to build, highly manoeuvrable, strong and fast, with a good field of vision, it was appreciated by all pilots who flew it.

Udet, who as usual thoroughly enjoyed his sojourn in Berlin, returned to the front, and scored his next victory on 18 February. Early in the morning he led his *Staffel* along the front, hoping to lure the enemy, then he turned eastwards. Flying into the sun, he blotted out the glare by holding his thumb over the sun's disc, and saw eight Camels about 50 metres above him. He quickly shot one down which crashed near Zandvoorde, four kilometres south of Ypres, while his *Staffel* tackled the remaining seven in a five-minute whirling dogfight without any successes. This Camel represented his 20th victory, and his last over Wynghene as leader of Jasta 37. It also brought him in line for the award of the Pour le Mérite.

A few days later he had his most ghastly experience of the war. He was flying at the head of his *Staffel* towards Ypres, several hundred metres below an unbroken pall of cloud, when suddenly a human body, limbs akimbo and turning over and over, fell past him hurtling to the earth and finally plunging into the ground just behind enemy lines. There was nothing else visible; neither aircraft or debris fell from the cloud ceiling.

Udet later wrote: 'I'll never forget that awful vision as long as I live.'

On 18 March Jagdstaffel 37 received an order to move to Le Cateau, a hundred kilometres further south. The German army was preparing for a massive spring offensive, hoping to obtain victory in the west before the arrival of American trooops in full strength in France. To provide air support for this land offensive Jagdgeschwader 1 was complemented by 80 other fighter squadrons, and two new *Geschwader* were formed; No 2 (*Staffeln* 12, 13, 15 and 19), and No 3 (*Staffeln* 2, 26, 27 and 36). Le Cateau, Jasta 37's new base, was only 22 kilometres south-east of Avesnes-le-Sec, near which Jagdgeschwader 1 had been stationed since 25 November 1917, under the command of Manfred von Richthofen.

On arrival at Le Cateau, after a nightmare road journey in drenching rain, Udet was busy helping his mechanics erect the tents, when he felt a tap on his shoulder. It was the 'Red Knight' – von Richthofen himself.

'Hallo, Udet, rotten weather today,' said von Richthofen.

Udet stiffened in salute.

'How many have you brought down, Udet?'

'Nineteen confirmed, one pending, *Herr Rittmeister.*'

Von Richthofen poked some dead leaves with his stick, pondering, then said, 'Hm, Twenty then. You'd seem ripe for us. Would you like to?'

'Yes, *Herr Rittmeister,*' replied Udet enthusiastically – to be selected for the Richthofen *Geschwader* was the ultimate ambition of every German fighter pilot. Von Richthofen merely nodded, then shook hands with Udet and clambered back into his car and left.

Udet almost never reached the Richthofen *Geschwader.* Still unfamiliar with this latest area of the fighting front, he set off with his *Staffel* in pursuit of nine RFC two-seaters returning from a sortie. He tackled one RE8 and forced it down from 3,000 metres to 500 metres, but then stalled. Assuming he was still within German lines Udet attempted to force the RE8 to land. The RE pilot actually started to land but his observer-gunner opened fire at Udet, hitting his engine and sending a jet of hot water into Udet's face. The RE8 then landed and was immediately surrounded by British soldiers

who set up a barrage of rifle and machine gun fire at the Albatros
– Udet was behind enemy lines! With great presence of mind Udet
decelerated his engine to give the impression that he intended to
land, floated along a few metres above the ground, and as the
excited soldiers ran towards him gradually accelerated again. He
floated on until, after some eight minutes he reached the front lines
and landed at Le Cateau, where German observers had already
reported him landing behind enemy lines.

Udet's arrival at Jagdgeschwader 1 on 18 March has been graph-
ically described by the *Geschwader* Adjutant, Karl Bodenschatz:

> In those days of heated battle a very cheerful young man joined
> the group, who had painted on his machine in delicate lettering
> the initials 'Lo'; he had up to that point already shot 21 enemy
> planes out of the sky, and was greeted by Richthofen with great
> warmth and sheer pleasure, because he knew that this cheerful
> young man was a fighter pilot of the very first order.*

The description by Bodenschatz was a fitting one, even though
he had awarded Udet one victory too many. After a meal together
Richthofen said he needed someone to replace his brother Lothar,
who had been wounded on 13 March, as leader of Jagdstaffel 11,
and offered Udet the honour. To be invited to join the Richthofen
Jagdgeschwader was a great privilege, but to be offered the command of what was known to be the Red Knight's favourite *Staffel*
was the accolade. . . .

On 21 March Udet was designated commander of Jagdstaffel 11,
which comprised the following pilots:
Leutnant Werner Steinhäuser (killed in action 26 June 1918)
Leutnant Esser
Leutnant Eberhardt Mohnicke
Leutnant Joachim Wolff (killed in action 16 May 1918)
Leutnant von Conta
Leutnant Friedrich-Wilhelm Lubbert (died 25 November 1966)
Leutnant Otto von Breiten-Landenberg
Leutnant Erich Just
Leutnant Siegfried Gussmann
Leutnant Krefft
Vizefeldwebel Edgar Scholz (killed in take-off crash, 2 May 1918)

---

* *Jagd in Flanderns Himmel;* published 1938 by Verlag Knorr & Hirth, Munich.

A few days later Leutnant Hans Weiss, a 16-victory ace also joined the *Staffel*, but was killed in action on 2 May 1918. The average age was twenty-one years, with Udet, their commander, among the youngest in years but the oldest in combat experience.

Despite his relatively vast combat experience, Udet now found himself in a new world. The four *Staffeln* of JG 1 were based only a few kilometres behind the front lines, and the pilots were quartered in wooden billets capable of quick assembly or dissembly for mobility of the unit. Activity was higher than with other *Staffeln* and JG 1 pilots often flew four or even five sorties in a day; being fully dressed and waiting near their aircraft on the airfield for the hours between flights. The group was now mainly equipped with Fokker Dr 1 triplanes; machines slower than the latest Albatros scouts but infinitely more manoeuvrable – 'the ideal machine for aerial combat', as Udet described it.

The great German land offensive commenced in the early morning of 21 March – 'Operation Michael' was under way. Significant successes were gained in the early stages, and Bapaume and Péronne were taken from the British. By 26 March JG 1 had also moved its base forward, taking over an airfield evacuated by the British RFC at Léchelle, nine kilometres south-east of Bapaume. The previous 'owners', 15 Squadron, RFC (RE8's) had left in a hurry and JG 1 found four hangars still intact and a cache of 1,500 litres of aviation petrol. The few shell-craters on the landing ground were soon filled in, and an 'air raid officer' was stationed twelve kilometres away on some high ground in the most advanced part of the German lines to inform the *Geschwader* of any enemy aircraft flying in their zone of operations. During the early days of the 'push' bad weather prevailed, restricting flying activity, but this situation quickly changed and on 27 March, in the early morning, Manfred von Richthofen shot down his 71st victim.

Following this von Richthofen took off again, leading four Fokker triplanes from Jasta 11, piloted by Udet, Scholz, Just and Gussmann – Udet's first sortie in a triplane. Over Albert Udet saw a lone RE8 circling slightly above him, left the formation and attacked it from head-on below the nose. The RE8 heeled over and disintegrated in the air. Udet then rejoined the triplane formation and followed Richthofen in a low-level strafe of Allied infantry, during which Richthofen destroyed a Sopwith Camel which failed to see the German formation diving on him.

After landing Richthofen congratulated Udet on his expert despatch of the RE8 and told him that from the following day Jasta 11 was his to lead in battle.* Next day, in company with Gussmann, Udet had a tough fight with a Sopwith Camel, which repeatedly attacked him from head-on. Udet finally caught the Camel with a burst in its belly and it crashed in German territory, killing its Canadian pilot Lieutenant C. R. Maasdorp. Udet returned from the fight soaked in sweat, with his nervous system jangling. To add to his state there was a dull penetrating pain in both ears.

Greeting Udet's return was a telegram from the General in Command, of the Luftstreitkräft, congratulating the Richthofen brothers on chalking up 100 victories between them, and which went on to say, 'To Leutnants Udet and Löwenhardt, who, through their exemplary energies and efforts, are continuing day by day to raise the number of their victories, I send my warmest appreciation.' Erich Löwenhardt had 15 victories at this date, and Udet 23, but Udet was ill, troubled constantly by stabbing pains in his ears. The *Geschwader* had no doctor, only a medical orderly, who probed Udet's ears, asserted that they were suppurating, and sent him to Military Hospital 7 in Valenciennes. Udet could not face staying in the cloying atmosphere of a hospital and, despite continuing pain, returned to his *Staffel* on 6 April. During his absence a cousin of Richthofen, Wolfram, had arrived in Léchelle, and was posted to Jasta 11, while the whole *Geschwader* then received orders to move base to Harbonnières, two kilometres east of Amiens alongside the old Roman road leading to St Quentin. Here the *Geschwader* was only eight kilometres behind the most forward line of the 2nd Army. Immediately on arrival at Harbonnières Udet took off for a war patrol, during the course of which he claimed his 24th *Luftsieg* (victory) – a Sopwith Camel in flames – but on his return the pain in his ears was almost crippling. Richthofen immediately ordered Udet back to hospital in Munich, and next day, reluctantly, Udet was flown in an old LVG two-seater to the nearest rail station and made his way home.

In Munich he was met by his parents and sister, and by Lo who was working as a junior nurse in a hospital in Schwabing. The family doctor inspected Udet's ears, then said, 'No more flying for

* Though Udet was the official commander of Jasta 11, this appointment did not necessarily mean he was yet judged to be the best *fighting* leader in the air. Most German fighter units often 'appointed' their own 'combat leader' irrespective of rank; usually the most experienced pilot.

you'. Udet protested vehemently, and after careful treatment his ear infection was eventually cured. At home he received a telegram, notifying him of his award of the Pour le Mérite – the Blue Max, as all pilots termed the decoration – and Udet managed to purchase the cross from a Berlin jeweller. His father brought out a bottle of Steinberger Kabinett 1884 from the cellar to celebrate, while his fiancée, Lo, took a childish delight in parading Udet, with the cross around his neck, up and down in front of the local barracks' guards; for the guards had to turn out in full salute to any wearer of such a high award.

Those weeks at home in Munich were 'days made of blue silk. I have never had another spring like it', Udet was to write later. Above all he needed to forget the war for a while, but well-meaning locals pestered him for stories of the fighting. 'I can't talk over beef stew and dumplings about men who have met their deaths at my hand,' summed up Udet's feelings about such matters. His worst moment was when he visited the parents of his boyhood friend Otto Bergen, who had been killed the previous year. In Otto's attic room, which had remained exactly as Otto had left it to join the war, Udet found the accounts book of their 'flying club', aeroplane models they had built and flown, and even letters he had written to Otto from the front. Gustav Otto invited him to his country house. At first Lo declined to go with Udet – 'What will our parents say?' – but then allowed herself to be persuaded, and the young couple spent some carefree days together at Lake Starnberg.

One amusing, if ironic, episode was an invitation from the Bavarian Army to join them. As victor in more than 20 combats, and wearer of the Pour le Mérite, Udet would have automatically received the Royal Bavarian Order of Max-Josef, which carried with it a knighthood; he would then have become Ernst Ritter von Udet. However, he declined: 'I stay with the Prussians who accepted me in 1915. The Bavarians rejected me then.' He did agree to go to DELKA, the German exhibition of captured spoils of the aerial war, which was being held in Munich at this time. Here he was photographed by the press alongside the exhibition's director Ernst Friedrich Eichler, standing in front of a DH4 shot down in 1917 by Vizefeldwebel Lautenschlager of Jasta 11.

Eichler then suggested to Udet that he should publish a book of his war experiences; Udet had merely to relate them and Eichler would arrange all details of publication. Udet agreed to do this; after all, several other leading German fighter aces had already had books published, including Manfred von Richthofen, Max Immelmann, Oswald Boelcke and Adolph Tutschek.

On 21 April, five days before Udet's 22nd birthday, the German high command reported the loss of their greatest fighter ace, Manfred von Richthofen, who had failed to return from combat over the Somme. The shock of this news unsettled Udet who could not bear to stay in Munich any longer. With his ears almost healed he returned to the front. The Richthofen Jagdgeschwader – so titled now by Imperial decree – was now based at Guise, north of St Quentin, in support of the 7th Army at Chemin des Dames. For this purpose two advanced landing fields had been prepared at Puisieux, eight kilometres north-east of Laon.

Richthofen had left a will which asserted in a single sentence: 'If I don't come back then Reinhard (Jasta 6) is to assume command of the *Geschwader*'. High Command had acceded to this last request, but the choice had caused some consternation within the unit. Willy Reinhard, born in 1892 and a 12-victory ace was popular enough, but was not considered to be a good judge of men and certainly no leader in the Richthofen mould.

Other appointments included that of Löwenhardt to the command of Jasta 10; with 24 'kills' he was now slightly ahead of Udet. The *Geschwader* had by now been re-equipped, exchanging their Fokker Dr 1 triplanes for Fokker D VII's. The D VII was faster than the Dr 1, but less manoeuvrable. It also had a slightly inferior rate of climb at low altitudes but was vastly superior at height, thanks to its 160 hp high compression engine. The pilots were delighted with their new steeds.

On 21 May Udet was officially appointed commander of Jagdstaffel 4. His pilots were Leutnants Heinz Graf von Gluczewski, Graue, Hertz, Viktor von Rautter, von Winterfeld, Heinz Drekmann, Egon Koepsch, Heinrich Maushake and Karl Meyer. On 30 May Leutnants von Puttkamer, Bender, Jessen and Kraut were added to the *Staffel* strength. None had more than one or two victories credited, with the exception of von Rautter who had 12, added three more in the next week, but failed to return from combat on 31 May. That same month Udet's old friend Walter Angermund was wounded in action as a fighter pilot, and was later transferred to the observers at Schleissheim.

The third phase of the great German offensive began on 27 May. The Richthofen Geschwader had landed the previous evening at the advanced airfield at Puisieux, where they would be facing French air opposition instead of British. At 2 am the German artillery barrage commenced and at 4.20 am the infantry over-ran positions held by the British 50th Division and the French 20th Division. Enemy activity in the air was minimal and the *Geschwader* scored few victories. The initial advance went so smoothly that within three days a new airfield, evacuated by the French, was spotted at Beugneux, 44 kilometres west of Puisieux and 16 kilometres south-east of Soissons. However, at this stage 31 May the field was still within artillery range, and the *Geschwader* utilised two fields at Arcy and Rugny, a few kilometres east of Beugneux as advanced combat grounds, flying back to Puisieux each evening. That day Udet shot down his first adversary since returning from leave, and his first as commander of Jasta 4; a French Breguet 14 which crashed south-west of Soissons.

On 1 June the *Geschwader* was able to occupy Beugneux. It was a well-constructed airfield, previously used mostly by night-bombing *escadrilles*, but the French evacuation had been hurried. The wrecks of a Breguet and ten Voisin bombers, as well as twelve Spad scouts, still lay around the field; while the unit adjutant, Bodenschatz, was particularly delighted to find a flock of 300 sheep still grazing on the edges of the field.

Taking off from this new base on 2 June, Udet shot down his 25th victim at about 1300 hours north-west of Neuilly. The same day Löwenhardt claimed his 25th victory, and received a telegram awarding him the coveted Blue Max. That evening there was a party to celebrate this unique but friendly rivalry between Udet and Löwenhardt – both were *Leutnants*, both *Staffel*-commanders, both victors in 25 combats, and now both holders of the Pour le Mérite. Each had been born in April, Löwenhardt a year before Udet, in Breslau; and each flew a Fokker D VII – Löwenhardt's painted yellow and Udet's red.

In June the rivalry became intensified. Udet destroyed a Spad each day of June 5, 6, 7, 13 and 14, followed by a Breguet on the 23rd and another next day; while Löwenhardt only achieved three victories in the same period. On 18 June Udet took over temporary command of the *Geschwader* when Reinhard and Leutnant Kirschstein (Jasta 6) left to go to Berlin where, on 21 May, the second series of fighter aircraft designs' comparative trials had begun. Air activity had increased considerably, a fact noted in the *Geschwader* diary somewhat prosaically:

Appearance of numerous enemy bomber groups. Air supremacy is to be secured by Geschwader 1 and 3. Three enemy bomber groups are systematically bombing the Fère-en-Tardenois area. . .

On 25 June Udet achieved his second 'double' victory, his 34th and 35th victories, when returning from a second evening sortie, by shooting down two Spads. His personal Fokker D VII, 4253/18, was a striking-looking machine. The fuselage was painted red, the upper surface of the top wing was candy-striped in diagonal white and red stripes, his fiancée's name Lo painted in white on the side of the fuselage, and on the upper surfaces of his tail elevators, in white, was the slang phrase '*Du noch nicht!*'*

Udet's apparently charmed life was particularly exemplified on 29 June. Recently some German fighter pilots had begun wearing the new Heinecke parachutes, including Udet. His report on that day's escapade reads:

On the morning of 29/6/18 I took off at 7.15 with my *Staffel* on a hunting mission. At 7.40 over Cutry I attacked a plane which was flying at an altitude of 800 metres over an area under artillery fire from the French. On my first attack the Breguet turned towards me and flew past below me. I then noticed that its observer was no longer standing to his gun, and therefore assumed I had already hit the observer. Contrary to my usual habit, I attacked the enemy plane from the side. Suddenly, however, I noticed the French observer re-appearing from the fuselage and at the same moment was hit by several rounds, one low down in the machine gun, another in the (petrol) tank. At the same time my elevator and aileron cables must have been shot through for my Fokker D VII was plummeting down out of control.

I tried everything I could, partly using the throttle and partly the rudder, to bring the plane under control again, but in vain. At an altitude of about 500 metres the plane went into a vertical nose-dive and could not be pulled out. It was high time to get out. I unfastened myself and stood up on the seat. Next moment I was blown backwards by the immense pressure of the air. At the same time I felt a violent tug and noticed that I had caught my parachute harness on the front edge of the rudder. With a

* Literally: 'Not you!', but which was really the idiomatic equivalent of the English slang expression, 'You and who else?' – a taunt.

final supreme effort I broke off the tip and in a rush was free of the plane, tumbling head over heels several times behind it. I thought at first that the parachute had failed me when I suddenly felt a gentle deceleration; shortly afterwards I hit the ground.

It was a fairly violent landing and I sprained my left leg. I had landed under an artillery barrage to the west of Cutry. Shortly before and after landing I came under heavy machine gun fire from my opponent. I freed myself of my parachute and ran off in an easterly direction. Directly after this I received a heavy blow on the back of my head and was thrown to the ground by the air-blast of a heavy calibre shell. Shortly afterwards I got a small stone in my left buttock. It must also have been thrown up by one of the numerous explosions around me. I summoned my remaining energy and ran on. Fortunately I reached the edge of the gorge to the north of Missy, where I was taken in by the 16th Infantry Regiment. I suffered violent coughing and retching as I had covered some three kilometres without a gas mask. After about three hours the gas bombardment slackened and I was able to reach the Paris road. From there I got to Courmelles where I informed the *Geschwader* by telephone what had happened. I was picked up in a car and by afternoon was able to take part in a happier sortie.

Certainly, Udet's nerves were unaffected by this hair's-breadth escape from death, and the very next day he was in action again and shot down a Spad for his 36th victory.

At about this time the Richthofen Geschwader received a visit from Carl Zuckmayer, who was serving as an observer with a 15 cm gun battery and had been taken off duty to undergo special training as an aerial observer. In his memoirs* Zuckmayer wrote of his visit,

... and met there a short, restless, wiry, ebullient and unusually humorous, often extremely witty flying lieutenant who had been honoured with the Pour le Mérite – Ernst Udet. We hit it off after our first few words, drank our first bottle of cognac together, and didn't lose touch till shortly before the Second World War.

The *Geschwader* had only recently received nine new Fokker D

* *Als wär's ein Stück von mir* – (A piece of me, as it were).

(*Left*) BLUE MAX – Udet in early 1918, wearing the *Ordre Pour le Mérite* at his neck. (*Right*) *Jastaführer* – Udet as commander of Jagdstaffel 37, early 1918, in front of his Albatros D V Scout.

Informal moment in the Richthofen Jagdgeschwader. From left, Löwenhardt; Schäfer; Udet (at wheel); Meyer; Karl Bodenschatz.

(*Left*) Testing new fighter designs, Berlin, 1918, Udet (left wearing flying kit and Heinecke parachute harness); Bruno Lörzer: Heinrich Bongartz.

(*Right*) Udet poses with Bruno Lörzer at Coblenz, 1919. (*Far right*) Post-Armistice discussion. From rt: Franz Hailer; Udet; Lothar Freiherr von Richthofen.

(*Left*) Udet with his Fokker D VII, summer 1918.

(*Left*) Galaxy of German fighter aces as guests of the Pfalz firm in the Adlon Hotel, Berlin, January 1918. Personnel identified here include Alfred Everbusch of the Pfalzwerke (standing centre rear); while seated, from left are Josef Veltjens; Hans Klein; Hermann Göring; Bruno Lörzer; Ernst Udet; Jacobs. Front centre is Paul Bäumer.

Aces attending the final series of aircraft designs, Adlershof, Berlin in November 1918. From left: Walter Blume; Josef Veltjens; Josef Jacobs; Oskar Freiherr von Boenigk; Edouard Ritter von Schleich; Ernst Udet; Bruno Lörzer; Paul Bäumer; Hermann Göring; Heinrich Bongartz. All are wearing a 'Blue Max'.

Udet in the cockpit of the Fokker V 35 — a two seat conversion of the wartime Fokker D VII Scout, 1919.

Udet with his wife 'Lo' Zink in 1919. They finally married on 25th February 1920, but divorced three years later.

Udet demonstrates the U U-2 at San Isidro airfield, near Buenos Aires on 10 June 1923.

VII's fitted with 185 hp BMW IIIa engines. Udet's praise for this engine was unqualified:

> We were at Beugneux airfield at the time of the push from Rheims to Soissons when the first BMW machines arrived at the front. To start with 22 of them were allocated to Jagdstaffel 11. There was general mistrust, especially from the chief mechanics and riggers, which is typical attitude from battle-wise frontline fighters faced with innovations tested only at home. During test flights I'd already noticed markedly significant reserves of power in this engine. It operated impeccably and was particularly responsive to the throttle. Next day I used a BMW machine for the first time flying over the front and could see an enormous difference in comparison with the Mercedes-Fokker. I could only use half-throttle if I wasn't to outclimb or outpace my *Staffel*. Its speed, particularly when flat out, was substantially higher at low altitudes, and rose rapidly in comparison with other planes at higher altitudes. At about 5,000 metres the machine was nicely balanced. Even so there were still tremendous reserves of power that could be brought to bear any time the need arose. In battle it's very reassuring to know you've got power to spare. The rev-count stayed constant at 5,500 metres, and at this altitude, with high octane fuel, rose by about 60-80 revs.
>
> Thanks to the reserves of power I could afford to attack from below; a tactic I employed in most cases. However, since the more powerful engine meant that I separated too easily from the other planes in my formation and they couldn't follow me, I gave the second BMW-Fokker to Leutnant Drekmann, with whom I then flew on many joint sorties until he was eventually reported missing in action.* As a rule we now flew at about 6,000 metres over the front, which wasn't possible with other engines, keeping 10-20 kilometres behind enemy lines without ever being spotted by the enemy. Most of our attacks were successful due to the element of surprise.
>
> Within a short time of the BMW engines arriving and being put into service, there was a noticeable increase in the number of planes shot down by the *Geschwader*; Reinhard (20 kills) Löwenhardt (53) and Kirschstein (27) etc achieved the majority

---

* Leutnant Heinz Drekmann was killed in action 30 July 1918.

of their victories with the aid of the BMW engine. The performance details of my Fokker D VII, 4253/18 with a BMW IIIa
engine were:

0 to 2,000 metres in 6 minutes
0 to 3,000 metres in 9 minutes
0 to 4,000 metres in 12 minutes
0 to 5,000 metres in 16 minutes
0 to 6,000 metres in 21 minutes

As my *Staffel* was later fully equipped with BMW's I reckoned
on about 22-23 minutes for the *Geschwader* to reach 6,000 metres.
After 82 flying hours I had my engine overhauled during leave.
There was very little wear and tear on the bearings and other
parts; it was just a matter of reseating valves and renewing piston-
rings. Certainly it is beyond dispute that the BMW engine con-
stituted a peak and pinnacle of performance in the last stage of
the war. Its sole 'fault' was simply that it was born all too late.

Udet achieved another double victory on 1 July, shooting down a
Breguet and a Spad scout, and next morning, though not scheduled
to fly, on hearing the sound of anti-aircraft gunfire he pulled his
flying suit over his pyjamas and took off. At 8.15 am, near Bézu St
Germain, he shot down a Nieuport scout of the 27th Pursuit Squadron, USAS, piloted by Lieutenant Walter Wanamaker. The American had been chasing Löwenhardt's yellow Fokker, which was on
the tail of another Nieuport, when Udet attacked him. Udet landed
near his victim, gave the wounded Wanamaker a cigarette, and
asked him to autograph the patch of fabric with the Nieuport's
serial number which had been cut from the aircraft tail. Next day
Udet brought his victory tally to 40.

On 4 July came a telegram from the High Command saying that
Reinhard had been killed during a test flight at Adlershof. Oberleutnant Hermann Göring, commander of Jagdstaffel 27, had flown
a brief test of the new Zeppelin-Lindau D I cantilever biplane scout,
then handed over to Reinhard for further testing. At 1,000 metres
the upper wing had broken away and Reinhard had crashed to his
death. For the second time in less than three months the Richthofen
Jagdgeschwader was without a leader. Udet was given temporary
command and for the next few days there was speculation as to
whom would eventually be officially appointed.

Then, on 8 July, a telegram announced: 'Oberleutnant Hermann
Göring is appointed commander of the Richthofen Jagdgeschwader.'
At this date Göring was a 21-victory 'ace' and a holder of the Pour

le Mérite. The day before this appointment JG 1 received examples
of the latest Fokker fighter, the E V, later redesignated D VIII. A
high-wing monoplane, the E V was not received with any great
enthusiasm by the Richthofen pilots, who felt (with good reason, in
the event) that the fragile-looking 'parasol' wing was not strong
enough for modern combat stresses.

Udet, meanwhile, had left the front, detached to attend a supplementary fighter evaluation trial in Berlin, where some forty differing
designs were on display for testing. At Adlershof the testing pilots
were given three specific tasks; to fly every design and report their
flying and fighting potential, secondly, to fly a maximum speed trial
at specified altitudes, and finally to attend a general debate and
discussion of the various aircraft. Udet was particularly impressed
with the new Pfalz D XII biplane. He knew personally the directors
of the Pfalz firm, founded in 1913 by Gustav Otto and the brothers
Ernst, Alfred and Walter Everbusch; a relationship which led to
rumours that Udet had been bribed by one of the Everbusch brothers to express a preference for the D XII.

From Berlin Udet visited Munich and made use of this leave
period to dictate an account of his war experiences, which was later
published by Ernst Eichler under the title *Kreuz Wider Kokarde*
('Cross versus Cockade'). Udet's name and fame had by then
become well known even outside Germany. On 25 July 1918 the
French aviation magazine *La Guerre Aérienne* published his photo
with the caption; 'The current ace-of-aces of the Boches to replace
Richthofen and pass Fonck; 40 victories'. By coincidence Udet was
later to shoot down a Frenchman who carried a cutting from the
magazine with Udet's picture.

He was deeply affected by the many indications of shortages and
general moral decline on the home front. In his black notebook,
which he always carried with him to jot down any impressions, he
recorded notes on a couple who advocated free love, a black mar-
keteer in foodstuffs, and a ponce who said: 'For 50 pfennigs you can
'ave me sister. . .'

When Udet returned to the *Geschwader* it was stationed near
Courcelles-sur-Vesle, sixteen kilometres south-east of Soissons,
where an airfield had been prepared near Monthoussard Farm.
However, the German front was being pushed back and the *Geschwader* was on the point of withdrawing to Puisieux again. Udet's
quarters with the unit at Courcelles were in a castle, which was to
be blown up on departure. Before doing this the Richthofen pilots

invited the men of a nearby *Staffel* and decorated the ancestral halls. They cut holes in the various portraits, in the gentlemen's jabots and just between the ladies' hands, and stuck in fresh flowers from the greenhouse.

Udet later described all this to Elly Beinhorn, who described it in her book *So Waren diese Flieger* ('Such were our airmen'), along with Udet's apologetic explanation;

> We were so young that we would dearly have liked to cry for our mothers in our first fights – many of us actually did. We saw blood and death, we were pierced by the cries of the wounded – we simply *needed* something like this. And whom did we harm by it? The ancestors? The owner and servants had long since fled. Perhaps the female ancestors up in Heaven even enjoyed our floral tribute. . .

Udet had still not met his new commander as Göring had gone on leave on 26 July, and the *Geschwader* was under the temporary leadership of Lothar von Richthofen. Udet wasted no time in getting back to work, and on 1 August shot down three enemy aircraft in one day – his first 'triple'. At 9.30 am he shot down a Nieuport; at 12.15 pm a Breguet; and at 8.30 pm a Spad. Three days later he added another Spad, bring his tally to 44 – three behind Löwenhardt's latest figure.

During the night of 7/8 August the pilots heard the rumble of a heavy bombardment and in the early morning Lothar von Richthofen was summoned to the 2nd Army headquarters. When he arrived there, accompanied by Löwenhardt, he was told that French, Canadian and Australian forces had broken through the German defences east of Amiens with massive tank support. Accordingly, Lothar led the *Geschwader* to Péronne, sixty kilometres northwest of Puisieux. There refuelling was a slow process and the pilots were not able to join the fighting until the afternoon. Udet, Löwenhardt and Lothar then shot down three enemy aircraft apiece, bringing Udet's tally to 47, Löwenhardt's to 51, and Richthofen's to 35.

The sky was filled with Allied aircraft and on the ground the attacking tanks moved steadily forward – 'like gigantic steel turtles, they crept and crawled, crept and crawled. . .' as Udet later wrote. General Ludendorff in his war memoirs indicated the significance of the day in these words:

August 8 is a black day for the German army in the history of this war. August 8 enlightened both high commands. The fate of the German people was too high a stake in a game of chance. The war had to be brought to an end.

One of the three enemy aircraft brought down by Udet on 8 August was a Sopwith Camel, D9481, piloted by a young Canadian, Lieutenant R. E. Taylor of 54 Squadron, RAF. Udet had unknowingly collided with the Camel at the top of a loop, his Fokker's undercarriage shattering the Camel's upper wing. Taylor, a student from Ontario, had been dropping pamphlets which called on German soldiers to surrender or desert to the Allies.

On 9 August the battle continued. Udet scored again, shooting down two Camels and thereby bring his victory tally to 49; while Löwenhardt, who was promoted to *Oberleutnant* that day, destroyed his 52nd victim. Next day the Richthofen Jagdgeschwader moved base to an ill-prepared advanced landing ground near Falmy, twelve kilometres south of Péronne, in order to be in the forefront of the desperate fighting. The same day Udet shot down two more Camels, while Löwenhardt sent down an SE5a as his 53rd victory; but only minutes later the yellow Fokker was rammed by Leutnant Wentz of Jasta 11. Both pilots took to their parachutes, but Löwenhardt's failed to open and he plunged to his death like a stone. Udet, with 51 'kills', was now Germany's leading fighter ace.

On 11 August the *Geschwader* moved base again, this time to a large site near Bernes, twelve kilometres to the north-east. On his first sortie Udet brought down victim No 52.

In view of the heavy enemy air activity the Richthofen Jagdgeschwader was now flying in concert with two other *Geschwader*, commanded respectively by Robert Ritter von Greim and Emil Thuy. On 13 August it flew alongside Jagdgeschwader 3 commanded by Bruno Lörzer. However casualties were so high that the Richthofen Geschwader, led by Lothar von Richthofen in Göring's absence, was finally reduced to little more than single *Staffel* strength. Then, on 13 August, Lothar was seriously wounded and hospitalised for the remaining months of the war. Udet took over temporary command.

By then he was scoring almost daily; a Spad piloted by the Frenchman Cael on the 10th, an SE5a on the 12th, a Bristol F2b on the 14th, and a Camel next day. Cael, his victim of 10 August, became a prisoner of war and Udet took time out to visit the

Frenchman in Cambrai prison. Cael described their meeting two years later in *La Vie Aérienne*:

> Udet told me he was going to fly to Munich on leave in a Spad, which was his favourite aircraft in which he always travelled. At the same time he promised me that one of his pilots would drop a message over the lines to say that I was safely in captivity. As he was leaving he hesitated. It seemed to me that he was in two minds about offering me his hand. Finally he held it out, and I held mine towards him. We had no reason to withhold this sign of mutual esteem, as we had faced each other in battle with mutual respect.

The misgivings with which the Richthofen pilots had received the first Fokker D VIII's now proved justified. On 19 August Leutnant Rolff of Jasta 6 fell to his death when the wing of his D VIII fell off at a height of 300 metres. Udet immediately forbade any other D VIII's to be flown. On 21 and 22 August Udet brought down two enemy aircraft on each day, bringing his tally to 60 – 22 of these since 1 August. On the 22nd Göring finally returned from leave, but Udet only saw him for a few hours. Handing over command of Jasta 4 to Leutnant Koepsch, he climbed into his personal white Spad S VII and flew off to Munich for a month's leave. There his book *Cross versus Cockade – the Fighter Missions of Lieutenant Udet* was awaiting him; published by Eichler in the publishing house of Gustav Braunbeck. The book contained 37 illustrations by the artist Erpf, and the cover by Claus Bergen.* Udet's leave brought him further honours. On 24 August he was given the Lübeck Hanseatic Cross; on 14 September he was promoted to *Oberleutnant*; and three days later received the Hamburg Hanseatic Cross.

During Udet's leave the *Geschwader* was again on the move. In the train of the German strategic withdrawal, it moved to Busigny nine kilometres south-west of Le Cateau; then on 19 September moved yet again, to Frescaty, near Metz in the south. There, after four hours' artillery bombardment, and supported by about 1,500 aircraft, 13 Australian and eight French colonial divisions attacked, taking more than 13,000 prisoners by the end of the first day. Udet arrived at Metz on 25 September, and next day shot down two more

---

* The brother of Otto Bergen, Udet's pre-war friend, who had been shot down on 26 September 1917. Claus Bergen later became a successful marine painter.

adversaries; a pair of DH9's flown by American pilots. He allowed a possible third victim to go home so that '... at least there was someone to take back the sad tidings'. His combat report – his last of the war – read:

> After shooting down the first DH9, I attacked the group again, which on its return flight now consisted of only four or five. I fired at the DH9 in the middle of the group, which at first smoked and then began to burn. The fire died down a bit but then flared up again. It crashed south of Metz.

One of the required eye-witnesses for confirmation of his claims was Göring.

These victories, his 61st and 62nd, were his last of the war. Since becoming its commander on 22 May, Jagdstaffel 4 had claimed a total of 71 combat successes; 39 of these – more than half – had been his own. In this his last air combat he was slightly injured by a bullet which grazed his arm, and he was taken to a nearby field hospital, returning on 3 October. The German front in the west was now broken and in general retreat, with the superiority of the Allies bringing even greater pressure. Even the latest fighters received by the Richthofen Geschwader could do nothing to change this situation. These were the stubby little Siemens-Schuckert D III biplanes, fitted with 160 hp Sh III engines; small, manoeuvrable, with phenomenal climbing ability. Udet's machine was, as usual, painted red, with the white letters 'Lo' on its fuselage flanks. The type was so successful that on 15 October the *Geschwader* ordered twelve more of the latest D IV version, with the intention of ordering a further dozen later. The orders were never fulfilled.

In these last days of the war Udet finally had an opportunity to get to know the *Geschwader*-commander, Göring. He flew with him to visit Jagdstaffel 90, commanded by Oberleutnant Rudolf Nebel, equipped with Pfalz D VIII's. Nebel had once served alongside Göring in a *Staffel* and had little time for his autocratic manner. He therefore ordered his chief mechanic to 'keep a watchful eye'. The man took him at his word and when, after landing, Göring ordered him to have a car brought round, the mechanic calmly told Göring that he would need to ask Nebel first, and stuck to this even when Göring threatened him with a court-martial. As commander of a *Jagdgeschwader* Göring was too proud to ask a mere *Staffel*-leader for permission, and therefore walked the six kilometres to the nearest town which was his actual destination. As Udet later said to a friend: 'You know Hermann. If he doesn't want to, he won't. He'd rather walk'. . .

On 9 October the *Geschwader* moved base to Marville, 32 kilo-metres north of Verdun, in the 5th Army's area; but Udet's days as a fighter pilot were over. Two days later he was officially transferred to the post of Inspector of the Flying Corps, and assigned to Flieger Ersatz Abteilung 3 – a reserve unit at Gotha. In this capacity, from 15 to 18 October, he was ordered to visit the Rhemag-Rhenania engine factory, which was building the Siemens Sh III rotary engine under licence. His fiancée Lo joined him in Mannheim for the three days. His next job was to attend the third and final fighter evaluation trials at Berlin's Adlershof. There 15 types were being tested. The trials ended on 31 October with a communal dinner at the Bristol Hotel. The general mood was sombre. Throughout Germany there was famine, and signs of dissolution appeared everywhere; the first mutinies in the forces had begun. After the meal Udet was taken aside by Anthony Fokker, who asked him if, after the inevitable end of the war, he would like to fly for him.

Came November – that grey, fog-shrouded month which Udet always hated so much – and on the 11th armistice terms were signed in a railway carriage in the Forest of Compiègne. The greatest war in European history was over. The German flying services no longer existed, yet out of their ashes rose a new future. On the same day that Germany's representatives signed the armistice terms, the first civilian flight in Germany took place. The Austrian-born engineer and pilot Dr Ing Josef Sablatnig flew from Berlin to Kiel with government officials and important documents aboard. This event passed unnoticed in the catastrophic chaos of ruined Germany, yet it was the spark of a new era in German aviation.

A week after the armistice, on 18 November, Ernst Udet, Ger-many's highest-scoring, living fighter pilot, was sent back to civilian life, after serving through every month of the whole war.

CHAPTER FIVE

Just a Pilot

On 10 January 1919 'Kneckes' was officially released from the Army Air Service in a gloomy, uneasy Munich. Since the bloodless November revolution Bavaria was no longer a kingdom but a republic, with a president, Kurt Eisner, a Berliner, noted for his hatred of Prussian traditionalism. Food and coal were scarce. Ex-officers were highly unpopular with those now in power and were having a hard time finding employment. In this Udet was lucky; through his friendship with the Otto family he got a job in the automobile department of the Gustav Otto Werke, where all work on aeroplanes had been halted. Living in Munich again, he once more had time to devote to Lo.

Though the Army Air Service was officially disbanded, this did not mean an end to all military flying in Germany. Several units continued to operate; some along the Polish border, others with the many *Freikorps*, and still others as police units – the *Polizeistaffeln*. And surprisingly in view of the chaotic state of affairs in Germany then, civil aviation was already developing. The first official permission to operate an airline had been granted on 8 January to the Deutsche Luftreederei GmbH, a firm which had been incorporated in 1917. The first regular airlines began in January, by Ernst Schlege, between Konstanz and Stuttgart, Berlin, Freiburg, Friedrichshafen and Munich. Then, in rapid succession, different firms started a series of internal airlines throughout Germany. The German aircraft industry, now deprived of its massive wartime orders, attempted to adapt to peacetime conditions by developing transport aeroplanes; many of which were simply ex-war designs transformed to offer some rudimentary form of passenger comfort. New designs were being projected by firms like Junkers and the former Fokker works at Schwerin, while most of the wartime manufacturers continued to plan building 'peaceful' aircraft.

As the general political situation throughout Germany became explosive, Udet began to spend some evenings with his old friends, ex-pilots like himself – men like Robert, Ritter von Greim, ex-commander of Jagdgruppe 9 and a Pour le Mérite holder, and Hermann Göring, final commander of the Richthofen Jagdgeschwader. They had to be careful – the workers' councils now in power did not like such meetings – so they met more or less in secret, usually in the back room of a beer hall. Invariably the conversation turned to flying; longing for the time when they might again hold a 'stick' and look at the earth again from above. For the moment this was imposs-ible in Munich; food had never been so scarce, milk could only be obtained on a doctor's prescription; while armed 'workmen', proudly displaying their red armlets, incessantly 'patrolled' the streets. Discontent with the rule of the Workers' Councils rose steadily.

Then, on 14 April, a Bavarian Militia was formed in Bamberg, the seat of the legal Bavarian government, specifically to restore order in Munich. Part of this militia were four *Staffeln* with late-design Fokker and Pfalz fighters, and when, on 30 April, the militia surrounded Munich, leaflets were dropped over the city as an ulti-matum. On 2 May Freikorps Epp marched into Munich – the *Räterrepublik* ('Soviet Republic') was over, and joyful citizens filled the streets.

'The aircraft of the Freikorps have landed at Oberwiesenfeld' – nothing could prevent Udet racing on his motorcycle to the field; he simply had to see the aircraft. There they were, still wearing their colourful wartime markings. Quickly he returned to the city to pick up von Greim and together they tried to get to the aircraft. They were to be bitterly disappointed; flying was out of the question, even the Freikorps' own pilots were grounded. Their fuel had run out. . .

If flying was no longer possible, at least now life was no longer so bleak. Having been a hero was no longer something to be hidden. No more secret meeting in dingy back-rooms; Munich now offered many light-hearted spots eager to receive a crowd of young carefree war heroes as their patrons. Ernst quickly established a solid repu-tation as an extrovert blade, who thought nothing of entering a select nightspot in Schwabing on his motorcycle and riding in circles around the tables – 'dogfighting on the ground' as he laughingly termed this pastime. One of Udet's favourite spots was the Maxim Bar, another the Odeon Bar which he cynically termed the 'Reptile House' – the 'reptiles' being the female beauties ever willing to drink at any *Kavalier's* expense. Several of these had their carica-tures drawn by Udet, who was becoming more engrossed in this hobby. He still had a black-covered copy book which he'd bought during the war at Mrs Seiffert's stationery shop in Mülhausen, and in it he drew Else of the Maxim, as well as wartime friends, war profiteers and many other subjects, some of these accompanied by a witty rhyme.

Nearly every Bavarian ex-wartime pilot then was a member of the Bayerische Fliegerclub, whose president was Freiherr von Könitz, a pre-1914 pilot who later became first commander of the Riesenflugzeug – Ersatzabteilung – the 'Giant Squadrons'. Many prominent pilots attended the club's weekly meetings and Udet regularly met Franz Hailer, Karl Braun and many others. By 1921 the club boasted a 1,500-membership. In May a number of US Air Service officers visited Udet, among them Major Fred Zinn, a resident of Koblenz and a representative of the US Receiving Commission. In the same month Udet climbed back into a cockpit, albeit briefly, when he 'tried for size' the Fokker V-40 'Baby' – virtually a scaled-down version of the famous Fokker D VIII single-seat monoplane fighter. Only one prototype was built by the former Fokker firm, now named Schweriner Industrie-Werke.

After the various 'workers' councils had been broken up, the *Freikorps* were disbanded individually. Those which possessed aircraft hid these away or put them in storage. A new German army, the provisional *Reichswehr*, was in the making to succeed the former Imperial Army and this took over some *Freikorps*, including flying units. On 18 May Hauptmann Wilberg of the Prussian War Ministry even proposed that the *Reichswehr* should have 16 air bases, each equipped with 100 aircraft. Then, on 28 June 1919, German delegates – having no other choice – reluctantly signed the Versailles Treaty. Convinced that they would be offered an 'honourable peace', founded upon the '14 Points' peace programme placed before the US Senate on 8 January 1918 by President Woodrow Wilson; the German delegates were shocked to discover that the Allies had other ideas. Particularly France and Belgium whose cities lay devastated and whose populations had suffered cruelly during the war. These insisted that the treaty was to be both a deterrent punishment and a guarantee against any future German military aggression; its clauses were harsh and drastic. Among many other clauses, the treaty stipulated that the German Army and Navy were no longer to have an air force, apart from 100 marine aircraft for mine-spotting at sea until 1 October 1919. Manufacture and importation of aircraft were forbidden for at least six months; while *all* military aircraft existing – not just those demanded at the Armistice – were to be handed over to the Allies within three months.

These terms not only meant the end of any hopes for a new German air service, but civil aviation suffered too and the resurgent aviation industry was brought to a complete standstill. Despite all such strictures Udet and his close friend von Greim undauntedly scoured the countryside trying to get their hands on one or more of the many secreted aircraft, in the hope of organising public flying displays. After many fruitless trips, the two pilots struck gold; a whole row of Fokker D VII's and D VIII's awaiting delivery to the Allies in an unused factory at Bamberg. They were soon able to talk their keeper into 'lending' some of the Fokkers; while Udet also visited the Pfalz works at Speyer, where he was presented with a brand-new Pfalz D XV.

Quickly organising their first public display, Professor Ludwig Hohlwein designed a colourful, eye-catching poster to advertise the event, which was seen all over Munich; an impressive placard depicting Udet and von Greim like demi-gods preparing to fly. The date set for this first meeting was 11 August, in Munich, at the Oberwiesenfeld, of course.

For the first time since the war Udet was flying again, practising with von Greim for the display. It was exhilarating to be in the air again, all cares forgotten, frolicking over meadows and skimming above picturesque Bavarian lakes, flying lower than the tree-tops. They practised dog-fighting again, so like the real combat flying they'd both done only a year before.

On the day masses of people streamed towards the Oberwiesenfeld; thousands upon thousands who wanted to see the two war heroes perform, though more people preferred to stay outside the roped-off area rather than pay an admission fee. . . ! Six aircraft were lined up ready. For Udet there were a Fokker D VII, a Fokker D VIII and his Pfalz D XV, all painted flame-red. Von Greim's D VII and D VIII's were silvery grey with two red bands across the fuselages. Spectators in their hundreds crowded excitedly around the aircraft, and when the time came for take-off, both men had to taxi in front of the crowds in order to clear a pathway.

First off was Udet, who then started dropping leaflets exhorting those who had not paid for admission not to forget the collecting boxes! – the display was in fact organised as a benefit for German prisoners of war. Flying before a huge audience was a new experience for Ernst Udet. Below he could see them, tens of thousands, massed around the airfield's boundaries. Reaching 300 metres height Udet began his programme – loops, rolls, Immelmann turns followed each other in tight, neat succession for ten minutes uninterrupted masterly flying. Then von Greim's silver aircraft shot into the air. Alternately each man took off in a different aircraft as the other landed. Then, at about 6 pm came the bouquet – the long-awaited dogfight. Both men then landed. It came quite spontaneously – the sound of an ovation from the throats of thousands of jubilant spectators – a new sensation to Udet, and one which Ernie liked!

Ten days later Udet and von Greim performed at Tegernsee on a warm, sunny day. Innumerable boats floated on the placid lake and the shoreline swarmed with people waiting to see the two pilots. At about 5 pm two aircraft arrived over the lake – just twenty minutes' flying time from Munich – and started their programme. Again, the finale was to be a dogfight. Von Greim, intent wholly on chasing Udet, failed to notice a power line which touched his under-carriage, causing him to crash-land into the lake. Within minutes the aircraft sank, but von Greim was saved by a motor boat and put ashore, where he was greeted with the ovation of thousands of spectators. Though he received only minor bruising, his aircraft remained at the lake bottom until salvaged on 31 October. That evening a get-together was organised and attended by both pilots. Their collection for prisoners of war yielded 3816 marks at Tegernsee alone.

The time when one could fly without a licence was now past, and even Udet had to apply for a flying licence. This was granted on 25 September, No. 172, and stated that Ernst Udet was employed by the Bavarian Rumpler Works at Augsburg. The active director of this works, Otto Meyer, wanted to organise a 'Rumpler Flying Display' at Augsburg which, apart from gathering funds for German prisoners of war, would bring good publicity for the regular airlines being flown by the parent works. The company had commenced such operations on 13 March when a Rumpler Ru C IV was flown from Berlin to Augsburg via Gotha; and in June aerial joyrides had been organised to the beautiful scenery of the Bavarian lakes and mountains. Slowly but surely the name of the Rumpler Works was becoming known; there was even a 'Rumpler Foxtrot', made popular by the well-known dancing pair 'Erry and Merry'. . .

On the day of the Augsburg display – a fine, warm autumn Sunday – Udet and von Greim flew over the city in the morning,

greeting the many church-goers to stir up interest; and long before
3 pm many thousands of the citizens flocked to the airfield in excited
anticipation. Just before three o'clock Udet sat waiting in an all-red
Rumpler D I, D-289, its Mercedes engine slowly ticking over. Then,
greeted by the 'A-a-ahs' of thousands of spectators, a white Very
light arced into the air and Otto Meyer personally waved the white
starter-flag as Udet brusquely gunned his engine to full power. The
180 horsepower quickly pulled the all-red biplane into the air. Again
Udet saw below him tens of thousands of spectators, massed along
the airfield boundaries and kept in check by two thousand *Stadt-
wehrmänner*, assisted by cavalry patrols. He started his programme. At times the red biplane skimmed so low over the audience
that they could almost touch it. A few final loops, then he cut the
engine and amid the hum of flying wires side-slipped to a perfect
landing, and to the usual ovation.

As the applause for Udet thundered von Greim took off in his
turn, and though his exhibition may have been slightly slower and
higher, he too was loudly acclaimed. After he landed aircraft from
the Rumpler firm began giving local joy-rides. The next event on
the card was the customary dogfight between Udet and von Greim.
Immediately after take-off they started chasing each other, sometimes climbing almost vertically, at other times only inches above
the grass. Breathlessly the spectators watched – so this was how it
was during the war! Finally Udet climbed slightly, then released a
black-white-red ribbon which fluttered to earth, just like an airborne
message bag during the war. At 4.30 pm both men landed among
a storm of 'Bravo, bravo' shouts and thunderous applause.

Following this display came Tony Ficklscherer's parachute jump
from a Rumpler C I, D-136, followed by joy-rides for those spectators who had won a free flight. Slowly the happy crowd began to
disperse. The Augsburg Infantry Band marched towards the city,
blazing away merrily, followed by the two thousand *Stadtwehr-
männer* in disciplined marching order. These marched past their
commander who took the salute outside the Kaiserhof Hotel. It
should have been a perfect finish to a perfect day, but as the last
joy-riders landed at the airfield, Ficklscherer, the parachutist, himself a 22 years-old ex-pilot, decided to show the last of the audience
that he too could fly, and took off in Udet's all-red Rumpler D I.
His first loop came off all right, but a second proved fatal – he hit
a wooden power magazine, the petrol tank exploded and Ficklscherer was killed instantly. Nevertheless the display had been an

immense success, with its proceeds going to the organisation responsible for helping German prisoners of war.

Winter was now approaching, but one more display was given. On Sunday, 12 October, the original venue was to have been the parade ground in Nuremberg but this proved to be impossible for safe landings and take-offs, so it was switched to Fürth airfield. Some 15,000 attended the display, which was flown by Udet and von Greim, who were joined by a local pilot ex-Unteroffizier Steiner.

Meanwhile in Munich, Udet's home town, numerous political meetings were being held; mainly small meetings, like the one held on 16 October in the cellar of the Hofbrauhaus, organised by a 'German Workers Party'. Its announced speaker was a totally unknown man, a certain Adolf Hitler. It was to be his first-ever speech to a German audience, and a total of 111 people attended. After speaking for barely half an hour he had completely mesmerised his audience, resulting in a collection of 300 marks towards the 'Party' treasury. Such things held no interest for Udet however; he knew of merrier ways to spend his evenings . . . and nights. At the end of one such boisterous drinking bout Udet and his friends visited a shooting gallery. Here 'Kneckes', without saying a word, handed the sleepy owner a 50-mark note, took the owner's gun, and calmly set about shooting every one of the numerous clay figurines, one by one. When they left not a single figurine was still in one piece. . .

In November Udet received a letter from an old comrade of the war, Hans Waldhausen, who had been a prisoner of war but had finally been released by the British. He wrote to say he would arrive in Munich at 8 am on 19 November. Though four hours late, Waldhausen finally arrived at Munich railway station, to be greeted by a resounding 'Horrido!' from his old friend 'Kneckes' Udet. Without further ado, Udet took Waldhausen's luggage, installed him in the Park Hotel in Maximilian Platz, and both went off on a *Grossstadtbummel* – a giant pub-crawl. . . Waldhausen barely had time to even wash his hands! They started with a champagne breakfast offered by Director Otto and his charming spouse, and by the time the *Bummel* finally ended, it was almost noon again.

As an interested reader of the French aviation journal *La Vie Aérienne* (which had originally started as *La Guerre Aérienne* in October 1916), Udet was irritated by every issue reaching him four to six weeks late, coming via Switzerland. So he wrote to the journal editor, Jacques Mortane, asking him to send future issues direct. He also wrote that he had no objection to the journal publishing as a serial a version of his *Cross versus Cockade*, which it had begun publishing without bothering to ask Udet first! Then, in a postscript, he offered to return the *Cigogne* ('Stork') insignia he had taken from the Spad of Lieutenant J. Cael, whom he had shot down on 16 August 1918. Udet's letter, written in German, caused some consternation when received by *La Vie Aérienne*, a journal not noted for its love of 'Les Boches', but it was decided to print it in full in the journal.

At the close of the year, while strolling with his latest girl-friend, from Dresden, Udet met Waldhausen and von Greim at the Hotel Vier Jahreszeiten. He presented his latest love as his official fiancée, then, after some pleasant talk, the twosome disappeared upstairs, to the great dismay of the ultra-conservative von Greim. . . There were some things one simply did not do in 1919!

CHAPTER SIX

Udet Aviation Begins

On 5 January 1920 Otto Meyer was married, but Meyer, the driving force behind the growing Rumpler Luftverkehr, could not spare the time for a traditional honeymoon. A solution was quickly found by Udet – one of Meyer's few '*Du*' friends – and he took each of the newly-weds for a flight over Augsburg in one of the Rumpler Works' machines. On the same day, in Paris, *La Vie Aérienne* devoted no less than four pages to Udet. Not only were some of Udet's letters to the editor printed in full, but also some of his caricatures, a translation of an article written by him for the *Illustrierte Motor Zeitung*, and Lieutenant Cael's story of how he was shot down by the chivalrous Udet, and the aftermath treatment by the 'Boches'. In one of his letters Udet expressed the hope that Germany might play an important part in the development of civil air traffic. This gave rise to a sharp rejoinder by Jacques Mortane; 'The conditions of the Peace Treaty cannot leave any illusions to the German ace of aces (sic)'. The deep wounds caused by the war had by no means healed as yet...

That the Allies meant to exact revenge was felt clearly by all German pilots when the Versailles Treaty came into effect on 10 January. Nearly 15,000 aircraft and 28,000 aero engines were surrendered and ordered to be destroyed. Fuselages were burned, wings hacked into firewood with axes, airscrew blades sawn off, and one million square metres of hangars were broken up. Virtually no aircraft could be saved; the officers of the Inter-Allied Control Commission who took up their task on 22 February saw to that. Those stationed in Munich, with their offices above the Cafe Fürstenhof, offered generous rewards to anyone giving information about hidden war material, including especially aircraft.

Udet and von Greim's plans for further flying displays came to nothing; they could no longer fly their ex-fighters. Udet's new Pfalz D XV went to Max Holtzem, a former Jasta 16 pilot and Pfalz test pilot, who took it with him to Argentina. Dejectedly Udet visited the large hangar at Schleissheim. It was filled with destroyed air-

81

craft, some brand new, the floor littered with torn fabric and smashed plywood . . . a sad sight. In a desperate attempt to salvage at least a few military aircraft seven German police units were provided with an aviation complement – a *Polizeifliegerstaffel*. The Army Air Service provided necessary material and personnel, one of the latter being a certain Hauptmann Erhard Milch, an ex-observer who had commanded the volunteer Fliegerabteilung 412 fighting on the Polish border from April 1919, and had recently become commander of the East Prussia police *Staffel*.

Despite the explosive and turbulent tide of politics inside Germany then, Udet remained aloof from such matters. On 25 February 1920 he married his teenage sweetheart, Lo Zink, and attended the celebration at the Regina Hotel in his full wartime uniform, complete with his impressive array of medals and decorations. And it would not have been Udet if he had not fired a pistol shot in the hotel room on his wedding night! After their honeymoon trip, in a Rumpler Works' aircraft, the young couple went to live in a simple, five-room apartment in Widenmayer Street, alongside the west bank of the river Isar. Marriage did nothing to change Udet's habits and he remained as carefree and rash as ever. As a young war hero he was well known and loved in 'his' Munich, whose inhabitants were tolerant of his many pranks. For Udet it was nothing unusual for him to enter a bar and start to juggle with five or six glasses, or to enter a cafe where staid citizens were quietly playing billiards and, without asking, take a player's cue and demonstrate a number of difficult strokes.

In sharp contrast to Udet's carefree mode of life, the internal situation in Germany was poised on the brink of civil war, uneasy, threatening. On the day before Udet's wedding the German Workers Party organised a meeting of some 2,000 in the Hofbrauhaus, where the audience heard the party's new '25 points' from its most accomplished speaker, Hitler. A week later he was to force through a change of name for the party, which then became the NSDAP – Nationalsozialistiche Deutsche Arbeiterpartei – and adopted its future insignia, a swastika. . .

Amidst all the economic and social turmoil, however, the seeds of a future German air force were already being sown. In order to keep posted on military aviation matters a special branch – a *Referat* – was organised within the Truppenamt, the cover for the secret German General Army Staff under its chief, General Hans von Seeckt. Established on 1 March 1920, it was placed under the command of Hauptmann Wilberg by von Seeckt, who ordered him to study all matters pertaining to military aviation. Apart from Wilberg, the section comprised one sergeant and one employee. From such a tiny seed was to come – within 15 years – a new German air force, its aircraft bearing the swastika *insigne* so recently selected by an obscure political party. . .

For the moment, however, the Allies were still obsessed with destroying the old *Fliegertruppe*. Realising that Germany was delivering its war planes too slowly, the London Conference of Ambassadors decided on 22 June that manufacture and import of aircraft in Germany would only be permitted three months after Germany had fulfilled all its treaty obligations, and not, as previously decided, six months after signing the treaty. The Germans found a loophole. No mention was made in the treaty of gliders . . . ' if we're not allowed to fly with engines, then we'll fly without them'. From February to April 1919 *Flugsport*, a magazine published by Oskar Ursinus, had published a series of articles on gliding, and under Ursinus's initiative an initial gliding contest was organised for 15 July to 7 September at the old pre-war gliding site, the Wasserkuppe.

Gliding held no interest for Udet at that period; remembering his own short-lived experiences of ten years ago, he told his friend Waldhausen that he considered these latest attempts to be nonsense. Yet gliding offered the sole hope for Germans, including many ex-war pilots, who so passionately wanted to fly. Only a fortunate few could obtain a job flying converted war planes on regular air lines. Here again Udet was lucky, being asked by Meyer to fly for the Rumpler works. Severe limitations imposed by the Allies on German air traffic from June to September 1920 were then lifted, and Meyer set about expanding his aerial network. From 3 to 9 October special flights were set up between Frankfurt and Munich, Berlin and Leipzig, and more ambitious plans were afoot for eventual lines to Vienna, Rome and Constantinople.

Official inauguration of the Munich-Vienna route was scheduled for 20 October. Udet was to fly a Rumpler C I, D-138, with two passengers in an open cockpit. Gustav Basser, a veteran pilot also employed by Rumpler, was to fly a second Rumpler C I; while a third machine, D-103, was to be flown by Adolf Doldi. The latter aircraft had been converted to a 5A2 version, with the rear cockpit enclosed, and equipped with fabric and mahogany upholstery and furnishing. In front of each of the passenger seats a small mahogany cabinet had been provided, plus a speaking tube for passenger-pilot communication. A small ladder for easier access for passengers was always carried aboard. Otto Meyer had prepared for his new service carefully, obtaining permits from authorities in Berlin and Vienna; while newspaper publicity gave glowing accounts of the proposed flight.

During the morning the three aircraft, each painted in the Rumpler house colours of blue and black, were flown from Augsburg to Oberwiesenfeld, Munich, where a host of officials and onlookers awaited this first take-off of the new air line. Udet's passenger was his wife Lo; while the other passengers were three reporters and Rittmeister von Crailsheim. Edmund Rumpler and his director Otto Meyer proceeded by train to Vienna for the planned reception festivities.

Amid much solemn ceremony Ernie and Lo finally took off about 1 pm. Unforeseen strong headwinds plagued Udet from the start, slowing him down considerably; then, when still at least 100 kilometres away from Vienna, Lo suddenly spotted fuel streaming from a cock on the fuel tank. After several attempts to convey a warning to her husband Lo managed to get the message over, and Udet immediately planed down for a forced landing in a clover field near a small village at Blindenmarkt, some eight kilometres east of Amstetten. It was the following day before Doldi's Rumpler landed nearby with extra fuel for Udet's machine, and the news that his and Basser's machines had also been forced down through lack of sufficient fuel the previous day – none of the three had reached Vienna as planned! Both Rumplers then took off and finally reached Vienna and the reception committee of officials awaiting them there. Later the same day all three pilots flew briefly over the city, giving reporters flights and releasing leaflets publicising the new airline.

Then came the anti-climax – in the afternoon four officers of the Allied Entente arrived, comprised of Major Thomson (British), an Italian colonel, a Japanese officer and a French interpreter. These claimed forcefully that Allied authority in Berlin had not signalled any approval for the flight and that they had not even been asked for the requisite permission. In vain Edmund Rumpler denied these allegations; his aircraft were impounded in the hangar and refused permission to be flown out of Vienna. Furious and dismayed, the pilots and passengers were forced to return to Munich by train. Another two weeks were to pass before the aircraft were eventually allowed to be flown back, but it was the end of Rumpler's plans for international German airlines. And to emphasise the Allied determination to quash all forms of 'para-military' flying in Germany, all police squadrons were ordered to be disbanded from 8 November.

Many of those who had hoped to continue flying now left the various police squadrons, among them Erhard Milch who left his *Staffel* at the end of March 1921 to become a director of the Danziger Luftpost GmbH, a firm which a few months later was to become the nucleus of the aviation department of the Junkers firm. Resentment against the harsh terms of the imposed Versailles Treaty ran high throughout Germany, and it became the object of fierce hatreds. 'It is our duty to fight for Germany against the treaty; it is our duty to honour those that fought and gave their lives for our Fatherland' was a cry which rallied a vast majority of all Germans. Very few thought otherwise, especially not the many ex-wartime pilots in Bavaria who made up most of the membership of the Bavarian Flying Club. These regularly met on the second floor of the baroque Preysing Palace in order to honour old comrades and to give example to Germany's youth. In the evening of Thursday, 19 May, for example, lectures were held in the Lowenbräu Cellar. Last of the three speakers was the prominent Lothar Freiherr von Richthofen, brother of Manfred, the famous Red Knight, whose theme was, naturally, the Richthofen Jagdgeschwader. Lothar was to die on 4 July 1922 when his airliner, AEG D-148 crashed near Hamburg on a chartered flight from Hamburg to Berlin, carrying an American film actress and her manager.

The growing German nationalism became an ideal environment for the growth of a myriad of so-termed 'national parties' in political fields. Of these the NSDAP proved to be the most virulent, masterfully organised and led by its president Adolf Hitler. On 29 July he assumed full dictatorial powers within the party, and a few days later the NSDAP's mouthpiece, the *Völkische Beobachter* ('People's Observer') called him '*Der Führer*' (The Leader); the title was to stick. . . Much after the style of the defunct *Freikorps*, Hitler gave the party its own semi-military section; the SA (*Sturm-Abteilung*) whose members were virtually a personal bodyguard at the various meetings he addressed thereafter.

Ernst Udet had already proved his love for his country during the war, but chauvinistic nationalism was not for him. He had no desire to get involved with politics, and found more excitement in a fresh pastime; motorcycling. He loved motorcycle racing; driving fast cars was another hobby; but his greatest passion was for flying.

Aviation had been his lot, and aviation was going to be his lot; he was going to build aircraft! He had become acquainted with a fellow Municher Heinz Pohl, whose brother William had made a lot of money in Milwaukee, USA.

In the autumn of 1921 William telephoned Udet to arrange a meeting in Munich. Pohl saw a bright future for cheap light planes built in Germany, bearing the name of Germany's highest-scoring, surviving ace. Such a 'people's aircraft' might not only sell well in Germany but also in the USA. Udet cautiously accepted Pohl's proposal and rented a small workshop at Milbertshofen, near the Oberwiesenfeld. He then hired an engineer; lean-faced Hans Herrmann, a Rhinelander from Koblenz who had been a bomber pilot during the war. After the war Herrmann had studied engineering in Berlin, and now he started designing a simple single-seat, low-winged cantilever monoplane built entirely of wood. All strength and stress calculations were checked by Alfred R Weyl, an engineer of the German Experimental Establishment at Adlershof, who was to flee to England when Hitler came to power later.

All such work had to be carried out in secret as for the time being no aircraft construction was permitted in Germany, and officers of the Inter-Allied Military Control Commission were constantly on the lookout for any such clandestine activities. The workshop windows were curtained, wolf-traps placed in front of every window, and a bell installed which would ring as soon as the garden gate was opened. They were by no means the only people building aircraft secretly in Germany. In Bremen, for example, Heinrich Focke and Georg Wulf were constructing an aircraft in the cellar of the Focke Museum.

Then, on 1 February 1922, the Allies decided that construction of civil aircraft in Germany could commence from 5 May. The announcement of this decision included the reminder that the German government had, on 11 May 1921, taken upon itself an obligation to draw up a set of regulations, the famous *Begriffsbestimmungen*, distinguishing between pure civil and military aviation. Udet, anxious to expand his activities as soon as possible, consulted his friend Walter Angermund, German liaison officer with the Aviation Peace Commission in Munich. In the interim Udet had moved his 'factory' from Milbertshofen for the Allied Control Commission had got wind of it. Another friend and former pilot, Scheuermann, had a small workshop at Ramersdorf, a south-eastern Munich suburb, where since 1919 some 30 workers had (among other items) fabricated fuselages for gliders designed by Willy Messerschmitt. Scheuermann suggested that he become a partner in Udet's business and offered the hospitality of his Ramersdorf works.

Udet accepted this offer and began moving his stock. Finished parts, including wing spars, were hastily loaded onto a horse-drawn wagon and covered with a tarpaulin; then, in the middle of the night, rumbled through the deserted Munich streets with Udet and two others walking alongside to ensure nothing fell off! Finally 5 May arrived – Germans could build aircraft again, and openly. However, the terms of the *Begriffsbestimmungen* were crippling to initiative and possible real expansion. Among other stipulations these Rules laid down:

> Any single-seater with more than 60 horse-power is considered military and thus a war implement.
> Every aircraft that can fly without a pilot (sic) or with armour or provision for armament are considered military.

Then followed the excessive limitations on pure civil designs:

> Maximum ceiling under full power to be 4000 metres. Any aircraft equipped with a supercharger to be regarded as military.
> Maximum speed at 2000 metres under full power: 170 km/hr
> Maximum quantity of fuel & oil to be carried must not surpass 800 × 170/V grammes, V being the max speed at 2000 metres.
> Maximum useful load, including crew and instruments: 600 kilos.

Airships were also limited to certain maximum sizes.

The Allies' intention was plainly not only to prevent Germany ever building 'disguised' military aircraft, but also to seriously impede all progress in aeronautical development and thus air traffic within Germany. Fortunately for Udet, his harmless, if advanced design of sports single-seater was not affected by these stipulations, and on 12 May it was rigged for a final check. Only then did Hans Herrmann realise that his original calculations were astray – the engine should have been 47 cm further away from the centre of gravity! Hastily disassembling the aircraft – just eight bolts secured the fuselage to the wings – the wooden fuselage was lengthened, and by 16 May the modifications were completed. The finished U-I was then transferred, by road, to Oberwiesenfeld, where Udet – who had not flown for many months – was eager to test the red and white contraption. Despite a wildly vibrating engine, he taxied the U-I several times across the vast green field, then got airborne, made one wide circuit, and made a perfect landing. The first aircraft to be built by the Udet-Flugzeugbau had flown! Subsequent testing and fairly extensive press and magazine publicity augured well for the future. Professionally, Ernst's gamble on building aircraft in secret had paid off.

Udet's marriage, however, was less successful. Life with Udet was not easy. Throughout the war he had been constantly close to mortal danger, and simply could not now be serious about everyday living. Above all he had to be free, free to do as he pleased, whether married or not. In truth he was not suited to conventional married life; Ernie and Lo therefore decided to separate – amicably, for they continued to see each other thereafter. Lo's father had been loth to see his daughter marry a man of uncertain financial standing, and Ernst often jokingly claimed it had been the story of 'Des Vaters Fluch – 'The Curse of the Father' – and paraphrasing a Bible parable, sometimes described his wife Lo as 'Father Zink's Prodigal daughter'. Strange as it may seem, Udet never met Lo's father in his whole life.

Udet therefore vacated their apartment in the Wiedenmayer-strasse and, with Bulli, his black-and-white spotted dog, went to live in two rooms of the Hotel Vierjahreszeiten; the rent being paid by his firm. Here Udet's war souvenirs were soon adorning the walls. A machine gun, pieces of fabric from enemy aircraft brought down, cockades, serial numbers, the remains of propellers, dedicated photos and the like. He also installed a practice butt behind one door for his air rifle, being passionately fond of shooting. Many an unsuspecting visitor was dared to shoot a cigarette from Udet's mouth as he stood in front of this target. Few dared, but when it was Udet's turn to shoot he never missed.

His aircraft firm was registered on 23 October 1922 by Udet, together with the financial backer, Heinz Pohl, the designer Hans Herrmann, and Erich Scheuermann. The original capital put up was 100,000 marks – though these were by then worth only one-hundredth of their pre-1914 value. At Ramersdorf the work continued undisturbed. In December a second design was completed; the U-2, a two-seat development of the U-I, equipped with the same engine type, a 35 hp Haacke. Though no plans were made for building more U-I's, a small series of U-2's was started.

On 1 January 1923 Germany once more became master of its own skies. In accordance with Clause 320 of the hated treaty, Allied aircraft no longer held exclusive rights to land in or fly over Germany at will. Though certain restrictions were still put on actual construction of aircraft, people at the German Defence Ministry, in the utmost secrecy, sought contacts within the German aircraft 'industry'. Nevertheless, the general economic atmosphere in Germany was rapidly worsening. At the end of the war an American dollar could be bought for four marks. By January 1922 it cost almost 200 marks; in July, 4,000 marks; and in January 1923, a staggering 7,260 marks . . . and worse was to come. Such escalating inflation meant that Germany was simply unable to pay its imposed war debts, thereby incurring the wrath of the Allies. France decided to force Germany's hand by occupying its most industrialised area, the Ruhr; while Belgian troops entered Germany on 11 January. The German reaction was not long in coming; passive resistance, total shunning of the occupiers, and government-ordered strikes in the rail and postal services. All economic life in the Ruhr area broke down completely, while the rest of Germany suffered seriously. Inflation, already extremely serious, now rapidly assumed proportions never seen before in the world.

Unknown to the French, their act had another consequence. General Hans von Seekt immediately contacted the German Defence Minister, emphasised Germany's defencelessness against such foreign threats and actions, and persuaded him to order 100 Fokker D XIII's – one hundred of the world's finest fighters, powered by British Napier Lion engines! Paid for with money originally destined for impoverished workers, the aircraft were ostensibly for an unspecified 'South American' country. For the German navy, ten Heinkel He 1's were ordered equipped with British Rolls-Royce Eagle engines. These were to be assembled and test-flown in Sweden, then sent crated to Germany.

February 1923 also saw the end of Udet's marriage to his beloved Lo; a divorce was officially registered at the Landgericht I (County Court) of Munich on the 16th. Meanwhile work continued diligently in the modest wooden sheds at Ramersdorf. The Udet 'low-winger' had been the 28th design to be approved for manufacture in Germany under the rules of the Inter-Allied Control Commission. In April seven U-2's had already been built, as had the first example of the type's development, the more powerful U-4. The Haacke engine had proved to be under-powered for the U-2. Fortunately

Siemens and Halske AG, the engine firm of Spandau, had been developing engines for sport aircraft since 1921, and the U-4 was fitted with the 55 hp Siemens and Halske Sh-4, five-cylinder, air-cooled radial.

It was, of course, not enough to build aircraft; they had to be sold too. Due to the disastrous economic climate this became increasingly difficult to do inside Germany, so thoughts were turned to export. William Pohl's original idea had been to build cheap aircraft in Germany for sale in the United States, but this deal had not gone through. Now an invitation from the Argentine's *Circulo Aeronáutico Alemán* to participate in the 'Coppa Wilbur Wright' handicap race on 5 August drew attention to South America. Scheuermann was wildly enthusiastic. 'Why not demonstrate our aircraft in South America like Professor Junkers does?', he asked. Indeed in November 1922 Hugo Junkers, having made a fortune manufacturing hot water boilers, had sent an F-13 cantilever air liner to La Havanna, and it was slowly working its way along the South American east coast towards Buenos Aires, being demonstrated along the way.

Initially, Heinz Pohl did not like the idea. Demonstrating Udet aircraft so far away would cost him plenty of money. But eventually, after much discussion, he agreed. Ernst would go to Argentina, taking with him two aircraft, a U-2 and a U-4. As the latter would be entered in races it could be equipped with a streamlined upper decking to become a 'U-3' single-seat racer. Udet would give a number of public stunt-flying exhibitions, while Otto Heinecke, the well-known parachute manufacturer – a Heinecke parachute had saved Udet's life in June 1918 – who was also going to Argentina, would perform exhibition jumps at the invitation of the Aero-Club Argentina. Naturally, Udet would try to sell the aircraft, and would also investigate the possibilities of establishing a branch of Udet-Flugzeugbau in Argentina where the limitations by the Allies could not hamper development of modern aircraft.

It took a staggering amount of marks to pay for the gold pesos needed for the trip, but on 11 April Udet, as a first class passenger, sailed from Hamburg aboard the *Cap Polonio*. Two weeks later Otto Heinecke left on the *Antonio Delfino*. It was a long trip, more than three weeks, but finally the *Cap Polonio* arrived in Montevideo, Uruguay – the last stop before Buenos Aires – where Udet was effusively greeted by Max Holtzem who had come from Buenos Aires to escort Udet into that city. The two pilots had first met at

Le Cateau in March 1918, and also two years before at the Pfalz factory at Speyer where Udet had obtained the new Pfalz D XV used in his original flying displays, and which Holtzem was now using for displays in Argentina.

On 3 May the *Cap Polonio* docked in Buenos Aires, and Udet was welcomed exuberantly by two 'gentlemen' who introduced themselves as Senor Mayenberger, manager of the Circulo Aeronáutico Alemán, and Senor Pablo Salomon Leube, representative of the 'American Press'. Holtzem was puzzled. Though well-known in Argentina's aviation circles, he had never heard of these two men before. Yet the pair had made big plans for Udet, explaining these with eloquent gestures while pacing the deck. 'The very finest hotel in Buenos Aires, the Plaza, Senor Udet, the very finest. We have booked you in there.' '*Mein Gott!*', thought Udet, 'What's that going to cost me?' Life in Argentina was going to be very expensive if one had to pay its gold pesos with nearly worthless marks.

'We will take your aircraft to the Escuela de Aviación Militar at El Palomar airfield, the centre of the Servicio Aeronáutico del Ejercito. We'll pay the freight, of course, then you will demonstrate them at various airfields.' The two men spread out the red carpet for Udet with such superlatives that Udet took an instant dislike to both men.

Fortunately, there were other people who had come to welcome him, including many notable names in Argentina's aviation and sporting circles. After the greetings Udet went to the palatial Plaza Hotel. Next day he was driven to the offices of the 'Circulo Aeronáutico Alemán' – an organisation which proved to exist mainly on paper only – and there he was dismayed to hear the two men dictating his 'contract' as 'general representative of the Udet-Flugzeugbau', and was shown printed advertising posters. Udet was disturbed by all this but said little. For the next three weeks Udet was received by various organisations in aviation; then on 28 May the *Württemberger* docked in Buenos Aires, carrying the two Udet aircraft, and the real work could begin. The machines were transported by rail to El Palomar airfield and erected. Next day pilots of the Escuela and the navy formed an attentive audience as Udet lectured on aerial combat tactics; then all went to watch a demonstration parachute jump by Heinecke, followed by some aerobatics by Udet.

Various official receptions and invitations followed, and on 10

June Udet formally presented his two aircraft at San Isidro airfield, twenty kilometres north-west of Buenos Aires, at a well-prepared public demonstration. In front of a very large crowd, including the most notable aviation figures in the country, Udet and Heinecke, assisted by three local pilots, gave a brilliant display of aerobatics, including a mock dogfight. The press coverage did not please Udet and he told his 'managers' Leube and Mayenberger so in no uncertain terms. They made some thin excuses, then went on to suggest that Udet should fly some publicity flights. Already dismayed by the pair's so-called 'organisation', Udet refused point-blank, saying that he would only demonstrate his aircraft with a view to selling one or both machines.

Leube's reaction was threatening; 'May I remind you that we paid 1200 gold pesos rail freight charges, and that the freight papers of your aircraft are in the name of our organisation. When you repay this money, the freight papers will be yours; otherwise you will advertise a brand of cigarettes for us.'

Udet was stunned; he was caught in a trap. White with rage, he left abruptly.

Thinking over his dilemma, Udet then remembered one man who had welcomed him, Tornquist, an influential banker and a member of the railway board. Hopefully Udet approached him and Tornquist replied, 'Herr Udet, your birds have been the guests of the Argentine railways. I'll see to it that you get the proper papers, made out in your name'. Udet had been 'rescued' from his plight; he was again master of his 'birds', as Tornquist had jokingly termed the aircraft. Further flying demonstrations of the Udet aircraft received good press coverage, and he was approached by a wealthy local sportsman, Jorge Luro, who suggested that he (Luro) become the Argentine representative of the Udet firm, and also offered to pay cash to purchase the U-2 and U-4 on the spot. Udet's mission was thus complete, and he returned to Germany.

In Udet's absence in South America the Udet works had been forging ahead steadily. A second U-4 (D-203) had been built but it was to be the last of its type; its successor, the U-6 (D-325) was also completed. Retaining the Siemens and Halske engine, Herrmann had converted it to two separate cockpits and generally improved the lines of the wing and control surfaces. Maximum speed had been raised to 145 km/hr. In addition the finishing touches were being put to a fresh venture in Udet designs – a small air liner, or 'limousine' in contemporary language. The pilot sat in an open cockpit in front of the high wing, while its two passengers were enclosed in a 'cabin' under the wing. Udet-Flugzeugbau was by now a growing concern, employing a staff of twenty. Sales rights for its aircraft were obtained by a Hamburg-based firm, Bäumer-Aero; a firm founded by the wartime 43-victory ace and Pour le Mérite holder Paul Bäumer.

The attempt to sell Udet aircraft in South America was now followed by an effort to make them known in Europe. The first U-6 was exhibited by Bäumer-Aero in the aeronautical section of the Swedish Tercentenary Exhibition (ILUG) at Göteborg from 20 July to 12 August; the first truly international aviation exhibition since the war. Asked by *Aircraft Yearbook* for information on his firm and its products, Udet's reply gives an insight on the firm's progress, policies, and his personal views in general:

> The fundamental idea of Udet-Flugzeugbau is to make flying as cheap – and as profitable – as possible. The wonderful performance of the 40 hp Avro Baby proves that an aeroplane with a low-powered engine is capable of a good performance. The restrictions imposed on construction by the Commission of Control did the rest, and so in May of last year we brought out a small single-seater with a 30 hp engine. Its performance being completely satisfactory, we started series' production of our little parasol (sic) monoplane in July. Our weekly output at present is one machine. I believe we are the only firm apart from Junkers and Dornier to be constructing in series in Germany. Financially Udet-Flugzeugbau can be considered as one of the safest and best-established concerns of its kind in Germany. The pre-war pilot, Dipl Ing E Scheuermann, who during the war was managing director of the Bayerische Flugzeugwerke, Munich, is our technical manager, whilst I act as test pilot and carry out the experimental work on new machines. Designer Herrmann, at one time of the Aeronautical Experimental Department in Berlin, is head of our Experimental Office. . . . We are at present engaged in production of a three-seater limousine, with a 55 hp five-cylinder Siemens radial engine, with which we hope to achieve a speed of 160 km/hr. The price of a production machine of the small type is about the same as that of a British motor-cycle with sidecar.

Optimistic as this survey was for the Udet firm, the general economic situation in Germany was at this time going rapidly from bad to worse. The value of the mark was now diminishing not merely day by day but hour to hour. All wages, usually expressed in the current food prices e.g. 'three loaves of bread' were paid twice a day; marks paid in the morning were worth very much less by the afternoon! Prices were now expressed not in millions but billions. French and Belgian troops still occupied the Ruhr area, and the resistance offered by Germans was not always entirely passive. Germany had to give in. The general strike of all railway staff had failed because the Allies moved in a total of nearly 10,000 railwaymen from France and Belgium who effectively replaced the 170,000 German workers on strike. On 20 September Berlin finally ordered a cessation of the 'passive' resistance. The strike action had utterly failed and merely plunged Germany deeper into the economic depression.

In Bavaria resentment at being subservient to the wishes of Berlin ran high and plans were put into being for Bavaria to become independent from Germany, headed by its president, von Kahr. Such separatism was not to the liking of Hitler, who dreamed of one united Germany. At various large meetings Hitler manoeuvred for power, constantly proclaiming his ultimate desire to see Germany under one dictatorial regime – his. As a stepping stone to such power plans were made for a coup in Munich, and on 8 November the Nazi supporters were strategically placed all around the city, poised for a take-over. Next morning Hitler and his aides Hermann Göring and Rudolf Hess marched at the head of their troops into the city; only to be met by a hail of fire from the Munich police. Hitler fled and was later captured, while Göring was badly wounded and escaped to Austria along with Hess. The attempted coup d'état was over – at least for the moment. . .

Relative peace returned to Munich, where by now a US dollar was worth four billion marks. Then, on 15 November, the German government finally took effective steps to halt the galloping inflation by having all marks converted to *Rentenmark* – each worth one billion old marks. The financial nightmare was over and the shattered German economy slowly began to recover.

Winter was now on the scene, with all airfields carpeted in snow. Udet thought it was time for relaxing. Climbing aboard D-325, a U-4 fitted with ski undercarriage, he took off and flew towards the Alps. Here he leisurely enjoyed himself, cavorting among the mountains, around the Zugspitze, the highest peak of the Wetterstein range.

To export aircraft proved to be very difficult for the Udet-Flug-zeugbau, despite favourable comments on its products by foreign trade press. Neither was the initial success obtained by Udet in selling two aircraft in Argentina followed by further orders, even when Luis Luro won the Coppa Gobernador Cantilo with his U-4 on 24 May at Castelar airfield. In April a new type was rolled out at Ramersdorf, the U-8, a further development of the U-5 'Limousine'. Powered by the more powerful 100 hp Siemens & Halske Sh 12, three examples had been ordered by the Deutscher-Aero-Lloyd for use on its Hannover-Hamburg/Bremen and Munich-Garmisch/Berchtesgaden services. Other orders for this new design also came from Mexico, which in the meantime placed an order for a U-6 to be used for flying instruction at Enrique Schöndube's flying school. The Udet low-wingers, to a limited extent, were generally popular for schooling, being used too by Relakraft GmbH at Königsberg, Ortloff AG, Berlin, the Arbeitsgemeinschaft EV, Würzburg, Compania Argentina Aeroplanes Udet in Buenos Aires, and indeed by Udet himself in Munich.

On return from his Alpine sojourn, Udet decided to enter for a new race – the Ostpreussischen Samland-Küstenflug, at Königsberg airfield – flying a U-6. He was accompanied by his latest 'conquest', Gräfin Margot von Einsiedel, whose elegance and connections had brought a new dimension into Udet's life. Together they flew from Munich to Königsberg, via Leipzig, Berlin, Köslin and Danzig; a distance of 125 kilometres taking only ten hours' actual flying, less than half the time such a journey would have taken by train, and at approximately one-third of the cost per person. The event itself was a triumph for Udet-Flugzeugbau, with the first two places going to U-6's; Udet (1st) and Hailer (2nd). It had been hoped to enter the glider and motor-glider competition which preceded the race; while the intention to enter a new design, the U-7, 'Kolibri', piloted by Heppner, was frustrated by its lack of engine, a British Douglas motor-cycle engine which took three months to be finally delivered. On 31 May Udet tested the U-7, and next day attempted an airborne endurance flight; achieving a sustained flight of two hours and two minutes, thereby claiming a new record in this context, and incidentally collecting a prize bonus of 2,000 marks for his feat.

In early July the first U-8 airliner ordered by the Deutscher-Aero-Lloyd concern was ready for delivery. Udet decided to show what

D-417 could really do and, with Scheuermann as his passenger, left Schleissheim and streaked towards Fürth where, after a quick stop-over, he continued to Berlin. He reached the latter after three hours, twelve minutes' flying time at an average speed of 141 km/hr – the German press took notice. Though Udet-Flugzeugbau could see a future in building airliners, it did not abandon the light aircraft field. The low-wing, two-seat line had been constantly improved, and in July the latest development, the U-10, stood ready.* Exter-nally similar to its U-6 predecessor, the U-10 had increased wing surface and an increased useful load. Cockpit comfort had been improved, while a change in wing section resulted in a very short take-off and landing run.

The annual gliding contest – already assuming a very special place in German aviation – was about to be held for the fifth time, at Rhön centre. The 'soul' of such contests, Oskar Ursinus, in order to stimulate wider interest in ultra-light powered aircraft or powered gliders, decided to hold a special contest for these classes of aircraft. Here was a chance for the 'Kolibri'; Udet decided to enter, while his friend Paul Bäumer entered his B1 '*Roter Vogel*' specially built for this contest. Among others entering powered gliders was a young man from Bamberg, Willy Messerschmitt who, at the end of the previous year, had founded Flugzeugbau Messerschmitt Bamberg. He entered two powered gliders, the S-16a 'Bubi' and the S-16b 'Betti'; but in the event both were dogged by bad luck; the 'Bubi' being written off after losing its propeller, and the 'Betti' forced-landing after its drive chain broke.

Though plagued by bad weather and continuous rain, the meet-ing's main event commenced on 28 August. Winning both that day's contest and the following day's competition, Udet collected the 3,000 marks first prize, and a gold bowl offered by the *Landes-hauptmann* of Nassau. Udet-Flugzeugbau was quick to try to take advantage of the 'Kolibri's' good showing, and shortly after adver-tised the design, selling for 7,500 marks, as the 'undisputed victor of the Rhön Contest', but only two 'Kolibris' were eventually built.

Germany was by now rapidly recovering from inflation, and there was even hope that relations with its former enemies of the war would soon improve. Nevertheless the Allied powers first wanted reassurance that Germany was not re-arming, and on 8 September

* The U-9 design had been an amphibious flying boat project, the construction of which had by then been abandoned.

bout to set out in Rumpler C 1, D-138 from Munich to Vienna, 20
ctober 1919. Udet (bare-headed, centre) and his (then) fiancée
.o' (in white bonnet).

elow) The Udet U-2 converted for ski-undercarriage. (*Right*) Udet
th his friend and manager Walter Angermund, 1926 at Innsbruck.

Udet and Erhard Milch, in the cockpit of the U-II, Kondor airliner, the newly created
Lufthansa's first four-engined passenger design. The occasion was a press facility at Berlin's
Tempelhof on 6 April 1926.

'SCINTILLA'—Udet's Flamingo D-822 on the frozen Eibsee.

Marga von Etzdorff, Udet and Gerhard Fieseler at Staaken, April 1928.

Ace meets Ace. Udet with René Fonck, France's highest-scoring fighter pilot in WW1, in Paris 1928.

started a short but searching 'final' examination to ensure that Germany's military potential had not been altered since January 1923.

At Ramersdorf things were progressing well, and in October four U-10's and three U-8's had been built; the latter design, with the help of Dr Gustav Lachmann, an airliner equipped with wing slots of Lachmann's own design. Udet-Flugzeugbau were thus the first German firm to obtain licence rights for what became known as the Handley Page-Lachmann slotted wing.

On 12 October 1924, the day the Zeppelin LZ126, built at Friedrichshafen on the war reparation account for the US Government started its trans-Atlantic flight; Udet was in Rome. Flying a U-10, D-460, he had entered the classic Italian contest, the Coppa d'Italia – a competition for two-seat sports designs with engines of 80 hp maximum power. He gained an overall third placing among the four German, three Italian and one French participants. A few weeks later, in reply to a request for details of the Udet-Flugzeugbau's production figures to date, Scheuermann listed the exact number of Udet aircraft built at Ramersdorf:

One U-1 .... May 1922
Seven U-2 .... Dec 1922 to April 1923
Two U-4 .... April/May 1923
One U-5 .... July 1923
Seven U-6 .... July 1923 to May 1924
Two U-7 .... May 1924 to December 1924
Three U-8 .... April 1924 to October 1924
Four U-10 .... July to October 1924

Thus, in slightly more than two years, the firm had built 27 aircraft, an average of better than one per month.

At the same time Scheuermann elaborated on the firm's plans to build a series of large transport aircraft, military machines, and instructional designs. Sports designs, the activity upon which the firm had been initially launched, were to continue to be built despite the lack of a large market for such machines. And in the design stages already were the four-engined U-11 'Kondor' and the U-12 'Flamingo'. He next disclosed that, shortly, a prototype fighter was to be constructed, with a cantilever wing level with the pilot's eyes. It was hoped to employ a plywood fuselage and fabric-covered wing; if not, an all-metal construction was mooted. Its rather low power was to come from a six-cylinder BMW engine. The firm's policy was to aim for standardisation of as many parts as possible – control surfaces, engine mountings, etc – and much experience had already been gained in the design and construction of wooden propellers.

The firm seemed to be going from strength to strength, and its works were enlarged by the acquisition of a building bought from the Munich Zoo. An airline firm, the Süddeutscher Aero-Lloyd, had already ordered the first U-11 'Kondor'. This high-wing monoplane, fitted with four nine-cylinder Sh 12s engines of 100 hp each driving 'pusher' propellers, was overtly capable of transformation with ease to a four-engined bomber – indeed, it was secretly hoped that the Reichswehr might be persuaded to take an interest in such an 'Udet-bomber'. . . The U-12 'Flamingo' was quite a different aircraft; the first biplane designed by Herrmann built by the Udet firm. The rather limited success of the Udet low-wing monoplanes had been ascribed to the fact that most German flying instructors were ex-war pilots who preferred a biplane configuration rather than mono-planes. Further impetus for biplane designs came from the fact that during this year a total of ten civil flying schools had been inaug-urated throughout Germany by the Sportflug GmbH. Ostensibly to train civilian pilots, such schools also permitted ex-wartime pilots to keep their hand in; while the whole movement was heavily sub-sidised by the Ministry of Defence in Berlin. Thus, with high expec-tations, Herrmann commenced the design of what was to become the classic German trainer of the late 1920's and early 1930's.

Udet-Flugzeugbau was now an important firm, with plentiful plans – and, of course, plenty of money for Udet himself. He could well use the extra funds. Gräfin Einsiedel had moved with her two children and their maid into the Hotel Vierjahreszeiten, where Udet was in residence, and all her bills were promptly sent to him. Spending money came easy to Udet, though the lack of it on occa-sion never worried him at all. Life in the hotel was never dull when Ernst was about. A practice butt for shooting always hung behind his door and was used frequently – to the dismay of the hotel proprietor, especially when Udet exchanged his compressed-air rifles for real pistols and ammunition!

By the close of the year Udet had already had several disputes with Heinz Pohl, usually about matters of policy for the firm, and the types of aircraft to be built. In this Udet was not alone; Herr-mann also failed to see eye to eye with Pohl on occasion. In fact Udet was seeking a way out – he really wanted to devote himself solely to flying in future. Knowing that his long-time friend Walter

Angermund, whom he affectionately nicknamed 'Dicke' ('Fat One'), had grown disenchanted with his job at the Junkers Luftverkehr, Udet proposed that they got together – Udet to fly and Angermund to organise flying displays. 'Well, I might give the idea some thought,' replied Angermund coolly, but his mind was already busy, organising. . . .

Just before the end of the year, on 20 December, a certain political revolutionary was released prematurely from Landsberg gaol, instead of completing a five years' sentence for high treason. An unimportant event, perhaps, to the vast majority of the German population, but the man concerned was Adolf Hitler. . .

CHAPTER SEVEN

Displays

At 4 pm sharp three loud bangs reverberated over the vast plain, cannon shots signalling the start of the Rundflug 1925. The starter's flag went down and the first competitor was away, Nopitsch flying Udet Kolibri D-621, followed in quick succession by the other seven aircraft in Class A, among them another Kolibri, D-621, piloted by Ferdinand Schulz. Next to start were the 25 aircraft in Class B, including two U-10's, D-640 (Paul Billik) and D-660 (Hochmut). Finally, 16 aircraft in the heaviest class, including U-8, D-670 (Polte), two U-12 Flamingos, D-661 (Erich Kern) and D-681 piloted by Udet.

Dressed in a tweed suit, maps under his arm, Udet was about to climb aboard when he received a warm handshake from the Crown Prince, while all around a host of camera shutters snapped. Immediately after leaving the ground Udet made a sharp, low turn to the right to go on course, not bothering to gain height.

On take-off the weather had been fine, but it quickly deteriorated with high winds, violent rainstorms lashing at the tossing aircraft, forcing them lower and lower. Soon several were forced to land, lacking fuel, but Udet continued in the teeth of winds reaching 70 km/hr, until near Osnabrück, his engine failed completely and he forced-landed, standing the Flamingo on its nose and shattering the propeller. A frantic telephone call to Berlin for help resulted in Udet eventually arriving at Tempelhof the following day; with all hopes of winning gone, though he still intended to finish the various stages.

The second circuit, starting 2 June, was completed by Udet, but was won by the ex-commander of Jagdgeschwader 3, Bruno Lörzer, in a Daimler L-21, D-623 twin-engined light plane specially designed for the Rundflug, and designed by the brilliant young engineer Hans Klemm. The third circuit saw a total of 40 entrants get away, of whom only 14 completed the stage on the same day; forced landings claiming the remainder, including Udet who spent the night at Bamberg. On 6 June, from Tempelhof, 35 competitors took off for the fourth circuit and Udet managed to return to Berlin the same day on completion; ready for a planned flying display next day, in which his immaculate exhibition of aerobatics drew huge applause from the assembled crowds. Finally, on 8 June, came the start of the final circuit of the Rundflug competition, with 37 competitors still in the running. At the end of the day 32 aircraft had flown the prescribed 5,242 km. Though only awarded a minor prize, Udet had made many new acquaintances, and renewed a host of old wartime friendships throughout the competition.

The 1925 Rundflug was over, but Udet's flying displays continued. On 19 July he flew at Leipzig; then Naumburg; and on 27 July gave a daring aerobatics demonstration at Bamberg where a trade fair was in progress. A novelty at the latter display was Udet's demonstration of picking up a load in full flight. Then on to Wurzburg to participate in the 3rd Bavarian Flyers' Memorial Day. This occasion was tragically marred when 38-year-old Hauptmann Nopitsch, while attempting a flying mail-bag pick-up, crashed and died in hospital the same evening. Thursday, 3 September saw Udet giving a breathless display of superlative flying at the Bavarian town of Rosenheim* in front of a crowd of some 5,000 local spectators.

Three days later Udet, flying Flamingo D-733, gave a memorable display at Vienna's Aspern airfield before an audience of at least 50,000; drawing high praise from the local press. But, after the Rundflug, the year's second most important aviation contest of 1925 was scheduled to take place from 12–14 September at Udet's 'home' – Munich. No less than 61 pilots put in their participation application forms, including Udet who was to pilot Flamingo D-681. Twelve of the aircraft being flown were Udet-Flugzeugbau designs, including a U-10 to be flown by the firm's new test pilot, Alexander von Bismarck, a distant relation of the legendary Iron Chancellor. This Munich meeting was of great personal importance to Ernst, who wanted fervently to show 'his' city that Udet was the very best pilot around. In the event he came only third in the aerobatic display placings, to his bitter disappointment.

Undaunted, however, Udet demonstrated his ability at Böblingen on 27 September; then returned to Innsbruck in Austria for the Tyrol capital's Autumn Fair on 4 October. The weather that day was fine but turbulent with gusting winds, and as Udet commenced

---

* Rosenheim was the birthplace of Hermann Göring, who, only two days previously, had been committed to a lunatic asylum at Langbro; suffering from severe drug addiction.

a series of successive and ever-lower loops the winds tossed his aircraft about. After the fifth loop Udet came out of it a mere three metres above the ground, where a down draught pushed him into the earth. The propeller hit the grass and the Flamingo tipped on to its back, trapping Udet underneath. At the first touch Udet instinctively shut off the fuel cock, and there was no fire. Rescued from his wrecked machine, Udet was only lightly injured, a few bruises, and that evening he took a full part in the customary celebration banquet.

On 24 October Udet took off from Schleissheim, accompanied by his mechanic Bernard Johnen, in the repaired D-733, heading for Graz in Austria, where he was due to participate in the Austrian Aeroclub's display next day. Angermund, of course, was already there, making all necessary arrangements. The flight proved to be a dangerous, difficult one. Violent headwinds, fog and low clouds forced Udet to land after barely 100 kilometres, at Bad Reichenhal. Taking off again, he was forced to fly low, and about thirty minutes later a steep hill suddenly appeared through the mist, forcing him to bank steeply and barely avoid a crash; the forbidding Trisseler-wand near Alt-Aussee had almost claimed another victim. Udet was now lost again, and decided to land to establish his whereabouts. He spotted a likely-looking meadow, but stood the Flamingo on its nose, shattering the propeller. It turned out that they were at Aussee, near the Totes Gebirge – 'Dead Mountain'. . . Luckily the engine appeared undamaged, and they replaced the broken prop with the spare carried, and were soon off again. Keeping very low in the Ennsvalley, Udet barely scraped over the Schoberpass to follow the Liesing and Mur valley. Shortly after 2 pm Thelerhof airfield, near Graz, hove into view and an uneventful landing completed the flight. The route through the Alps taken by Udet had never been flown before.

The students at the flying school – who were mainly responsible for the organisation of the Graz display – quickly made friends with Udet, and he accepted an honorary membership; thereby entitling him to wear the special *Fliegerschaft* cap of their association. Sunday, 24 October dawned bright and clear, and at noon Udet took off to distribute 20,000 leaflets advertising the display, and eventually some 12,000 spectators were massed expectantly on the airfield. Again, Udet was the hero of the day with his usual masterly flying exhibition; while in the intervals aerial joyrides were available in two Junkers F-13's, and Herr Duschner jumped by Heinecke parachute for the 68th time in his career. Prizes were offered – 50, 30 and 20 schillings – for those spectators who could accurately judge Udet's height in his Flamingo when a Very light was fired – only one winner was accurate in guessing 350 metres. Only when the first long shadows crept across the airfield did the spectators begin to leave – another working day was over for Udet.

That evening a large banquet was held in the Hotel Wiesler for Udet and the various organisers and local dignitaries. The last speech was by Generalkonsul Müller who concluded his comments by saying 'Udet is a symbol for all of us'. Next morning Udet prepared to return to Munich but found that the *Benzol* fuel needed for his Siemens Halske engine was scarce in Graz. The problem was solved by his friends, who set out on a begging hunt for the precious liquid – a litre here and a litre there – until sufficient had been gathered in. In gratitude Udet proceeded to give them – two at a time – free flips in his aircraft, including an occasional loop. Then, at 1 pm, the red and white Flamingo disappeared towards the north-west.

On 9 November Udet again left Schleissheim, this time in a new Flamingo D-563, with Johnen as passenger, bound for Italy to take part in the Coppa d'Italia series of races. Atrocious weather conditions turned the trip into a long series of frustrated attempts to complete the journey through the Alps, and he eventually arrived in Rome five days later. After the competition Udet had to make an emergency landing during his trip back to Germany, but then realised he had no money on him to pay his necessary expenses. In a typical Udet solution to such a situation Ernie unloaded the 'singing saw' he was carrying aboard the Flamingo, walked to the nearest *albergo*, gave a mini-concert of 'saw music', and returned half an hour later with sufficient cash to enable him to continue his journey. . .

By this time Germany's international status was markedly improving. The spirit in which the various treaties signed at Locarno in October signalled the start of an era of confidence and understanding between the more powerful European countries. Germany was no longer the outcast. Hitler still ranted against the Versailles Treaty terms which continued to restrict the size of any army to 100,000, and forbade the formation of a German air service; and on 9 November an autonomous formation within the Nazi Party came into being; the *Schutzstaffeln* – SS – which now became the personal bodyguard of the self-styled *Führer*.

A few days after the notorious SS was formed Germany brought
home the body of its most illustrious flier of the recent war, Rittmeister Manfred Freiherr von Richthofen. He had been buried in
April 1918 in Fricourt Cemetery where more than 18,000 German
soldiers lay. Now he was brought home in a special train, and
throughout Germany all flags and banners were flown at half-mast.
A catafalque was set up in the Gnadenkirche in Berlin, and thousands of Germans filed past to pay their respects to the dead hero.
On 20 November they gave Richthofen a state funeral; his coffin
being borne on the shoulders of eight former pilots, each a holder
of the Pour le Mérite, including Udet, to the final resting place set
aside in the Invaliden Cemetery. Just sixteen years and one day
later Udet too was to be buried here. . . .

Though Udet himself was no longer with the Udet-Flugzeugbau,
the company was going well, employing some 130 people, and was
the third largest aircraft manufacturing company in Germany. The
ambitious U-11 Kondor was nearing completion and taxying trials
were imminent. It was a four-engined airliner of modern concept,
capable of carrying 11 passengers, and a giant design, with provision
for two pilots in an open cockpit. It was in fact a dual-purpose
design; perfectly capable of conversion to a bomber, and there were
secret hopes that the Defence Ministry would show an interest in
such a development. There was also a promising future for the Udet
Flamingo design, as a training aircraft for the clandestine German
air force. The firm's future was indeed bright, reflected in the large
royalties being paid to Udet for each aircraft sold.

Even without these generous royalties Udet had had an outstanding year financially. His flying had brought in some 140,000 marks,
including 80,000 from 17 displays, 38,000 from prize monies, and
some 21,000 from publicity and other flights. In addition Udet was
by now recognised as Germany's most outstanding flier – virtually
a legend in his own lifetime, and an accepted authority on the
subject of aerobatics. After his first public demonstration of the
Flamingo, in April at Regensburg the press had hailed Udet as 'the
symbol of the old fighting Germany'; while Angermund, Udet's
constantly active manager, saw to it that Udet's name was publi-
cised where and whenever possible.

In January 1926 Udet, flying a Flamingo fitted with ski undercarriage, was one of the first to make use of a new airfield – the frozen

lake at St Moritz, the fashionable winter resort. Meanwhile Hitler's NSDAP organisation, some 27,000 members strong by the end of 1925, was hopelessly divided internally due, mainly, to Hitler's absence in prison. To remedy this Hitler organised a party meeting at Bamberg on 14 February, and in a brilliant display of demagogy he succeeded in uniting his party again, and at the same time had himself recognised and acknowledged as the sole *Führer* to whom all party members were to owe allegiance – a unique position he was never to lose until his death almost twenty years later.

On a lesser level another man of the future, Erhard Milch, also consolidated his status. The Lufthansa had been officially founded on 6 January 1926, though during the winter months all flying was cancelled in order to smooth out its organisation. When, on 6 April, flying was resumed, Milch used the occasion to hold a huge press facility, attended by many dignitaries. He addressed them standing in the open cockpit of the recently-delivered U-11 Kondor, the Lufthansa's first four-engined airliner.

In the spring Udet finally obtained his own Flamingo, D-822 (c/n 269), its fuselage painted all red, with silver wings. The first display in the new season was at Halle at Easter. Here his new Flamingo was rammed by another aircraft landing, and Udet had to borrow another Flamingo, D-829 owned by the Krone Circus for his Easter Monday display at Staaken airfield, Berlin. On 18 April it was Jena's turn to see Udet and his D-822, where an audience of many thousands watched Udet's display of aerobatics, and the feats of a parachutist Meisterknecht. After Jena came Ernst's 'home' town, Munich. The event here, organised in aid of the Haunersche Kinderspital – a children's hospital – took place on the Oberwiesenfeld and drew some 30,000 paying spectators – and an estimated 50,000 non-paying onlookers outside the enclosure. . . Several Lufthansa aircraft, including the U-11 Kondor, gave joy-rides throughout the day, while another attraction was a lady parachutist, Miss Nelly Tussmars.* But the star of the show, as ever, was Udet – the 'red air-devil' as he was described in the press reports.

On Thursday, 13 May Udet participated in a large flying meeting at Sterkrade airfield near Holten, one of Germany's first flying venues. Spectators were offered a formation flight, followed by aerobatics by a trio of Dietrich DP IIa's from the Auffahrt Flying School,

---

* Three years later, on her 71st parachute jump at Chur in Switzerland she was killed.

including one flown by the ex-30 victory ace Harald Auffahrt himself. These were followed by more aerobatics from Udet in Flamingo
D-822 and his close friend Paul Bäumer in another Flamingo D-
296. The highlight of the day was the mock dogfight between Udet
and Bäumer in their Flamingos; a superb exhibition of tightly-con-
trolled twisting, turning manoeuvring as each attempted to fasten
on his 'opponent's' tail. The day closed with joyrides for paying
spectators in the various Junkers and Focke-Wulf aircraft in
attendance.

That evening a banquet was waiting for the participating pilots
in the Kaisersaal, laid on by the display organisers. Udet entered
the banquet room with Fräulein Thea Rasche, a former pupil of
Bäumer's who was now Germany's first woman aerobatics pilot.
On each seat at the festive tables was an *Esskarte*, entitling each
guest to one supper, one bottle of wine, cigars, cigarettes etc. Udet,
with a twinkle in his eyes, immediately collected each card and gave
them to the head waiter. 'How much are these worth?' he asked.
'Give us ten bottles of champagne instead'. From that moment the
well-organised reception turned into a highly boisterous evening of
celebration. . .

Three days later Udet was en route to Budapest. Earlier in the
year the Hungarian government had ordered five Flamingos for
evaluation alongside five Bristol Type 83 primary trainers at the
Hungarian Central Flying School where pilots received initial training for national airlines and, in secret, military flying. Later this
order was augmented by seven more machines, and later still twelve
more. At first some difficulty was met in finding suitable pilots to
ferry the Flamingos from Munich to their destination at Szombathely, Hungary, but this was soon solved. One ferry pilot was
Waldemar Kenese who, ten years later, was to become director of
the Royal Hungarian Aviation Bureau; while another was an ex-
wartime observation pilot Hans Baur, one of the first pilots in the
Lufthansa.

On 21 May he was in Vienna again, performing above a crowd
of 30,000 paying spectators – and unnumbered free-wheelers. Two
days later, the Austrian Aero Club awarded Udet their Gold Sports
Medal in appreciation of his services to aviation. While he was
thrilling the Viennese crowd, in Paris on 22 May, an agreement was
signed between representatives of the Allied Council of Ambassadors
and the German government to bring to an end the restrictive
Begriffsbestimmungen order which had so severely limited past con-

struction of aircraft in Germany. The new agreement was made public on 16 June. Henceforth all types of aircraft could be manufactured, with certain reservations on construction and import of modern 'racing' designs; these being subject to special sanction by the German authorities. On the reverse side of the picture, however, the government could no longer directly subsidise sports flying, and this meant the end of the *Sportflug GmbH* whose flying schools had previously been financially supported officially. Seventy-two officers of the Reichswehr (Armed Forces) were permitted to take part in sports flying at their own expense, and the services could take an official 'interest' in the subject. This was modified later to allow potential officers to learn to fly at government expense before commencing military careers.

By June the flying season was in full swing, with Udet appearing at virtually every important display and meeting; Krefeld, Würzburg, Karlsruhe, Baden – all witnessed the red Flamingos piloted by Ernie in his normal superlative manner. While all this was going on, the rising Nazi Party took a further step towards its future; on 4 July the Hitler-Jugend – the Nazi youth organisation – was officially inaugurated during the Party Day of that date.

Also looking to its future was the German navy. The lifting of the construction ban on aircraft allowed the air staff of naval higher command to organise a competition – the *Seeflugwettbewerb* – at Warnemünde from 11 to 21 July. Officially it was a competition for civil postal seaplanes, but in reality it was a trial for naval reconnaissance aircraft of all types. Prize monies totalling 360,000 marks enticed a batch of 17 entries and the trials were won by D-937, a Heinkel HEa, equipped with British 450 hp Napier Lion engines, and flown by Oberleutnant zur See a. D. von Gronau. The competition interested most German aircraft manufacturers – future naval contracts might result – and firms like Dornier, Rohrbach, Heinkel, Junkers, LFG and the Udet-Flugzeugbau all began preparing special designs to participate. At Ramersdorf Hans Herrmann set out to design the U-13, but only one example was built, D-945, equipped with a 600 hp BMW VI engine. It was to be the last aircraft built by the firm.

Design difficulties, particularly with the propeller, delayed U-13's completion and it failed to take part in the naval trials; a bitter disappointment for its makers. Nevertheless, plans for the immediate future of Udet-Flugzeugbau hinged on the selection of another, more suitable base for the works – Ramersdorf had no airfield within

reasonable distance – hence it was decided to abandon Scheuermann's original factory site. A number of municipalities were
approached where suitable airfields existed. Munich appeared to be
disinterested, but finally Augsburg was chosen. A contract was
drawn up to the effect that the town of Augsburg would acquire the
old Rumpler works and then sell the workshops to Udet-Flugzeugbau, while the adjacent airfield would remain the town's property,
leased for 99 years to the aircraft firm. Before any signatures could
be put to this contract, financial tragedy struck.

Development and construction of so many diversified types as the
U-11 and U-13 had eaten up large amounts of money, necessitating
recovery through substantial orders. These, with the exception of
the Flamingo, were extremely doubtful in forthcoming. Cash had
run out, large debts had been incurred, and the bank Merck, Fink
& Co alone had invested 800,000 marks on which no dividends
could be paid. There was also no hope of repaying the subsidies
paid by the Bavarian State Government and the Defence Ministry.
The bank, government and ministry held a series of talks and then
decided to form a new firm to take over the financial ruin; on 30
July this was founded, the Bayerische Flugzeugwerke AG (BFW)*.
Series production of the Flamingo was prepared at Augsburg, the
testing of the U-13 continued under the aegis of BFW on the Starn-
berger lake until the aircraft was destroyed during these tests later
in 1926. The shareholders then decided to liquidate Udet-Flugzeugbau on 24 August 1926. For Udet it meant the end of the flow of
royalties – he now had to earn his whole living by flying.

This Udet proceeded to do; on 1 August he was in Mannheim;
the following Sunday at Chemnitz; the next week-end at Villingen
– he became extremely busy. The last venue was almost impossible
– Udet was in bed with a high temperature, and the doctor even
had to resort to pumping out his stomach. It was only on the Sunday
morning that his red D-822 appeared over the town, dropping
publicity leaflets for an exhibition at Dusseldorf. On Sunday, 29
August it was the turn of Fürth to watch Ernst's immaculate flying.

'The master-flyer, the artist of the air, the man who shot down
62 aircraft, and the man who makes flying a delight. . .' burbled the
local press announcing his display at Fürth-Nürnberg airfield.

---

* Not to be confused with the defunct Bayerische Flugzeug-Werke established in
1916 by the Albatros Werke GmbH in Munich which had been closed down shortly
after its foundation.

Sunday, 8 September brought what was in all probability the largest flying display ever held in Germany to date. The venue was Berlin's Tempelhof aerodrome. Spectators were estimated to number 200,000, among them Udet's friend the Crown Prince. By noon the airfield was already flooded with thousands, and the display opened with the release of 3,500 carrier pigeons. Among other novel demonstrations was the flight by Frank T. Courtney in Juan de la Cierva's revolutionary 'Autogiro'. The unique aircraft intrigued Udet who immediately expressed a wish to try his hand at its controls. Courtney, however, had private doubts on the craft's blades' reliability and therefore discouraged the idea. This event was followed by no less than six aerobatics pilots – Udet, Bäumer, Poss, Weigel, Joachim von Hippel and Fräulein Thea Rasche. Of these Udet drew the loudest applause when he performed his now-famous engineless inverted flying, and when he looped around a cable suspended between two balloons.

A display at Karlsruhe on 20 September proved to be a black day. After completing his full programme of flying, Udet then took off carrying a demonstration parachutist, Otto Fusshöler, a 20 years old student from Landau studying in Leipzig. At a height of 380 metres the boy clambered out onto the lower wing, sat for a moment, then jumped. His Heinecke parachute failed to open and he plunged to his death.

In Germany generally there was now the prospect of a few prosperous years ahead. Though the working classes were still in an unenviable position, for those with money it was a golden era; investments brought rich returns and quickly. In September 1926 Gustav Stresemann, the German Foreign Minister, saw the fulfilment of a personal dream when his country was admitted to the League of Nations. It was also a period of expansion for Hitler's NSDAP which, by the close of the year, could boast 108,000 members; four times its previous year's membership. Hitler's awareness of the influence of public orations had the NSDAP organise its own school for orators before the end of this year.

Udet too was aware of the necessity of publicity; it was his bread and butter. As long as he remained in the public's eye, he was in business – well-paid business. It would obviously benefit him if he could make a really spectacular flight of some sort. One constant temptation was the 25,000 dollars' prize offered by Raymond Orteug, hotel owner and philanthropist, some seven years before for the first pilot to make a non-stop flight between New York and Paris, a distance of about 3,600 miles. No serious attempt had been made on this for some time, although the French 'ace of aces' René Fonck was preparing for just such a flight at this time. However, Fonck's second attempt to take off in the Sikorsky S-32 on 21 September ended in a crash and the deaths of two crew members in the flaming wreckage of the huge aircraft.

In Germany serious thought had been given to a trans-Atlantic attempt by Dr Ing Adolf Rohrbach, an ex-Zeppelin engineer who founded his own aircraft firm in 1922 in Copenhagen; an arrangement which obviated the treaty restrictions on aircraft design and construction. Like most specialists, Rohrbach was convinced that the ideal aircraft to fly the Atlantic must be a flying boat. Such an attempt would require an excellent pilot – Udet perhaps? For the moment, however, Udet had too many commitments to fulfil.

Hof, a small town on the river Saale, had a number of flying enthusiasts, all members of the DLV, and these had long hoped to get Udet for a local flying display. Finally a date was agreed, 10 October. Together with Kern, Udet set out on the week before but made a stop en route at Heinersgrün where they became the guests of Freiherr von Feilitzsch; then flew to Hof next day. The town reminded Udet of a wartime friend in the Richthofen Jagdgeschwader, Leutnant Hans Weiss, who had been born in Hof, the son of a sculptor, and who had been killed in action on 2 May 1918. His subsequent display on the 10th led the local papers to write that it was a never-to-be-forgotten spectacle to see Udet's red machine cavorting against a background of black clouds crossed by a brilliant rainbow.

Nevertheless the day had not been successful from the financial point of view for its organisers, with little more than 1,000 marks being paid at the ticket booths. According to their contract with Udet they owed him 3,000 marks for his fee! Udet, who with his many friends was celebrating in the Hotel Strauss that evening, the problem was simply solved. When the organisers showed him the actual amount collected, he merely took the 1,000 marks, gave half to Kern, then returned to his table and drank the health of all present. . .

The 1926 display season was by now virtually over, and Udet began investigating the possibilities of forming another aircraft manufacturing firm. The Frankfurter Flugplatz-Gesellschaft invited him to build his works at their airfield, while the local press reported that Udet was seriously considering the possibility of leaving Munich for the town where he was born. The end of the display season also brought relief for the various police forces all over Germany – Udet was becoming notorious for his flying pranks! In particular he had a penchant for flying under bridges; across the Rhine at Dusseldorf, across the Isar at Munich, where he even flew between the twin towers of Frauenkirche and Ludwigskirche. Came December and Ernie made his first trip to France since the end of the war. Though mainly to visit the 10th Salon International de l'Aéronautique, he had also been invited to address the Union of French Civil Pilots (UPCF) on the subject of the state of aviation in Germany.

Due to take place on 13 December in the lecture room of the newspaper *Le Journal*, the announcement of this talk produced threats of demonstrations by local Frenchmen who still hated the '*Boches*'. The UPCF President, Claude Marcel Haegelen, a 23-victory wartime ace, and now Hanriot's chief pilot, made it clear that no hostile demonstrations would be permitted. Thus anyone wishing to enter was closely scrutinised. Udet spoke of the various aspects of Germany's aviation scene – the revival of the industry, gliding, powered gliding, metal construction methods, seaplane trials at Warnemünde, Prandtl's theories, etc. Then, as a finale, he showed his attentive audience two films, the first showing Udet flying his Flamingo in every facet of his normal aerobatics display programme, and the second showing the Udet Kondor flying majestically over the Alps.

When the lights went on again, the applause was warm, and many of those present wanted to shake his hand. It was strange to Ernst – just eight years before they had been shooting at each other, now they were chatting gently together.

Financially the year 1926, in which his old friend Otto had died, had been a good one for Udet. Before taxes he had earned a quarter of a million marks; from publicity flights for firms advertising chocolate, soap, matches, oil, toothpaste etc, royalties on Flamingo sales, and not least the actual displays which alone brought in some 170,000 marks. Yet there were still times when Udet was practically broke! His friends quipped that when Ernst had 3,000 marks, he spent 4,000. . . Udet's free-spending was exemplified by the occasion when a well-known toy aeroplane manufacturer paid him a 500-mark advance royalty for the use of his name for their products. Ernie immediately took some friends to a *Lokal* (public house), collected some girls, and spent the lot. He then returned to his benefactor, obtained a second advance of 500 marks, and when dawn broke next day this sum had also 'disappeared'. . . . His latest mistress was only too willing to help him to spend all his earnings; indeed, Udet spent vast amounts on her, in return for small scraps of paper bearing her signature, the amount and the date – worthless receipts.

Udet found a new winter airfield in the Alps, the frozen Eibsee; a beautiful small lake of only 1.8 square km, nine kilometres from Garmisch, with the Zugspitze forming an impressive background. It had been privately owned by the Terne family since 1884, was surrounded by tall pines, with only the one hotel on its shores, also Terne-owned. It was all so convenient. The Flamingo was left on the lake while Udet and the Countess stayed at the Alpenhof in Garmisch, along with Angermund and his other friends. On a particular night in February the nightly celebration was more exuberant than usual – his mistress, without explanation, calmly left Udet and drove away with a new *beau*, a racing car driver! Two months after her disappearance, however, Udet's good friend Angermund also left Munich and moved to Berlin, where he became the new head of the Lufthansa's publicity department. The two parted in good friendship, but now Udet had to fend for himself.

Around this time the publishers of the *Münchener Illustrierte* devised a huge publicity stunt. Germany's best-known pilot was to take off from Germany's highest peak, the Zugspitze. A glider had been specially built for this – designed by the ever-smiling P. Zarbl and built at Ramersdorf by a small team headed by Kern. On 7 April the machine was completed and transported eventually to Ehrwald, a small Austrian village at the foot of the Zugspitze. It had been particularly designed for Alpine conditions, having a smaller span than was usual, but with a safety factor of 12; twice the normal factor for gliders. The sponsors' name was painted in large letters on the fuselage side, while on the top of its nose was the winged-U *insigne* of the Udet-Flugzeugbau.

Udet planned to have himself launched by shock-cord from the Zugspitzplatt, an inclined plateau sloping eastwards from 2700 metres to 2000 metres. Ideally he needed a good easterly wind which would create an up-draught over the snow-covered incline, enabling him to gain altitude and fly northwards and eventually crossing the Alps to reach the plains below. The whole project was to be filmed

by a Munich kinematograph firm. Starting on 14 April the various
sections of the glider were taken up the mountain, but a series of
accidents and weather conditions delayed the actual gliding attempt
until 29 April. As that day dawned bright and clear, with hardly a
breath of wind, Udet and his maintenance team set to work to
retrieve the glider from the thick layer of snow which covered it; the
aftermath of two days of snowstorms. Once clear, the glider was
dragged to the top of the incline and Udet prepared for his flight.
The lack of an east wind was worrying; would there be any up-
draught at the edge of the plateau? Below lay an abyss some 1,500
metres deep. . .

Udet climbed into the snug cockpit, then gave the order to let go.
The four men holding the cord splayed out into a Vee as quickly as
possible, down the snow-covered slope, parallel with – and only
yards from – the gaping precipice. Behind the glider three strong
men, mountain guides from Ehrwald, held the rope holding back
the glider. At Udet's command the rope was cut and the glider shot
forward . . . slowly gained speed . . . began to get airborne . . .
reached the edge of the plateau. Immediately Udet did a tight left
turn – then the earth suddenly fell away beneath him; one minute
he was sliding over snow, the next flying over a yawning drop of
1,500 metres . . . it was a peculiar sensation for Udet.

The slight up-draught allowed Udet to circle and gain a few
metres' height, but any prolonged flight was out of the question.
After a few S-turns over the cheering crews below, he began to glide
downwards, circling the Zugspitznase and reaching the north side
of the mountain, from where he flew over the frozen Eibsee. Then
southwards again towards the green valley, circling above the lower
cable car terminal at Ehrwald, and making a smooth landing after
a 32-minutes' flight on a meadow behind the Drei Mohren Hotel
between Lermoos and Ehrwald. The stunt was successful.

There now came a big change in Udet's life; he moved from
Munich to Berlin. The Berlin of the Golden Twenties, one of the
spiritual and cultural centres of Europe where new ideas and new
'art' forms blossomed in an ultra-liberal climate. Berlin with mem-
ories of the *Adlershof-Vergleichsfliegen* and being pampered by the
magnates of the aircraft industry of 1918. Berlin where high-priced
whores slapped their riding boots with leather whips as they saun-
tered elegantly along the streets. Berlin where Georg Grosz made
biting caricatures of the 'new way of life' in the big city where age-
old taboos had been thrown overboard. Berlin – where his seven-

year-old illegitimate son lived. . . Udet soon found accommodation
in a two-room, furnished apartment at 6 Bendlerstrasse. Alongside
the doorbell he put a plate with his name and occupation: Aerobatic
and private pilot.

Here he met his old friend Walter Angermund, now with the
Lufthansa publicity department, and also renewed his friendship
with Walter Kleffel, the aviation columnist for the huge Ullstein
publishing concern from whose presses poured millions of newspapers and periodicals. Each time Udet had visited Berlin in the
past he had always called on Kleffel; he attached great importance
to good relations with the press. Kleffel knew his way round Berlin
and immediately introduced Udet to the favourite haunts of Berlin's
'Upper Ten'. There was the very fashionable Horcher Restaurant,
the Russian restaurant *Medwjed* (polar bear), the wine business of
Julian Ewest on the corner of Behrendstrasse and the Friedrichs-
trasse. At these and many other 'high spots' Udet soon became
famous for his pranks; like thrusting a long needle through his lips,
and especially his excellent cartoons. Patrons at nearby tables
always looked on in admiration each time Udet requested a clean
plate, held it over a flickering candle until it was black with soot,
then drew one of his funny caricatures in the soot. Nobody ever
doubted that Udet could just as easily have made his living as a
cartoonist.

From the Bendlerstrasse Udet moved to the Fehrbelliner Platz,
and later to Pommerschestrasse where he was to remain for many
years. He quickly made himself at home in Berlin but often went
back to Munich, each time visiting his mother. Then, on 13 May
1927 – ever after known as Black Friday – the Berlin Stock Exchange
crashed, and the German economy collapsed.

Eight days later, however, the world was acclaiming a young
American pilot, Charles Lindbergh, who had flown non-stop from
New York to Paris. Udet based his all-red D-822 at Berlin's Tempelhof aerodrome, which had opened in 1923 and had recently
completed many of its modern buildings and hangars; and from
here he flew to his various air displays. At every airfield where Udet
performed he was greatly admired by the local pilots who considered
it an honour and a pleasure to have such a well-known aviator in
their midst. After one display at Munster in June the glider pilots
of the Ring der deutschen Flieger offered him a flight in a glider
they had built themselves, an invitation Udet duly accepted to
everyone's delight.

At another meeting, at Graz in Austria, Udet could not resist the temptation to fly under the bridge across the River Mur on his return to Germany; and while flying in the neighbourhood of Innsbruck he noticed below him some Austrian mountain artillery practising firing. Immediately he dived and flew low over the heads of the toiling soldiers. He was always on the lookout for some form of fun. A broken-down car below? Udet swept down and dropped an empty cognac bottle. A peasant working in the fields? Again Udet would sweep down while the frightened peasant took hasty refuge. At times Udet might chase a hare for miles on end; at other times he would engage in mock combat with a stork or a bird of prey which had by chance crossed his flight path. Once, on a trip from Munich to Leipzig, he even made a mock attack on a Czech-oslovakian student pilot who had lost his way and was over German territory. Not that his jokes were always welcome. At one banquet he was sat next to his friend Kleffel's mother. Having arrived already slightly drunk, he started telling jokes, then said, 'Just imagine, *gnädige Frau,* when Thea Rasche sits in an aircraft with her fat behind. . .' – then he stopped as he noticed an icy-cold stare! Such things were not said in good company. . .

Udet had to make his living out of flying, so it was natural that he was always trying to think of new ways of doing so. His latest idea was the *Udet-Schleppschrift* (towing gear) for aerial advertising banners. First thoughts had been to tow aerial targets for the army, or the secret air force. Hans Herrmann designed the system, which consisted of a banner chute fitted between the undercarriage legs, and a winch wound by a large wheel mounted on the right side of the fuselage in front of the forward cockpit. Through this wheel the steel cable, which carried the banner and was ballast-weighted, carried any target – usually an aircraft painted on a silk banner. Udet decided to develop the device for pure advertising purposes. Instead of a target, banners, each carrying a single letter one below the other, could be air-towed. Prior to take-off these banners, care-fully packed, were wound into a funnel and later lowered in the air on the cable. At first, to advertise the scheme, the letters U.D.E.T. were used. To exploit the scheme he set up a special firm Udet-Schleppschrift GmbH, and its account was opened in the C. N. Engelhardt bank.

In fact very few deposits were made into this account, and Udet was forced to borrow money from Ernst Hoffmann of Lausanne, Switzerland. This debt was then taken over by Thea Rasche, who recently had purchased her own Flamingo, D-1120 with part of the 50,000 marks given to her by her father after Thea had rejected a fiancé a mere thirty minutes before their projected wedding early in 1927! Thea and Udet were good friends, and the debt amounted to 13,000 marks, which Udet undertook to repay within one year. As security for this loan, Udet's D-822 was legally made over to Thea but remained at Udet's disposal to use freely. When both pilots took part in air displays the profits were to be split, while, as long as the debt remained unpaid, Thea was to get 15 per cent of all profits made by Udet-Schleppschrift. This contract was duly signed on 23 June in the Hotel Adlon in Berlin.

From Berlin Udet often visited Copenhagen where, with his old friend Paul Bäumer, he test-flew the all-metal Rohrbach IX 'Rofix' fighter. Here he became well acquainted with Kurt Tank, an engineer with Rohrbach since 1924 and whose influence on Rohrbach designs was increasingly evident. Udet and Bäumer were almost legendary as a drinking duo – neither man was ever known to refuse a good bottle. Then came 15 July. At eight o'clock that morning, despite the anxieties of his friends who felt that the effects of Bäumer's celebrations the evening before had not yet dispersed, Bäumer set off in the 'Rofix', intending to test-spin the fighter from height for at least 1,000 metres. Climbing above the water between Denmark and Sweden, he started his prolonged spin – and never came out of it, plunging straight into the water. Divers who salvaged the aircraft could find no technical defects, while Bäumer's body was still strapped to his seat, apparently uninjured. That same day Dr Rohrbach burned all the plans of the 'Rofix'. . .

Udet continued to visit Copenhagen, spending less time on flying displays after July. Among other reasons, he was busy preparing for the projected trans-Atlantic East-West attempt. At Copenhagen he test-flew Rohrbach's latest design, the Robbe II flying boat, fitted with twin BMW VI engines of 700 hp each. The first such test was flown with Kern, and when flying about 50 metres above the water the aircraft slowly lost height until it reached stalling point, then went into the water like a brick. Very little damage to the aircraft resulted, but when the spray died down Udet and Kern could be seen – and heard – sitting on the wing, shouting at each other, blaming each other for flying too slowly. The Robbe II was repaired and preparations were continued for the trans-Atlantic flight; scheduled for early October. With Kern, Udet planned to fly from Copenhagen to Cuxhaven, then to Portugal, the Azores, Bermuda, and eventually New York. As a preliminary, Dr Rohrbach wanted his Robbe II to beat a weight-carrying record over a distance of 2,000 kilometres. On 9 September the Robbe II, its rather heavy lines lightened by its two-tone paint scheme, was ready for the record attempt. Udet climbed aboard, followed by Kurt Tank as second pilot, and an air mechanic, Schnell. The load to be carried weighed 1,000 kilograms.

It took a long time to get the heavily-loaded flying boat off the water, but once airborne everything ran smoothly. Tank wanted to fly at 1540 rpm, but Udet thought this figure rather too high and, surreptitiously, tried to lower the revs. In the event, it was academic – a sudden explosion, and they were lucky to get Robbe II back on to the water. One of the four-blade airscrews had worked loose and friction had burned out the resulting hole, until the propeller had flown apart and destroyed the other prop. Heavily damaged, the Robbe II's state meant several months' delay on any record or trans-Atlantic ventures. Accordingly, Udet returned to Germany.

On 9 October, for the first time since the war, a flying display to include foreign participants was planned in Germany. It was to be held at Neuostheim airfield, near Mannheim, and the highlight was to be an aerobatic 'duel' between Udet flying his Flamingo and Michel Detroyat, the French 'aerobatic king' flying a Morane Saulnier parasol, Type 130 two-seater. After the more normal preliminary items, the time for this contest arrived and Detroyat took off first.

The local press reports described his flying as, 'His movements were short and sharp', but thought that, ' . . . this is probably caused by the powerful engine which makes manoeuvres seem too rigid. . .' Of Udet's performance the same paper said, 'It was Udet's motorless soaring that will remain unforgettable. In this Udet is unconditionally superior to Detroyat.' Both pilots received a huge ovation on landing. After the close of the display Udet got to know Detroyat on a friendly basis, an acquaintanceship which lasted until the start of World War Two.

CHAPTER EIGHT

Shirts and Safaris

Almost silently the tiny low-winged monoplane glided towards the glittering expanse of snow. Its two-cylinder engine – designed by Ferdinand Porsche – barely ticked over. Lightly loaded, its ski-undercarriage gently touched the snow, raising two fine white plumes. Udet was back on, top of the Zugspitze! He was flying D-1122, a Daimler L-20 B1 from the Klemm works, mounted on skis, powered by a 20 hp Daimler-Benz F 7502 engine. Udet made two consecutive landings, having taken off from the frozen Eibsee, and was only the second man ever to accomplish this particular feat of flying.

The L-20 was the first design of Klemm to be series produced, and was more successful than the sporting aircraft manufactured a few years previously by the Udet-Flugzeugbau. The latter appeared to have a relatively short life. By the end of February 1928 only five Udet machines were still on the German civil register, all Flamingos; Udet's D-822, D-681 and D-953, both registered to the Bavarian State, and D-865 and D-905 registered in the name of Deutsche Luftfahrt GmbH, Berlin. Thirty-three BFW-built Flamingos were also on the register, though not a single Udet low-wing type. Of the original Udet-built Flamingos, five were put onto the register during the remainder of 1928; D-883, D-813, D-909 and D-787 by the Deutsche Luftfahrt, and D-764 by the DVL, Adlershof. In November D-813 was struck off the register when it was burnt out. The Flamingo continued to be manufactured by BFW, and of the 450 aircraft on the German register on 1 February, thirty-four were of this type.

Among the happy owners of a brand-new Flamingo was Erich Kern, Udet's friend, fellow-pilot and mechanic. With his D-1206 (Wk Nr 358) he wanted to strike out on his own, but this meant Udet was without a permanent mechanic. Johnen, his former mechanic, had left to work for Siemens; as a married man he wanted a more settled mode of life. To find another mechanic Udet approached the directors of Siemens-Halske at Siemensstadt, asking

them to 'loan' him an air mechanic to accompany him during the
1928 display season.

One of the two young men selected was Erich Baier who had
been working for 4½ years in the Siemens experimental air-cooled
engines' workshop. He was an eager young man who had spent 3½
years attending evening classes on machine engineering; four hours
a day, with six months still to go. His interview with Udet that
evening pleased Udet, despite Baier's admission that he'd never
flown as yet. The job was Baier's if he wanted it – it was up to
Baier. It was the youngster's big chance – for a long time he had
looked longingly at the flying scene, wishing he was part of it. His
remaining evening classes could wait – he accepted. Little could he
suspect that the 'six months' job would last six years; the most
exciting years of his life. . .

Baier's first experience was not long coming. The first Easter
'People's Flying Display' – it was to become a traditional occasion
– was planned for 8 April at the Staaken airfield. More than 100,000
Berliners came to see such famous aviators as Antonius Raab, Gerhard Fieseler, Thea Rasche – '*Die Rasche Thea*' ('Fast Thea'), and,
of course 'Ernie' Udet. After the display press photographers
crowded around Udet, wanting particularly to take shots of Udet
with Thea Rasche; it was by now generally known that the pair
were completing preparations for a proposed flight from Europe to
New York at the end of the month. Their hopes for this trans-
Atlantic project were defeated on 13 April, when a Junkers W-33L
crash-landed on Greenly Island, off the coast of Labrador after a
nightmarish flight of 36½ hours, piloted by Hermann Köhl, the ex-
commander of Bombengeschwader 7, a Pour le Mérite holder and
chief of Lufthansa's night-flying division. There was now no point
to Udet and Rasche's proposed attempt; the plans were dropped.

Returning to his display 'circuit', Udet next flew at the small
town of Sagan, Silesia, the birthplace of his latest mechanic Baier.
The latter thereby made his first-ever flight in the front cockpit of
the great Udet's Flamingo, and over his home town. Further displays in May and June were flown at Bonn-Hangelar, Mannheim,
Leipzig and Kassel. Udet got to know Baier well; what had at first
been 'Herr Baier' soon became 'Baier' and eventually the more
familiar 'Baierlein'. Never far from Udet's side at the Kassel meeting
was Antonie Strassmann, a stately woman, one of Germany's earliest female pilots, and Udet's latest flame. The jewellery she so

proudly wore was reputed to be the same as that given to each of the women he 'liked' by the Crown Prince.

Another member of the old royal family, the Kaiser's nephew Prince August-Wilhelm, known usually as 'Auwi', had other interests. His leanings were more towards politics, to the Nazi Party, to be exact. Together with Göring, he saw to it that the Nazis were accepted in the highest circles. Göring, back from Scandinavia, was by now one of the dozen Nazis in the Reichstag. Göring's personal income was augmented every month with the 600 marks paid to every *Abgeordnete* (parliamentarian), but more important was the 1,000 or so marks quietly paid to Göring by Erhard Milch for being the Lufthansa's 'secret counsellor'. . .

Udet's income, on the other hand, was augmented by royalties of a book. He had not written a book, but drawn one. More than 70 of his amusing cartoons had been selected, each captioned with a short rhyme by the late C. R. Roellinghoff. Titled *Hals und Beinbruch* – the traditional greeting of all German flyers – it illustrated mainly the latest events on the flying scene, including many famous names. From Icarus to the tailor of Ulm, Santos Dumont, Graf Zeppelin, Thea Rasche, Heinkel, Rohrbach, Lindbergh, Chamberlain, Junkers, von Hühnefeld, Könnecke, Fieseler, Doret – ending with a cartoon of himself in his Flamingo, with the couplet, 'Who is it that flies so early in the morning wind? That's Udet, the happy child'. The book, soon to become a minor classic, was published by the Traditions-Verlag Kolk & Co in Berlin. It once more proved that he was as handy with a pencil as he was with a joy-stick.

Of the 33 candidates for the German Aerobatic Championship – part of the Rhineland Flying Tournament held at Lohausen airfield starting 30 June – only four were still in the running at the end of the day, able to take part in the finals next day; Gerhard Fieseler, Peschke (director of the Raab-Katzenstein flying school at Dusseldorf), Willy Stör (a DVS aerobatics instructor), and Udet. Next day, flying D-822 fitted with a special carburettor for inverted flying, faced the competition of Fieseler's D-1212, Stör's DVS Flamingo, and Peschke's Raab-Katzenstein. A crowd of 20,000 spectators, including Lufthansa director Erhard Milch and the minister Koch, watched each pilot demonstrating his personal style of aerobatics, until the championship became virtually a duel between Udet's all-red Flamingo and Fieseler's all-silver *'Schwalbe'*. The latter's flying was extremely precise, while Udet's showed more daring, more showmanship. In the event it was Fieseler's outside loops which clinched the day for him, and he was proclaimed champion, with Udet second, Stör third, and Peschke fourth.

Performing at displays had by now become almost routine. Many of the details were taken care of by Baier, who obtained the necessary flying maps at the Lufthansa, paid all bills and meticulously kept the accounts in a small note-book. He was responsible for preparation of the Flamingo, including ensuring all necessary spares were aboard such as cylinders and pistons for the special engine fitted to Udet's machine. Another regular chore for Baier was fitting the special carburettor for inverted flying, with its own 20-litre-fuel tank and hand-pump mounted in the cockpit; this tank having to be changed after any display for the normal fuel storage tank. One important task for Baier was to ensure that Udet's talisman was always aboard – an old clay sphere depicting a bat clasping the earth, wrapped in a small square of silk. This was invariably carried by Udet either in his pocket or in a tiny locker in the Flamingo's cockpit head-rest. It had been a present from Lo while she was still a nurse in Munich, and unless it was aboard his aircraft Udet would refuse point-blank to fly. If Baier's airfield duties were few he often visited Udet at home, more or less filling the role of secretary and taking care of paper work. Udet gradually came to trust Baier completely, and often sought his valued opinion on many tricky problems. When dedicating a portrait to Baier on 29 August, Udet did not hesitate to sign it, 'To my dear Baier in good friendship'.

Udet was becoming increasingly popular with people from many circles; film stars, sportsmen, writers – he knew them all. Often after a display he would take a party of friends home and indulge his passion for shooting. A practice butt always hung somewhere in his house, on which he tried out every shooting trick. He was an excellent host, superb raconteur, including a knack for speaking many different German dialects, and could be wildly exuberant and as boisterous as a young boy. At every party his talent as an artist was guaranteed to have a fascinated audience. Though realistic, even slightly cynical about some people, Udet would often go to great lengths to help a friend or others in need.

In the International Aviation Exhibition held at the Kaiserdamm, Berlin on 7 to 28 October, no less than 23 different nations participated. Of the many interesting designs on show, including the Dornier 'Wal' and the Wright brothers' 'Flyer', one in particular intrigued Udet, the Cierva 'Autogiro'. Two years previously he had been unable to get a flight in this, but on 9 October he was invited to take it up by Cierva's test pilot, A. H. Rawson. His flight was later headlined in the press as 'Udet has wind-milled', and duly celebrated in the Adlon Hotel by Udet, Rawson and Juan de la Cierva himself.

One stand at the exhibition was that of the French *Armée de l'Air*. It had been hoped that René Fonck, the French 'ace of aces', would attend, but Fonck had demurred, not wishing to open old wounds with any Germans present. However, an invitation was expressly sent to Fonck, and on his arrival in his Berlin hotel, Udet went to meet him. The two men, the world's top-scoring surviving fighter aces, became friends quickly, and could generally be seen, elegantly dressed, strolling together through the streets of the city. In December Udet visited Fonck in Paris, where the two were received warmly by Les Vieilles Tiges – 'The Old Stalks' – a flying pioneers' association founded in 1920. French aviators simply could not do enough for Udet. There were dinners, laudatory speeches, toasts – each emphasising the chivalry Udet had personified during the war.

Fonck also took Udet to the French Aero Club where, in the extensive library, he showed Ernie a book *Sous les cocardes* – 'Under the cockades'. Like Udet's *Hals und Beinbruch*, it was a book of cartoons, drawn by Marcel Jeanjean during the war; a collection of delicate, almost childish drawings, but evoking life in the French *escadrilles* during the war superbly. When he saw the book, Udet was pleasantly surprised; here were the same scenes that he had lived through – only the uniforms were different. It astonished him, and he could only mutter '*Wunderbar, wunderbar. . .*'

In January 1929 Udet returned to the Eibsee lake on being invited to take part in the Eibsee-Rennen – a race between cars and aircraft at the end of the month, organised by the Bavarian Automobile Club. Having his Flamingo fitted with ski undercarriage, Udet flew from Tempelhof aerodrome, via Munich, to the venue, not forgetting to circle his beloved Zugspitze. Among the racing drivers who had gathered to participate were such internationally famous drivers as Carraciola and Udet's friend Hans Stuck of the Austro-Daimler works at Vienna.

On the lake an oval race-track of some 1,500 metres had been cleared. When the race started Udet had to complete 15 circuits to the cars' 12 circuits, and during the race he made a point of flying as low as possible during the straight sections. After the race Udet demonstrated some of his flying skills for the assembled company. A pole about four metres long was fastened to the balcony of the Hotel Eibsee, with a handkerchief loosely tied to its end. Udet then made a low, slow pass and retrieved the handkerchief with his wing-tip. Next he demonstrated the art of low looping, coming out of one loop in front of the hotel by only just missing the ice on the ground. That evening's celebrations ended in the hotel bowling alley, where the skittles were replaced by champagne bottles.

His acknowledged mastery was recognised by a contract to fly for a film, *The White Hell of Piz Palü*. On 25 February he flew to St Moritz, landing on its frozen lake, and joined the film team camped in the Diavolezza Cabin near the Morteratsch-Glacier at a height of about 2,600 metres. With this team were the manager Dr Fanck, and the actress Leni Riefenstahl. In the film an aircraft was used to find two people lost in the mountains due to a sudden storm. This was where Udet and his Flamingo came into the picture. From the frozen lake, where a temporary shack had been erected to serve as a hangar, Udet had to make a number of particularly daring flights close to the precipices, and several highly dangerous landings on the glacier. Some flights were by Udet on his own, while some carried a camera operator, Schneeberger, who covered the aerial views needed. During the actual filming Udet flew almost recklessly, achieving seemingly impossible feats of manoeuvrability; so much so that when the completed film was exhibited later many people could not believe that the flying sequences were real and not camera trick-shots.

When the filming was completed at the end of March, the Flamingo was put in for a major overhaul, while Udet and Baier went to Willy Messerschmitt's Bayerische Flugzeugwerke at Augsburg. Udet was considering replacing the Flamingo used so extensively in his displays, and had thoughts of an aerobatic biplane built to his instructions by the BFW. He had written to Messerschmitt about this project, which BFW subsequently designated as the M25. A month later the Flamingo's overhaul was finished, and it now looked new. The opportunity had been used to equip it with bench-type tabs above the ailerons, similar to the BFW 3, a type originally evolved from the Flamingo design. Udet immediately returned to the display 'circuit' with his revitalised D-822. On 19 and 20 May he was part of Hamburg's *Grossflugtage*; then on to Frankfurt, Munich, Landshut in southern Germany, Leipzig, then north to the famous naval base at Kiel where he was joined in the air by the wartime 'aces' Theo Osterkamp and Hagen over the heads of some 30,000 spectators.

Within Germany itself, despite the inauguration of the *Rentenmark*, prosperity was slow in coming. The national debt had reached alarming proportions, and there were over a million unemployed. Political unrest swelled and in northern Germany hordes of peasants terrorised the countryside during a series of revolts against their lot. The Nazis were making preparations for the fourth *Reichsparteitag*, when 60,000 SA were expected to parade before their *Führer*; while in the Reichstag Hermann Göring clamoured for the setting up of a strong German air force. Yet notwithstanding the crippling effects of the Versailles Treaty upon German aviation, of the 82 international flying records recognised by the International Aviation Federation, 33 were by Germans; 40 per cent. By this time Germany was undoubtedly the most air-minded nation in the world, and the Deutsche Luftsportverband already boasted 50,000 members. In 1928 100,000 people were carried by German airlines, as opposed to 60,000 in the USA, and 25,000 in the United Kingdom.

It was to Britain that Udet finally turned for a 'brother' to his Flamingo. Wanting another aerobatic aircraft for display work, preferably a design not yet familiar to the public, he selected a De Havilland DH 60 'Moth', and was able to buy one, second-hand, through the DH representative in Germany, Herr Friedrich. This was registered G-EBOU (c/n 271), a special lightweight version of the Moth built for the British light aircraft trials at Lympne in 1926, and fitted with a 75 hp Armstrong Genet I radial engine. With a red fuselage and silver wings, it was thoroughly checked and tested by the De Havilland engineers before Udet flew it from England to Berlin. In June 1929 the Moth was re-registered in Germany as D-1651. One very convenient feature of the design was its folding wings, permitting it to be stored in little hangar space. Wanting to employ both aircraft in his future displays, Udet hired a young pilot, von Suchotsky, to ferry the Moth to and from venues, while he flew his trusty Flamingo as before.

He was often approached by representatives of various commercial firms with proposals for pure publicity stunts, advertising the commodities manufactured by such firms. Udet's normal reply was to refuse such offers; he was always reluctant to mix pure flying with 'crass commercialism'. And when, while having dinner in the Tempelhof *Heldenkeller*, he was sought out by the manager and asked to see the publicity manager of the Rotbart razor-blade makers; he almost declined, but then agreed to meet him. Udet cut short the interview by making it clear that he had no wish to fly for publicity purposes; it was not 'dignified'. . . The publicity man however did not give up hope, and two days later joined Udet at his table. Udet patiently listened to his proposition. Mainly, this consisted of having Udet's aircraft marked with UDET in large letters on the top wings, then ROTBART and MOND EXTRA – the firm's trademarks – on the underside of the lower wings. He would then fly along the beaches, from Borkum to Kolberg, and later from Wannsee and the Müggelsee, releasing some large blue and red balls, printed with slogans.

'And how much would you pay for this?' asked Udet.

'My director-general, Herr Roth, would be willing to pay something between 200,000 and 300,000 marks' was the reply.

Udet almost jumped from his seat – 'Two to three hundred thousand marks? *Donnerwetter!* When can I meet him?'

'Right now, if you wish'. Udet immediately drove to the KaDeWe stores and bought several of the balls, and that same afternoon rubber balls fell from the skies over Tempelhof – Ernst was already putting in some practice. . .

On 24 July, with the Rotbart publicity chief as his passenger, Udet took off in his Flamingo, heading for Warnemünde. During the following three weeks he flew over many seaside resorts, beating up the crowded beaches, while Baier in the second cockpit inflated the rubber balls by mouth, then attempted to drop these overboard accurately to the huge number of holiday makers below running to catch them. Rotbart got its money's worth in massive publicity, while Udet normally added a few impromptu aerobatics to round out his performances. While staying with Ernst Heinkel by invitation at Warnemünde, Thea Rasche was another guest. She had been engaged in a similar publicity stunt; dropping tablets of Sunlight soap along the coastline, and not always too accurately. Udet pulled her leg by quipping, 'Thea, you're polluting the whole of the Baltic Sea. . .'

Having two aircraft at his disposal for displays had its advantages, particularly when, on 19 August, his Moth's engine quit during a demonstration at Wilhelmshaven. Making a safe forced landing just outside the airfield, he simply transferred to the Flamingo and completed his programme. The big money in display flying was now attracting more and more participants. Men like Hundertmark, the aerial trapezist, who was forbidden to perform at the Kaiserlautern meeting on 25 August because his act was considered too dangerous. And women like Fräulein Hoffmann, just nineteen years old but already an accomplished pilot and aerobat. Before her death she was to become the first female works-pilot in Germany, testing aircraft for the Bücker firm.

Later in the summer, during a round of displays in (mainly) eastern Germany, Udet met another remarkable woman pilot, Fräulein Elly Beinhorn. She was at the Königsberg-Devau airfield with her second-hand, white and blue Messerschmitt M-23b, D-1674, and it was her first aerobatic display. Udet, after watching her programme took it upon himself to give her some 'fatherly' advice, advocating caution and patience until she was more experienced. Then, typically, he cheered up the crestfallen Elly by partnering her at that evening's celebrations. . .

The year 1929 closed on a note of near-tragedy – the catastrophic 'crash' on Wall Street, New York on 29 October which precipitated the worst international economic crisis the world had ever known, bringing with it a wave of suicides.

With the return of deep winter Udet started his annual trek to the south, to the Alps he so passionately loved. On 5 February he flew the Moth – known to everybody as *Die Motte* – from Berlin to Eibsee by way of Leipzig and Nuremberg. Ice on the Eibsee was 30 centimetres thick, and some two hundred cars stood ready to participate in the Partenkirchen-to-Eibsee race, to be followed by the popular *Eibsee-Rennen*, the now-famous race on ice, including the aircraft-v-car races. Among the many friends waiting for Udet at the hotel was Frau Felsing, divorced wife of a Berlin jeweller, in whom Udet had more than a passing interest. . .

A more mundane reason for Udet's visit this year was to take part in another of Dr Fanck's films with an Alpine setting, *Storms over Mont Blanc*. The leading male role was to be played by the actor Sepp Rist, and the leading female part by Leni Riefenstahl. Third in the billing was Udet, playing the role of Thoreau, a pilot dropping supplies to the observatory on Mont Blanc, and rescuing his friend from sudden death in a hostile mountain world. For this film Udet chartered D-1450, a Klemm L-25 from the Klemm works, which he collected on 19 March. In the interim his Flamingo, D-822 was refitted with a new Siemens-Halske Sh 14 engine, and re-registered as a U-12a (Special) in Udet's name. Filming took a total of seven months, during which Udet, among other feats, succeeded in making one landing on the Orny Glacier at almost 4,000 metres altitude.

While in Switzerland Udet took the opportunity to give a flying display at Cointrin airfield, near Geneva on 15 June, where his skill was matched against the aerial artistry of the French aerobat Marcel Doret, who flew a red and white, 'candy-striped' Dewoitine D 27 with panache and precision. On the following Sunday Udet gave another display at Lausanne in front of some 20,000 inhabitants of the locality, where his rival for aerial honours was the Swiss pilot Glardon, flying a Raab-Katzenstein. By 26 June all flying sequences for the film were in the can, so Udet packed his gear and returned to Berlin.

July and August were booked up completely with a succession of displays – Dusseldorf, Hannover, Dortmund, the *Volksflugtag* on 9 and 10 August at Tempelhof, on to Bonn, then to Lachen-Speyerdorf (an airfield since 1912) where Udet was joined by Fieseler and Stör; an intensely busy programme which left little time for other activities.

Another busy man at this time was Udet's friend Kleffel of the Ullstein concern, who was on a six-months' tour of the USA. Ostensibly a normal 'reporting' journalistic tour, he was also using the occasion for taking note of all the latest military aviation developments in America at the secret request of the German Defence Ministry, and sending his observations back to Germany in a series of special reports. Germany was still not permitted an air force, but German higher authorities were already planning ahead towards this goal. Their secret rearmament plan foresaw a period 1931–32 during which 22 squadrons of military aircraft would be created. During a further stage this total would be sustained but the *Staffeln* would be re-equipped with modern aircraft. In the meantime three *Staffeln* would be created for use with army manoeuvres, equipped with Arado SC1 machines and camouflaged as 'aerial publicity' outfits belonging to commercial firms – hence their given title of *Reklamestaffeln* – 'Publicity squadrons'.

In particular Kleffel was much impressed by the various demonstrations given by the US Navy's dive-bombers, especially those which employed the Curtiss F8C 'Helldiver' aircraft with its 700 hp engine. The dive-bombing technique – though not originated by the American air arms – had been perfected by US Marine Corps Aviation pilots, involving a near-vertical diving attack pattern which produced almost perfect bombing results in the matter of spot accuracy. Kleffel's reports to the German Ministry emphasised the latter aspect as well worthy of study by the embryo German air force, and privately he gave an enthusiastic description of both the aircraft and the technique to his friend Udet on his return to Germany. Udet's imagination was fired at the prospect of such a powerful aeroplane, but only in the context of display and stunt flying; the dive-bombing aspect held little interest for him.

At this time came a proposal from Britain that Udet should undertake a new flying feat – flying over Mount Everest, and being filmed in the process. The idea appealed to Udet and arrangements were started, only to be nullified when the Nepal authorities refused permission for any such venture. Udet then turned to his friends Edy von Gontard and Willy Zeitz of the Reemtsma tobacco firm with a proposition that they combine to make a flying film in the sunshine of Africa this coming winter. The film, *Strange Birds over Africa* would use three 'birds'; Udet's Moth-1651, a Klemm L-26 IIa, and a BFW M-23b, D-1970. As second pilot Udet decided to take along von Suchotsky, with Schneeberger as the camera operator and his assistant Bohne. Stage manager was to be Junghaus, while Baier would become engineer in charge of all three aircraft. Von Gontard's wife and the actress Yvette Rodin would be accompanied by Udet's friend Frau Felsing. The plan was to leave for Africa at the end of October. All three aircraft were painted silver as part-protection from the sun's heat, and larger wheels and additional oil coolers were fitted in each.

On 18 October Udet's three aircraft left Hamburg aboard a steamer, while Udet and his company left Berlin by train for Genoa on 2 November, and then joined the ship *Adolf Woermann* en route to Mombasa in what was then Kenya Colony. Crossing into Tanganyika Territory (now Tanzania) with all their equipment, the party made Arusha their 'operational base', about 100 kilometres from the forward camp established on the north shore of Lake Manyara. At the latter site a windsock was put up, and a primitive hangar erected from bamboo reeds with a corrugated tin roof. The site was then named 'Udet Camp'; a title which continued to be used by the native population for many years after. Udet, as soon as the aircraft were ready, indulged himself by several flights over the beautiful and untamed territory; flying low over the huge herds of wild animals to be seen roaming everywhere, and thoroughly enjoying himself in this unfettered freedom of pure aerial joy. On the ground he pursued his other main passion, hunting wild game,

An international group of pilots competing in the National Air Races at Cleveland Ohio, USA on 31 August 1931. From left: Mario de Bernardi (Italy); Boleslar Orlinski (Poland); Alford ('Al') Williams (USA); Ernst Udet; Alois Kubita (Czechoslovakia).

(*Left*) Old enemies, new friends. Udet meets Eddie Rickenbacker the American 'Ace of Aces'!
(*Right*) Udet presents his former 'victim' Walter B. Wanamaker with the serial cut from Wanamaker's Nieuport Scout N6347 – Udet's 39th confirmed victory of the war.

(*Top*) *Die Motte* – the De Havilland DH60 Moth, ex-G-EBOU, registered in Germany as D-1651, which Udet bought, second-hand in 1929. Seen here in Greenland during Udet's 1932 'expedition'. (*Left*) Greenland's icy mountains, 1932, with Udet suitably attired.

(*Right*) Udet and his mechanic Baier.

Udet with some enthusiastic young model makers at Berlin's Tempelhof aerodrome on 2 June 1935.

and recorded everything with the three personal Leica cameras he had brought with him.

Udet's penchant for 'strafing' any batch of animals on the ground nearly had serious consequences on one occasion. Flying the Moth, Udet was accompanied by von Suchotsky in the Klemm on a general joyride, making use of the cameras fitted to various parts of the airframe to obtain background footage. While beating very low across one stretch of plain a large lion suddenly leapt at the Moth with claws extended, but just missed. Udet tried to warn von Suchotsky behind him of the possible danger, but too late. Von Suchotsky's Klemm slowly reached the lion which leapt again – and clawed a chunk out of the Klemm's starboard wing. The wing dipped, almost touched the ground, then as its pilot fought for control, slowly rose again.

On another occasion the two pilots, accompanied by another member of the party, Siedentopf, decided to land out in the savannah to film some wildlife, close to some grey rocks. Von Suchotsky was the first to land and as he was about to touch down one 'grey rock' got up – it was an angry rhinoceros. Von Suchotsky tried to bank, hit a termite hill, somersaulted, and the Klemm ended up on its back in a cloud of dust. Udet landed as quickly as possible, chased off the rhino with his gun, then hurried to the wreck, fearing the worst. Hacking away at the crumpled fuselage with a knife, he eventually got both men out, both, amazingly, little the worse for their mishap. The two men were air-ferried back to camp, where they recovered from their minor injuries. The Klemm, apart from its engine, was simply left to rot where it lay, being unrepairable in Baier's opinion.

Filming continued, and while Udet and Schneeberger were staying temporarily at the Fig Tree Hotel at Babati – a particularly 'civilised' encampment whose facilities included a small airfield, huts with thatched roofs, and a restaurant with a bar well-stocked with cognac – a sudden downpour of rain and high winds wrecked their Moth. With the help of two local resident German carpenters the Moth was patched up, and Udet was left with just the BFW to complete the filming. By the end of March 1931 all filming was finished and, with the rainy season imminent, the expedition came to an end. While the rest of the party and the equipment crossed to Mombasa and boarded a ship for home, Udet and Schneeberger decided to fly back in the BFW, via Cairo.

Crossing the 3,000 metres-high Mau ridges and subsequent jungle they landed at Kisumu to refuel, then followed the northern shore of the lake into unspoilt Uganda. Schneeberger, in the front cockpit spent much of his time filming the scenery below but was startled to feel the aircraft suddenly starting to vibrate. Dropping his camera he grabbed the fuel tank in front of him; its retaining strap had broken. In this position he remained until they finally reached Jinja without further damage to the fuel line. This effort exhausted Schneeberger who, that night, ran up a fever temperature.

Next day, after another refuelling stop at Juba, they set off for Malakai. Crossing the Nile near Bor, they were only some 180 kilometres south of their goal when Udet saw the fuel gauge indicator dropping fast. A fuel line had broken and fuel was pouring out of the tank. Finding a reasonably flat stretch of scrubland, Udet hastily landed. It was a completely deserted spot, but near the normal track to Malakai. Thus it should only be a matter of time before they were found by some passing transport.

What worried Udet most though was Schneeberger. He had a high fever and was becoming delirious, lying under the wing to shelter from the blistering heat. Also they had relatively little food and water provisions. To walk out was out of the question; they had to stay put and hope for rescue. For two more days and nights they sat it out, with Schneeberger getting noticeably weaker and even Udet began to feel the lack of sustenance.

Unknown to them the Shell representative at Malakai, when Udet failed to appear as scheduled, wired his colleague at Juba, and realised the two Germans must have forcelanded somewhere along the way. Accordingly the authorities in Khartoum were notified, among them Wing Commander Sholto Douglas, RAF who immediately arranged for three Fairey IIIF's of 47 Squadron RAF to be despatched to find the lost pair. Douglas also requested a friend, Campbell-Black of the Wilson Airlines at Nairobi to keep a lookout. Campbell-Black had just landed at Khartoum in a DH Puss Moth which he was ferrying from England to Kenya, and was about to fly to Juba.

Later the same day Campbell-Black spotted the stranded couple, landed nearby and provided Udet and Schneeberger with fresh water and cigarettes, then continued to Juba where he reported Udet's exact location to Khartoum. That same afternoon a Fairey IIIF landed alongside the BFW, bringing 16 gallons of fuel, and tools to repair the BFW's broken fuel line. As Udet was to jokingly but sincerely say later, 'I never imagined I'd ever live to see the day I would actually be glad to see RAF roundels above me!'

Udet now flew to Malakai (where he was received by the RAF with some ice-cold Bavarian beer), and then continued his flight next day to Khartoum, where he was the guest of Sholto Douglas and his wife and spent that evening 're-fighting the war' with him in a happy bout of reminiscences about their respective war experiences.

The next stage was to Atbara, then on to Wadi Halfa on the Nile. Next day, 31 March, he reached Cairo. Here it was very clear that Schneeberger was in no fit state to continue much further by air, so Udet made a short flight to RAF Aboukir, near Alexandria, where he requested facilities for dismantling the doughty BFW for transportation by road to Alexandria and loading on to a ship. In 35 flying hours the BFW M-23 had covered 4700 km from Arusha to the Mediterranean. Once aboard ship in Alexandria Schneeberger was able to receive much-needed medical care, but was still very weak when they arrived in Vienna. So Udet had him put aboard a train to Munich, while he himself flew via Trieste to Munich, arriving there on 9 April. The African safari was over. His welcome at the old familiar Oberwiesenfeld outside 'his' Munich was an occasion for a large crowd of important officials and a battery of camera men from the press. Ernie was home.

CHAPTER NINE

Hell-divers and Glaciers

It was a sombre Germany to which Udet returned in April 1931. Factory after factory was closing its doors, suicides among the middle classes were continuing, and the queues outside the public relief bureaux grew longer each day – nearly four million men on state relief without hope of employment. And as soon as these obtained their pittance they took to marching through the streets by their hundreds, some carrying banners emblazoned with the Iron Cross, some with a red hammer and sickle – and an increasing number bearing a black swastika. Yet still people flocked to watch Udet's displays, even if cash proceeds were now less than in previous years.

On 3 May Udet was back at Oberwiesenfeld, the day it was officially opened as Munich's latest airfield. Plans to equip the field as a modern airport had begun in 1927, and now the main structure was finished. 100,000 people came to the opening. A formation of Albatros L 75's from the DVS at Schleissheim flew over; Groenhoff was towed into the air in his Fafnir glider; Willy Stör astonished the crowd with his BFW M-23's manoeuvrability; and they were then deafened by four Lufthansa Rohrbach Rolands roaring over their heads. They gaped at Rawson's unique Autogiro – but most of all they wanted to see Udet and his Flamingo.

Further displays occupied Udet for the next few months though the diminishing returns turned his thoughts to the possibilities in foreign countries. In the meantime he redecorated his small apartment in the Pommerschestrasse 4. Cockades from his various war victims, models of the Udet works and others he had flown, with the recent additions of spears, shields, knives, native masks, arrows and even stuffed animals from his African sojourn – all adorned the walls of his four-room apartment. Then came news of the latest victim of the depression – on 1 June Willy Messerschmitt's BFW firm went bankrupt.

At Basle on 6 and 7 June – where Udet was billed as 'The King of Aerobatics' – he first met the American Captain Frank Hawks, the Texas Oil Company pilot, who was demonstrating his Travelair

'Mystery Ship' NR1313, which he called Texaco No 13. A month later, on 8 July he was introduced to another American, Alford ('Al') Williams, whose demonstration of a Curtiss 'Hell-diver' had so impressed Kleffel in the United States in the previous year. Williams was responsible for contracting foreign aerobatic pilots to perform at the annual American National Air Races, and had tried to procure Udet's services in 1930, but the German's commitments prevented him participating. This year Udet was free to accept and on 8 July signed a contract at the office of the US Consulate-General to appear in the NAR at Cleveland, Ohio later in the year.

First, however, Udet was invited to perform during the intervals of that year's King's Cup Air Race in Britain, by the Royal Aero Club. The race was due to be held on 25 July, and Udet, after some difficulties with arranging the financial aspect, flew with Baier across the Channel in D-822. The venue for the race was Heston, London's latest airport, and the day was part-spoilt by bad, rainy weather, but 40 aircraft started the 982-miles course, while Udet performed in the intervals between laps. His programme brought wide praise in the British aviation press, exemplified by the report in *Flight* magazine, dated July 31, which said, in part:

> His exhibition, which he made in his own machine called the Flamingo, was beautifully done, and all his manoeuvres showed a smoothness and steadiness, the like of which we have seldom seen.

Two more displays in July, at Würzburg and Königsberg, and then Udet began his preparations for the trip to America. He planned to shop around while there for one of the high-powered aircraft Kleffel had told him about. Finance might be a problem, though. Udet himself did not have enough money to buy what would undoubtedly be an expensive aircraft, but his friend Willy Zeitz might be persuaded into financing a new machine, especially a modern American machine. By mid-August it was time to leave and, after several farewell parties, Udet and Baier flew from Berlin to Hamburg. Next day they went to Bremerhaven where the Flamingo was disassembled and loaded onto a trailer, then taken aboard the *Europa* and stowed.

On 19 August the *Europa* sailed. The trans-Atlantic voyage provided a standard of luxury which astounded Baier who had never experienced its like before; while one diversion for the passengers was the launching from a Heinkel catapult of D-2244, a Junkers Ju 46 mailplane. On board Udet met another pilot bound for the Cleveland Air Races, Flight Lieutenant Richard 'Batchy' Atcherly, RAF, who had with him G-EBVO, a Blackburn Lincock single-seater bought from Robert Blackburn for the nominal sum of 10 shillings. On 25 August the *Europa* docked at New York and Udet's Flamingo was taken to Floyd Bennett airfield for assembly.

For the next two days the foreign pilots were entertained by their hosts, including a presentation to the President of the USA in the White House, and a luncheon given by the Washington Aero Club. Then, on 28 August, Udet and Baier flew to Cleveland's municipal airport. This year's NAR was scheduled to take place from 29 August to 7 September, and when Udet arrived over Cleveland the air was crowded with pilots putting in some last-minute practice. Among them was Atcherly in his diminutive Lincock. Each time Batchy attempted a snap roll, he could hear an ominous knocking sound, so decided to land. In fact an American mechanic had omitted to fit a vital bolt in the aircraft's undercarriage, resulting in one undercarriage leg and its wheel becoming detached and dangling loose. Unaware of this Atcherly crashed on landing, wrecking completely the Lincock and putting himself in hospital where 14 stitches were inserted in his facial injuries.

On the airfield were many of the world's fastest and most powerful aircraft designs, along with a host of internationally famous pilots and aircraft manufacturers. The press reporters had a field day. When they first saw Udet's Flamingo, they could barely conceal their amusement; imagine a pilot coming all the way from Europe with a six years-old, wooden, low-powered biplane to compete with the all-metal, high-powered monoplanes of the American entries! Indeed, even Udet began to be dismayed as he saw the many ultra-modern designs around him. His trusty old D-822 was hardly a match for such sleek, powerful aircraft. He needn't have worried. . .
Reporting on the first day's events, the local paper, *Cleveland Plain Dealer* said of Udet's display, 'Fascinated spectators are treated to the most startling aerial show ever given here as flashing Flamingo bounces about field to thunderous applause'; while another description read:

In the greatest exhibition of dare-devil flying ever staged in this air-thrill wise city Captain Ernst Udet, outstanding German ace, furnished the high spot in an afternoon and evening of thrilling aerobatics. Pitting his superb flying skill against the laws of gravity, Udet flew his German Flamingo plane in positions never intended by the Wright brothers and certainly never imagined possible by the wondering thousands of spectators in the air race stands. Like a crazily bouncing ball, the little craft went hopping here and there, now bouncing on one wheel, now dragging a wing-tip in the turf, now jumping a line of parked airplanes. Every movement was followed by the fascinated spectators, and long and thunderous was the applause as the German ended his marvellous exhibition by executing two loops in succession at low altitude with his motor idling.

Hardly had the ovation from the estimated 80,000 audience died down than Udet was presented to Captain Eddie Rickenbacker, America's top-ranking fighter ace, Vice-President and Sales Director of the General Aviation Company, USA. The two shook hands and posed for the cameras, while Rickenbacker whispered in Udet's ear, 'Have a drink with me', and tapped his trouser pocket significantly; America was still 'dry' under Prohibition. . . During the following week event followed event, including the Bendix Trophy Race for a coast-to-coast speed competition, with the cream of American aviation being displayed to the public.

On Sunday, 6 September, Udet finally met a former foe whom he had shot down during the war, and had been corresponding with occasionally in recent years; Walter B. Wanamaker, now a common pleas judge from Akron. On 2 July 1918 he had been Lieutenant Wanamaker of the 27th Aero Squadron USAS, flying Nieuport Scout N6347 on a patrol, when Udet led a Jagdstaffel 4 formation of Fokker D VII's down to attack the Americans. In the ensuing combat Udet had shot down Wanamaker as his 39th confirmed victory, and Wanamaker, wounded, saw the war out as a prisoner of war in Germany. Now the former enemies met and shook hands, grinning; then Udet produced the framed piece of fabric, bearing Wanamaker's Nieuport serial, which he cut from the aircraft in July 1918 and kept ever since as a souvenir of the fight. 'I now give you what I took away'.

That evening Udet went for a closer look at the Curtiss F8C 'Hell-diver' which Kleffel had described so enthusiastically before. Nearby was a line-up of the Curtiss F6C Hawk fighters. Udet climbed into the cockpit of one of these, trying it for size, imagining the sensation such a modern, high-powered aircraft would be for the German display crowds back home. He wondered – would Curtiss be willing to sell one to a foreign civilian? Next day brought the finale to the air meeting, and Udet had time to pursue his intention of attempting to buy a really modern machine. From Lloyd Child, the Curtiss test-pilot, he learned that Curtiss would be agreeable to such a sale; a Hawk, which would cost him 14,000 US dollars. Several other manufacturers also indicated that they would willingly sell examples of their designs, but the prices were staggering to Udet. He wrote a postcard to Angermund in Germany, telling him about the *wunderbar* aircraft he had seen, but accompanied the card with one of his cartoons showing himself with both trouser pockets turned inside out. By the side of each empty pocket he wrote, 'Do-laar' – meaning either 'Dollar' or '*da leer*' ('empty here'). . .

Before arranging for his return trip to Germany, Udet visited Akron to see the giant airship hangar being completed there, and took the opportunity to take up Wanamaker's invitation to visit him at his home, where the two men chatted amicably well into the small hours, fortified by several bottles of good Rhine wine. On 16 September he arrived in New York and stayed for ten days at the Ritz-Carlton Hotel; then left the USA on 26 September in the *Bremen*. A week later Udet stepped on to German soil again at Bremerhaven, meeting old friends and acquaintances to whom he described at great length the various aircraft and aviation events he had witnessed in America.

Shortly after Udet returned to Germany, Hermann Göring also returned. President von Hindenburg had at last been persuaded to grant the 'upstart' Hitler an audience, and Hitler wanted Göring by his side. Leaving his beloved wife Karin in Stockholm – a dying woman – Göring obeyed his *Führer*'s 'request'. Before the presidential audience, he attended a film evening organised by Lufthansa on 8 November in the Atrium in Berlin. Udet attended too; part of the film he made in Africa was to be included in the programme. Here Göring approached Udet. Göring was not popular with many ex-Richthofen Jagdgeschwader members, who (among other reasons) disapproved of his activities, especially his involvement with the Nazi SA. Udet had often, in public, made quite clear his personal aversion to Göring, his former commander in 1918. However, Ernst was never a man to carry a grudge and, through a mutual friend Paul 'Pilly' Koerner, who since 1928 had been one of

Göring's assistants in the Nazi movement, Udet agreed to a kind of 'reconciliation'.

After listening intently to Udet's descriptions of his American visit, and the aircraft there, Göring said, 'Udet, you belong to us, the Nazis.' 'No', replied Ernie, 'Politics don't interest me. They are just a noise in the background.' Göring persisted, 'Not just politics, Udet, flying, aviation. Things are changing in Germany. Soon I'll need men, men like you. Will I be able to count upon you when the time comes?' Absentmindedly almost, not really believing what he was saying, Udet replied, 'Yes, sure.' Göring ended the conversation by saying 'You should come and see me at home. We must talk seriously.'

Göring was talking 'seriously' two days later – to von Hindenburg. Contemptuously the 85-year-old President did not even reply to his or Hitler's diatribes. It was a disillusioned pair who left the presidential study. Göring might just as well have stayed in Stockholm to comfort Karin. He was still in Berlin a week later, on 17 October, when she died. It hurt Göring deeply; Karin had been *the* woman in his life.

During the course of the year Udet too had been bereaved; his father died in Munich. On the other hand a new woman had come into his life, a vivacious, black-haired creature. Reputedly of Spanish blood, Fräulein Elloys Illing – always 'Laus' to Ernie – was gay, full of life. In the rest of Germany something else had almost died too – the dream of a democracy. There were now almost five million unemployed, including more than 100 aircraft designers; while the Nazi Party could point to 806,000 members. . .

After his usual winter sojourn at Eibsee, Udet returned to Berlin at the end of February, where Dr Fanck invited him to fly in yet another film. 'Where to?' asked Ernie. 'Greenland' replied Fanck. 'Can I take Laus with me?' 'Yes, and three aircraft; we'll leave at the end of May. The film will be called *SOS Eisberg*.' Two months left Udet ample time to prepare, and in the meantime he began the year's flying displays. At Easter he was booked for the annual meeting at Staaken, and on 15 May at Tempelhof. Ever seeking to improve his programme with some innovation, Ernie instructed Baier to fix a short stick on the Flamingo's lower left wing, and to put an additional strut between the upper and lower left wings. Berliners who subsequently watched him actually dragging his wing along the ground in full flight went wild – such daring! Some of

Udet's friends thought he was taking chances, overdoing it; but Ernie's reply was succinct, 'I know exactly what I'm doing, don't worry'. It was a simple statement of fact, made without conceit or any hint of boasting.

One of those friends was a popular Munich film star Heinz Ruhmann who had moved to Berlin. He had learned to fly at the Oberwiesenfeld under instruction from Ritter von Schleich the famed 35-victory 'Black Knight of Germany'. Ruhmann had then bought a Klemm and this stood alongside Udet's aircraft in their Tempelhof hangar. Another close friend was the racing driver Hans Stuck. Hans decided to marry Fräulein Paula von Reznicek, and the best men for the ceremony were Crown Prince Wilhelm, 'Auwi', and Udet. Before going to the *Rathaus* (City Hall) of Charlottenburg, Udet and some friends 'fortified' themselves with a few cognacs. . . The registrar monotonously droned out his text until Udet, sitting next to the bride, fell asleep, his head slowly bending forward. When the time came for the best men to sign the necessary certificates, Stuck's bride prodded Udet, who woke suddenly and rather loudly asked, 'Who's dealing?'. . .

Despite a naturally ebullient nature, Udet could never stand being bullied. Indicative of this side of his nature was his encounter with a member of the air police at the Halle an der Saale display. While waiting to leave at the close of the display Ernie sat in his Flamingo, smoking a cigarette; nowhere near any buildings or hangars. The *Luftpolizist* spotted the cigarette and rudely ordered Udet to put it out. 'This is my aircraft, and I'll do what I like in it. I'm endangering nothing and nobody' was Udet's sharp reply, and he calmly continued to puff away. After having his flying log stamped by the control tower staff he taxied out to take-off point. There his friend the policeman stood waiting with his flag to give permission for take-off. Just before going Udet called the man over – then shouted at him, 'You're a very big boor!', then gunned his engine and left.

For his trip to Greenland Udet had three aircraft prepared; D-1651, his Moth, and D-1970, his BFW M-23b – both of which had been used in his African venture. The third was D-2269, a new Klemm L-26 powered by an Argus As 8, which Udet had recently purchased and to which he had fitted two floats. The BFW M-23b after its overhaul was also fitted with twin floats. He left his Flamingo in Berlin, along with 'Hannibal', a hawk given to him by friends; a joking 'compensation' for Udet's lack of money to purchase a Curtiss Hawk from Al Williams. The actual expedition started on 25 May when all concerned boarded a special rail coach at Berlin railway station. Dr Arnold Fanck was in charge of the party, which included Udet, Leni Riefenstahl (the star), Erich Baier, Franz Schriek (a second pilot, from the DVS), Schneeberger, guides and technicians. At Hamburg the party boarded a steam freighter, the *Borodino*, and set sail.

During the next four months Udet lived and flew in a new world, flaunting with icebergs, and having several narrow escapes from death or injury. Landing on a sea littered with invisible 'blue ice' just beneath the surface was a constant danger, and Baier was kept constantly busy repairing damaged floats on the aircraft. On the return to Germany a publicity display at the Kaufhaus des Westens department store in Berlin's Tauentzinstrasse included a selection of the best photo stills from the film, and Udet's BFW M-23.

For most of December Udet was confined to his apartment, having contracted a severe bout of pneumonia. His aversion to illness in any form led him to forbid his housekeeper, Grete, to allow any visitors while in this state, and eventually his mother had to come from Munich to persuade him to even see a doctor. Ill or not, Udet kept himself busy with correspondence and caricaturing. At Christmas the results of the latter became revealed to his circle of friends. He sent to each of them a small leather bound calendar for 1933. Inside each cover had been imprinted a caricature of Udet himself, smiling like an angel; while bound into the booklet were nine of his personal cartoons, illustrating some aspect of his African or Greenland ventures. In subsequent years these calendars were to become a yearly institution, cherished by his closest friends, of how Udet saw himself during the last years of his life. In addition that year his story of the African expedition was published under the same title as the film, *Strange birds over Africa*, including a selection of his best photographs. *Storm over Mont Blanc* had been published in book form the previous year.

When the year 1933 began the Weimar Republic had just 28 days to live. Behind the scenes the NSDAP expounded an enormous amount of activity, as if Hitler realised that it was now or never if the Nazis were to take power. In Berlin the people almost seemed to sense what was coming, and talk invariably turned to politics, to Hitler. Udet, now in full health again, gave a lecture on his experiences in Greenland at the Gloria-Palast on 22 January, on behalf of the Lufthansa. Five days later he attended the fashionable horse races at the Exhibition Halls. The last event he attended in a free Berlin was the annual Berlin Press Ball, held in the Zoo on 28 January. This was the most important social event of the Berlin year, and Udet was invited to sit in the Ullstein firm's box, next to the Government's box.

Udet, in the company of his friend Carl Zuckmayer, the author, spent a merry evening, drinking champagne alternated with cognac. Then, with a fair amount of both under his belt, he became slightly aggressive. Unlike former years, those attending the ball this year were festooned with medals, decorations and Party insignia; nationalism was rampant. Udet spoke; 'Just look at all these "chandeliers". They took their brass out of mothballs. Last year it wasn't the fashion.' In disgust he took off his Pour le Mérite, which he usually wore with evening dress. He turned to Zuckmayer: 'Let's both bare our asses and hang them over the edge of the box!' The pair had got as far as loosening the buttons of their braces before Zuckmayer's wife and Ehmi Bessel, an actress, expressed their dismay. This sobered Udet. Rather than stay there, Udet then invited his whole party back to his apartment to continue the celebrations in private.

In the morning of 30 January Hitler and his hierarchy were received in von Hindenburg's Palais, and the ageing president formally named Hitler as *Reichs* Chancellor. When Göring appeared on the balcony to shout the news to the assembled masses below, the Wilhelmstrasse reverberated with the cry '*Heil!*' The news spread like quicksilver and swastika flags and banners were soon to be seen unfurled all over Berlin. More and more people rushed to the city centre and from the Leipziger Platz to the Unter den Linden became one heaving multitude of people. Preparations were finalised for a mass torch march that evening.

Udet was at home during all this. The telephone rang; an invitation from the manager of his favourite Adlon hotel, offering to reserve a place at one of the hotel windows to watch the evening's parade. Udet accepted the offer. About seven o'clock that evening the spectacle began. With burning torches more than 25,000 uniformed men of the SA, SS and the *Stahlhelm* marched in close formation behind a myriad of flags and banners. It was like some fire-snake winding its way from the Charlottenburger Chausée, through the Unter den Linden, into the Wilhelmstrasse to march past von Hindenburg and Hitler – a personal triumph for the organisation of Göring. From his window seat in the Adlon Udet watched the parade with mixed feelings.

Next day Göring returned to Berlin from a visit, and twelve former World War One pilots, each a holder of the Pour le Mérite, assembled on Tempelhof aerodrome to meet him, with Udet selected to greet Göring in their name. Göring's Junkers stopped just in front of the pilots, and as he stepped out of the aircraft, Udet stepped forward to greet him. Göring ignored him and the other pilots, going straight to the SA guard of honour waiting nearby. The pilots were not in uniform, an item rapidly becoming indispensable in Germany. . .

On 1 February the German Aero Club rented the Kroll Opera House for a banquet and dance to celebrate its 25th anniversary. Anyone even remotely connected with aviation simply had to attend, especially since it was known that Göring would be coming. The official announcement of Göring's elevation to *Reichskommissar* for Aviation by von Hindenburg and Hitler had yet to be announced, but everybody knew of it and were convinced that it meant a big stride forward for aviation generally in Germany.

Shortly after Udet arrived, Göring arrived, bringing with him Erhard Milch, the director of Lufthansa, and Karl Bodenschatz, ex-Adjutant of the wartime Richthofen Jagdgeschwader and now a colonel in the Reichswehr. Göring had not come to dance; he was busy recruiting – ostensibly for his civil aviation bureau, but in reality for the still-secret German air force. In particular he wanted to enlist all surviving Pour le Mérite-holders, the well-known aces. There was Friedrich Christiansen of Dornier DoX fame, Edouard Ritter von Schleich, Robert Ritter von Greim, Bruno Lörzer – and above all, Ernst Udet. Such famous names would add prestige, not only to the reborn air force but to the Nazi party.

As soon as Göring saw Udet he greeted him jovially, 'Ha, Udet. I've been looking for you. Come with me, I have to speak to you.' Taking Udet by the arm he led them to a quiet corner where they would not be interrupted. 'You know, of course that I'm going to build a new air force. I need men to do this. Most of the pilots of the great war will help, but I need you most of all.'

'Well', Udet said, 'I'll do anything to help German aviation, but I don't like uniforms or being told what to do. I want to be able to fly how and when I like. Politics are not for me.'

'Of course, I know that' replied Göring, 'It won't be easy to tie you down, but you must realise that with your fame you simply won't be able to stand aside. You could be swept away. Anyway, I have time. I don't want to hurry or press you.'

Then, cleverly, he added, 'Your idea to go to America regularly is excellent. We have much to learn from them, and I'm very interested in their technical advances, especially the dive-bombers you told me about. To show you that I want to help you I'll give you the dollars you need to buy a Curtiss Hawk.'

Udet was taken aback with surprise. Göring then went on, 'In fact, you'll buy two Hawks. I'm curious to know what they can do and want them thoroughly tested at Rechlin; after which they'll be yours to do whatever you like with them.' Göring then left him.

Later, Göring invited all former members of the Richthofen Jagdgeschwader to see him. In the past he had been banned from the *Geschwader*'s Association; most members being upset that in his political career he continually emphasised the fact that he was the last wartime commander of the unit. The Association's president, Wolfram von Richthofen, the Red Baron's nephew, had been the chief instrument in having Göring banned. Now, leading the host of famous pilots into Göring's Palais was . . . Wolfram von Richthofen. Only weeks later the Berlin Reichstag was burned, and next day the Communist Party leaders were imprisoned, and all left-wing press prohibited 'for the protection of the people and State'. Things were changing rapidly in Germany. . .

On 25 March all sport-flying activities in Germany were grouped under a single organisation. The traditional aviation federation of independent flying clubs, the DLV, – Deutscher Luftfahrt-Verband eV, founded in 1902 – which included about a thousand local aviation groups involving some 60,000 members, was dissolved. In its place a second DLV – Deutscher Luftsport-Verband eV – was inaugurated, which also incorporated the Rhön-Rositten-Gesell-schaft gliding association, and the National Socialist Flying Corps, founded on 1 January 1932 and which was to be resurrected in 1937. Organised in 16 *Landesgruppen* – 'local groups', the new DLV also took in the SA- and SS-*Fliegersturmen* later in the year.

In this way the DLV became the camouflage organisation for the secret German air force, and at the same time a reserve for military pilots. All DLV members wore a standard blue-grey uniform. Naturally, the DLV came under the aegis of Göring, who named Bruno Lörzer as its president, with von Hoeppner as vice-president.

Meanwhile, Udet was having a good time in St Moritz, having flown there on 12 March to complete the final flying sequences for the film about Greenland. Staying at the plush Palace Hotel, he made the most of this semi-holiday, celebrating with friends most evenings at the nearby Café Hanselmann. By 2 April all filming had been completed and it was back to Berlin via Innsbruck, notwith-standing a raging snowstorm. In Berlin a brand-new grey-blue DLV uniform awaited him, along with an honorary title of *Fliegervize-kommodore*. In the interim Bruno Lörzer had engaged Walter Angermund to take care of all DLV propaganda.

Henceforth Udet intended using a Klemm L-25 C XI, D-2397 equipped with a British seven-cylinder Pobjoy engine for displays and demonstrated it in public for the first time at the annual Easter Flying Display on 16 and 17 April. Here Udet also gave a crazy-flying humorous demonstration as the mad 'Professor Canaros' – similar to an event flown by the British pilot Batchy Atcherly at the Cleveland Races previously. Four days later, however, Udet was in sombre mood when he attended the ceremony at the Invaliden Cemetery to lay a wreath on the grave of Manfred von Richthofen; the fifteenth anniversary of the 'Red Knight's' death in action. Others attending included Bruno Lörzer and another wartime ace Arthur Laumann; both proudly wearing their early-pattern DLV uniforms and decorations. Udet on the other hand wore morning dress and top hat – his 'monkey suit' as he called it; thereby bringing a reproof from Lörzer for not showing himself in his DLV uniform. And three days before Göring had set up the *Geheime Staatspolizei* – the Gestapo.

By this time Udet was quite used to seeing huge audiences at his various displays, but on 1 May even he was startled to see one and half million spectators! The venue was Berlin's Tempelhof aerod-rome, and the occasion a celebration of the National Labour Fes-tival, organised by the Nazi party. Hundreds of SA formed long lines, keeping the masses under crowd control. High above the Graf Zeppelin airship passed in silver majesty, while elsewhere aircraft formations and the aerobatic wizards, Udet, Stör and Achgelis per-formed for the crowds. It was an undoubted piece of masterly organisation. But the real star of the show was Hitler himself, who addressed the masses as evening came. The wholly impressive occasion was then rounded out with a giant fireworks display. That same day Göring was promoted to the all-embracing status of Reich Minister for Aviation.

Two days later, at the home of his friend Kleffel, Professor Gott-fried Feder, one of the original members and founders of the

NSDAP, was extolling the virtues of the Nazis. Quietly, Udet turned to Kleffel's mother and said, 'We remain what we are, red-white-black, eh, Frau Kleffel?' When Feder asked him if he would be prepared to undertake aerial propaganda for the NSDAP, Udet retorted, 'Certainly, it just depends on what you're prepared to pay me.'

Nevertheless, in spite of his former views, Udet acknowledged that the Nazis had fostered aviation, and apparently rejuvenated the country. He decided he would join the NSDAP. This was easier said than done. After the Nazi victory in January many thousands of opportunists had flocked to join – now one needed an introduction. Udet went to see Franz Dahlmann whom he had befriended when Dahlmann was an officer of the air police at Tempelhof, and who had since become an NSDAP member. The two men went to the NSDAP office on the Kurfüstendamm where they were at once ushered into the office of the *Ortsgruppenleiter*. This worthy was so overcome that the great Udet wished to join the party that he immediately offered him his own party badge! They left the flabbergasted *Leiter* later and went straight to the Café Künstlereck where, with the help of a few cognacs, Udet practised the Nazi salute. . .

On 4 and 5 June Udet was back at work, flying at the national Whitsuntide Aviation Display being held at Hamburg's Fühlsbüttel airfield. Afterwards he returned to Berlin where he had been invited to a dinner at the German Aero Club, given in honour of 25 members of both Houses of Parliament in Britain who were on a flying tour through Germany. Present was Pg.* Hermann Göring, and Udet sat opposite Lord Willoughby de Broke, one of 10 pilots flying their private aircraft on the tour. Udet, naturally, drew a caricature for Willoughby's scrapbook. When someone told Udet that he thought him very courageous to do such dangerous flying in his films, Udet replied jokingly, 'Courageous? Each time I take off I shut my eyes tightly and move any handle at random. It has to work then. . .'

Meanwhile Erich Baier was busy preparing for Udet's forthcoming visit to the USA. Ernie had again been invited to perform in the National Air Races, and was also contracted to fly and perform at

---

* Pg – Parteigenosse – Party-Fellow – an abbreviation put in front of one's name which, if not exactly indispensable, was 'useful' to have in the contemporary political climate in Germany.

the World Fair in Chicago. Udet took two aircraft, the Flamingo and a Klemm Kl-32 XIV three-seater. On 8 June Udet flew the Flamingo to Bremerhaven, where it was quickly dismantled and put aboard the *Europa*, along with the Klemm, and they set sail next day. The Klemm was to be used simply for Udet to travel around in during his stay in America, while the trusty Flamingo would provide all necessary display flying. Privately he had already placed an order for two Curtiss Hawks with the Curtiss Wright Corporation, and Göring had made arrangements for the requisite cash to be transferred to the US Consulate in America.

The *Europa* finally docked on 15 June and Udet and Baier checked in to the St Moritz hotel. Udet then telephoned the New York office of the Curtiss company and confirmed that the purchase money had been duly transferred; he could have his pair of Hawks whenever he wished to take delivery. While at the hotel he contacted several friends and acquaintances, including another wartime comrade von Barnekow, former commander of Jagdstaffel 20 who now worked for General Motors in New York. His reception by the Americans was somewhat chillier than on his previous visit; due perhaps to the increasing reports of Nazi brutalities in Germany. On 21 June he started flying south to Los Angeles, being well received and feted at the various stops en route.

During one overnight stop at St Louis he was interviewed by press reporters, who questioned him closely about circumstances in Germany under Nazi rule. His reply was curiously naive:

> The position of Hitler in Germany is not understood or appreciated in other countries. Whatever Hitler does is not his own desires but of the 40-million Germans who are behind him. There have been exaggerated reports of what is taking place in Germany today. One thing is certain, the Kaiser will never return to the throne, that day is past. There have been a few cases where the Jews got the worst of it, but these are terribly exaggerated. The German Jew who minds his own business and is a good citizen has not been molested, and is carrying on today just the same as he ever did. Those not in the Communist Party go along in their usual way and are not disturbed. Things reached a point where something had to be done to stop the growth and spread of communism.

A peculiarly uninformed viewpoint when it was only three months since it was announced publicly in Germany that a KZ (Concentration Camp) was being constructed five kilometres from the picturesque town of Dachau, near Udet's 'home' town Munich. It was built for 5,000 prisoners around the buildings of a wartime ammunition factory; 'for the good of the Fatherland'. . . .

Finally arriving at Los Angeles, Udet and Baier were welcomed very cordially. There was even a delegation of Germans living in California, wearing white shirts which had been dyed brown, and even carrying swastika flags! Both men booked in to the Biltmore Hotel. The National Air Races for 1933 started on 1 July and lasted just four days. Highlight of the races was indisputably Udet's performance, which drew the loudest applause from the 100,000 spectators. Throughout the four days Udet was beleaguered by the press and photographers, the latter especially requesting shots of him in front of the Flamingo, wearing the DLV uniform which he had brought along at the express wishes of Göring and Lörzer.

Once the races were over invitations were showered upon Udet from all sides. Actresses Mary Pickford and Lilian Harvey wanted him to visit their homes, as did Harold Lloyd, who invited Ernie to see his famous swimming pool – and walk along its bottom wearing a diver's helmet! A number of American pilots gave a huge dinner in his honour in the Biltmore Bowl, and Udet sat next to Le Roy Prinz, the American he had shot down on 21 August 1918 in an SE5a, near Hébuterne, France; his 57th victory. On 7 July he flew to Inglewood to visit the Northrop Corporation subsidiary of the Douglas Aircraft Company, and a week later he was at San Diego's military aviation field, by invitation. The following day he visited the Universal film studios where, among other things, he was offered a lucrative contract as adviser for a film about Manfred von Richthofen. Udet declined the offer – von Richthofen was too revered in Germany to be subjected to any Hollywood treatment.

The following weeks went by in similar vein; a round of various US aircraft manufacturers, interspersed with dozens of social invitations and occasions, each outdoing the other with lavish hospitality in the American tradition. By 1 September however Baier and Udet were in Chicago for the start of the World Fair there. Udet's flashing display earned him tumultuous applause for each of the first four days of the exhibition, and he became the darling of the crowds. Three weeks later, on 29 September, came the day Udet had longed for – the day he first saw 'his' Hawks. He had flown to the Curtiss works at Buffalo, and now here they were; beautiful, all-silver, brand-new, sparkling in the pale sunshine. They were Hawk II's, the export version of the US Navy's F11C, and could be fitted with twin floats. Curtiss had no objections to exporting Hawks to Nazi Germany – wasn't there talk of Germany re-arming? They would need aircraft, and business was business. . .

Udet could hardly wait to get his hands on the Hawks, and as soon as each had been test-flown by the Curtiss test-pilot, Lloyd Child, Udet was strapped into one and took off. Within minutes he was putting it through a series of aerobatic manoeuvres. Just like his first flight in his faithful Flamingo, it was a case of 'love at first sight'. He stayed at Buffalo until 5 October, then flew to New York's Floyd Bennett Field, where everything was dismantled and packed for the return sea journey to Germany. On the 7th and 8th Udet gave his final display in the USA, at a charity function at Roosevelt Field; then attended the premiere of his film *SOS Eisberg* in New York. Four days later he sailed aboard the *Europa*.

On the morning of 19 October Udet stepped ashore in Germany again. It was a warm reception waiting for him. A minister from Göring's bureau ensured that the crated Hawks (already arrived on a freight ship) went through the customs without any problems. 'Udlinger', as his friends were calling him now, had come home.

It was a bright day when Udet first demonstrated the Hawk to a party of RLM officials, a bitterly cold day with a wintry sun brightening the lake-studded woodlands surrounding Rechlin airfield. Taking off directly from in front of the hangars, Udet made four climbs in a row to 4,000 metres, each time hurtling down to within a few hundred metres of the ground. Yet when he taxied in again, hardly a word was said. The general consensus was that the Hawk was too slow, too vulnerable to anti-aircraft fire for its intended military role. Many of the high-ranking officials privately thought that this 'amateur strategist' had no place here anyway. And popular as he was, he was more of a filmstar than an officer. What's more they frowned on his pranks, his drinking, and his womanising.

On 16 December Udet demonstrated the Hawk again, this time at Tempelhof in front of Erhard Milch. While Udet had been in the USA, Milch had signed an order on 12 October setting up the first *Sturzkampffliegerverband* dive-bombing unit – at Schwerin airfield. Now he asked Udet to attend all future conferences at the RLM which concerned dive-bombing. After all, Udet was one of relatively few experienced pilots in Germany who really knew what it was like to dive in a high-powered aircraft. Until now Udet had only considered the Hawks as splendid aircraft for his flying displays; but his thoughts were gradually spreading to its application for bombing – he was 'getting involved'. . .

In his private life his friend Kleffel had several times suggested that he should write a book about Udet's career, but Ernie had always put him off. Now Ullstein was definitely interested in publishing an autobiography of Udet and they sent Dr Paul Karlsen to help him with it, in fact to ghost-write it for him. The two spent many hours together, talking and taking notes as Udet described the many facets of his past. When Kleffel heard of this he immediately went to the Ullstein director to protest – after all, he was Ullstein's aviation expert! However Kleffel was by no means popular with the Nazis – he was on his way out. The book, to be titled *Mein Fliegerleben* – My Flying Life – was to be published under Udet's name, but he was no writer – indeed, he read very little, preferring more active pursuits – so needed Karlsen to complete the manuscript.

While all this was happening Udet had met Inge, a cultured, good-looking, elegant woman who had been married to a member of the Stuttgart textile industrialist family Bleyle. Udet was soon confiding to his closest friends, 'This is the woman I want to marry'.

CHAPTER TEN

In Uniform Again

Erich Baier and Ernst Udet finally parted company on 6 January 1934. During the past six years Baier had come to mean very much more than just a mechanic to Udet. He had not only looked after the aircraft, but had done all kinds of work to help the flier. They had flown together, been in Africa, Greenland and America together. Udet had even taught Baier to fly. The two had become true comrades. Now Baier wanted to marry, settle down to a more staid routine in life. They parted on the very friendliest of terms; Baier going to work for the Bavarian Motor Works in Munich, while Udet also went south, to his beloved Alps at Garmisch. On 4 February, the motor-sport season was opened by races in the frozen Titisee in the Black Forest, while the general festivities began in the morning with the Horst Wessel song. In the afternoon Udet flew a display programme for the 15,000 spectators, in the Flamingo, and then won the car-versus-aircraft event at an average speed of 105 km/hr.

Returning to Berlin he then began to familiarise himself with the Hawk in preparation for the coming display season. His first public demonstration of the Hawk took place at the Easter *Volksflugtage* at Tempelhof. The only technical snags encountered with the high-powered aircraft was when German-made spark plugs were fitted, so it was necessary to import plugs from America. Easter Sunday, 1 April, saw 120,000 people swarm towards Tempelhof, where the crowd, after a varied programme of aerobatics by other pilots, parachute demonstrations, formation flights, and joy-rides, watched breathlessly as Udet shot across Tempelhof at 300 km/hr, then pulled up into two consecutive loops. Coming out of the second loop at 250 km/hr, he climbed straight up doing vertical slow rolls. When the air speed fell to 150 km/hr Udet did a flick roll, coming out of it on his back at a height of 800 metres. A last roll, then the vertical dive from that height, his speed rapidly building up until he roared across the airfield doing 550 km/hr with the huge Cyclone engine

149

at full revs. Then straight up again where a vertical bank was started. The crowd exploded in wild applause.

Among the horde of journalists and press photographers who wrote ecstatic reviews of Udet's performance was his old friend Kleffel, who wrote about Udet's 'dive-bomber'. He was promptly arrested by the Gestapo who charged him with treason for 'divulging a state secret that the Hawk was a dive-bomber!' Though he was soon released, Kleffel immediately went to the RLM to see Kapitän zur See Wenninger, chief of the Zentralabteilung (Central Office). Here he calmly said, 'It was through my efforts that you got these Hawks. I reported on them in 1930, always referring to them as dive-bombers. How can I be charged with treason and divulging State secrets, when I now use my own description?' Kleffel heard no more of the charge.

In April the RLM changed the German aircraft registration system. Instead of a 'D', followed by four figures, all registrations henceforth were to be 'D' followed by four letters. Thus when Udet flew one of the Hawks at Hamburg's Fuhlsbüttel airfield on 20 May it bore the new markings D-IRIS. Its wing leading edges were decorated in red, as was the engine cowling.

In between his demonstrations Udet was teaching Erhard Milch to fly. Milch, Göring's Minister for Aviation, was highly intelligent and a quick student. Udet and Milch, the latter recently promoted to *Generalmajor*, got along fine. After about six hours instruction Udet yelled to Milch, 'Right, you're doing fine. You can fly by yourself' – then promptly threw his joystick overboard! Milch, an ex-wartime observer, wasn't fooled, he knew this traditional joke. The control column Udet had thrown out was a spare which Udet had surreptitiously smuggled aboard. However, he went along with the joke, showing convincing alarm, and could hear Udet's roars of laughter above the noise of the engine.

Milch at this time was energetically building the clandestine German air force, though its 'secret' existence was virtually known by foreign countries by now. Milch's orders, in this event, were to make it impossible for any other country, especially France and England, to *prove* Germany had an air force. The Nazi propaganda machine worked hard to preserve this illusion, and one film was described by *Newsweek*, dated 19 May 1934:

Patriotic Germans dutifully shudder when the official Air Defence League flashes its terrifying propaganda on the screens. Mag-

nificent 'foreign' planes rain down gas and incendiary bombs on
the 'helpless Fatherland.' Then pretty girls pass among the
hushed audience holding out bomb-shaped collecting boxes for
pennies for the League. A storm trooper points to the moral;
Germany is forbidden to own such beautiful, death-dealing bombers. But few foreign statesmen doubt that Germany is building
them, and buying them abroad as fast as General Hermann
Wilhelm Göring, dynamic Air Minister, can arrange it.

In the previous week the London correspondent of the *New York
Times* had revealed some details of the Reich's recent purchases,
saying,

> Within a year Germany will be in a position to add to her air
> force by assembling practically overnight some 3,000 to 4,000
> machines. . . Theoretically such planes are for 'commercial use',
> others are for 'sport'. For 'sport' Major Ernst Udet, spectacular
> German ace, bought two Curtiss Hawk military ships. Also for
> 'sport' General Göring has outfitted young air enthusiasts in
> martial grey-blue uniforms. The 'sportsmen' do not fly at will.
> They are mustered into a national federation under leaders called
> Airmen Vice Commodores . . .

Already the 'Luftwaffe Legend' had been born. . .

Milch often invited Udet to attend conferences at the RLM, and
though Udet had no official status whatsoever, his influence on
official aviation circles was considerable. For example, he had been
able to have his friend Willy Messerschmitt's BFW – resurrected in
1933 – included with the Henschel and Focke-Wulf firms as recipi-
ents of a contract for three prototypes of a *Kampfzerstörer* – a new
concept for a heavy, twin-engined fighter with long range. The
outcome was the Fw 57, the Henschel Hs 124, and the design which
ultimately was built in large quantities, the Messerschmitt Bf 110.
Not all at the RLM were partisans of the dive-bomber concept.
Udet, who had become an 'addict' of dive-bombing, started an
enthusiastic crusade, getting full support from Oberst Wever, chief
of the *Luftkommandoamter*. The first Henschel 123's and Heinkel
He 50's were interim dive-bombers, due soon, but Udet pressed the
urgency for issuing specifications for the second phase of the dive-
bomber programme. He knew that Pohlmann of the Junkers works
at Dessau had started design of a modern aircraft which eventually

became the Junkers Ju 87; while the same firm were already experimenting with their K-47 design, while a mock-up of the projected
Ju 87 was under construction.

Another concept being pushed by Udet to the RLM was that of
gliders being used to land troops behind the battle lines. All research
in connection with gliding was being carried out by the Deutsches
Forschungsinstitut für Segelflug (DFS) at Darmstadt-Griesheim. In
1932 the Alexander Schleicher Flugzeugbau at Poppenhausen had
built a heavy, 28 metres-span, three-seat OBS glider, designed by
Dr Alexander Lippitsch. It was so heavy that a BFW Flamingo, D-
1540, had tipped onto its nose at the end of the small Wasserkuppe
airfield in its unsuccessful attempt to tow the glider aloft. Udet, on
hearing of this project, went to see the OBS at Darmstadt, and
foresaw the possibilties of a large glider being capable of transport-
ing ammunition and other supplies to beleaguered troops, or dropping troops behind enemy positions. He expounded the idea with
RLM officials, where it found favour.

Another advantage of Udet's close connections with the RLM
was that no aircraft manufacturer refused Udet a flight in his latest
product; indeed, many usually asked him to try out their newest
designs. Thus, among others, he was able to try the latest trainers
about to replace the ageing Flamingos, such as the Arado Ar 66,
Bücker Bü 131, Focke-Wulf Fw 44 designed by his friend Kurt
Tank, Gotha Go 145, and Heinkel He 72. Apart from Milch, Udet
had other friends at the RLM, including Major Karl Bodenschatz,
now Göring's adjutant, Oberst Wever and Oberst Kesselring.

On 12 June Udet was at Dübendorf in Switzerland. Though not
an official agent for the Curtiss firm, he could earn a handsome
commission if he persuaded the Swiss to buy Hawks. His demonstration of the Hawk, particularly its diving ability, impressed the
Swiss officials gathered to watch, but produced no firm orders. Two
weeks later Göring gave a speech at the close of the annual Aviation
Rally round Germany, ending with the words, 'The German people
has to become a nation of fliers'. Yet six days later, 30 June, he was
involved in the bloody *Putsch* in which Ernst Röhm, head of Hitler's
SA and one of the few able to address the Führer as '*Du*' instead of
the less intimate '*Sie*, was murdered, along with hundreds of other
followers.

That day Berlin was in a state of uproar, but Udet was driving
through the city, accompanied by Elly Beinhorn, intending to visit
friends at Grünewald. As he drove along the Kurfürstendamm he

was stopped by a young SS officer who curtly ordered Udet out of the car and reached towards the car's glove compartment. Udet barred his way defiantly, glowering at the SS man who was much taller.

'Get your hands off,' Udet shouted, 'Can't you see there's a lady sitting in my car?'

The SS man pointed his pistol at Udet and said, 'You'll have to come with me.'

'Oh no we won't,' Udet shot back. 'If you want anything from me then report to my office at the RLM!'

The SS officer stepped back, meekly, saying, 'Yes, *Herr Major*, my apologies'.

Udet's bluff had worked. Nevertheless he thought it wise to get far away from Berlin and quickly, so drove to the country house of a director of the Roth-Büchner ('Rotbart') firm at Blankensee and spent the night there. Next day he returned quietly to Berlin.

The Hawk D-IRIS was next demonstrated on 15 July, this time at the NS Flugschau (Nazi Flying Display) on the occasion of the opening of a new airfield at Altona. The clouds were low that day and Udet disappeared from view each time he climbed after a power-dive. Five days later disaster struck. Udet was climbing D-IRIS over Tempelhof aerodrome at some 1,000 metres when he rolled the Hawk and his seat collapsed, blocking the controls. The Hawk fell away in a vicious spin, leaving Udet no alternative but to get out. Managing to jump clear he parachuted down and hit the ground in some allotments south of Tempelhof – and promptly fainted. The Hawk meanwhile crashed right in front of Rudolf Müller coming in for a spot landing in a Klemm Kl 31. Siren wailing, the Sanitätswagen (ambulance) took Udet to hospital where he recovered quickly, being uninjured. His Hawk, however, had exploded into flames on crashing – little remained of it. Future displays would need to be flown in the other Hawk, now registered as D-IRIK and all-silver in finish.

Many Germans were now in some sort of uniform – SA, SS, Hitler-Jugend, DVL and many other recently-created organisations each with their own distinctive uniform and insignia, making the wearer's status clearly visible. The Nazi Party was tightening its grip on Germany. Five days after the Annual Party Day at Nurenberg – from 4 to 10 September – the Party ordered that all German aircraft were henceforth to bear a swastika on each side of the fin, replacing the old red-white-red national markings.

In October the Nazis arrested Kleffel and took him to the Kolumbiahaus in Berlin, then to Lichtenburg, and finally put him in the Dachau concentration camp. As a journalist and speaker on Radio Berlin, Kleffel had many clashes with the Nazis; now they acted to be free of him. He wrote to Udet for help, but Udet's influence within the RLM was powerless against the authority of the Gestapo. Also arrested was Alfred Richard Weyl, an engineer of the DVL, Adlershof, who had assisted in the design of the U-1 in 1921. Luckily for Weyl he was able to escape from Germany after his arrest and flee to England.

The Nazis wanted to make Udet's base airfield, Tempelhof, a showpiece for the modern Germany, and on 29 October 1934 Hitler came to the aerodrome for conference with the director and Commandant to finalise plans for renewing the air port. Professor Sagebeil was ordered to prepare plans for a completely new *Luftkreuz Europas* – the centre of European aviation. It was merely one facet of the Nazi desire to develop aviation nationally, typified by a decree on 17 November by the Minister of Education, Science and People's Enlightenment, Bernhard Rust. In future all schools were to integrate aviation in their syllabuses. Material, books and so on were to be purchased at once, model aircraft construction taught, gliding training made available, aviation subjects generally provided – as Göring had prophesied, Germany was indeed to be a nation of aviators. The DLV itself was doing everything possible to foster aviation, while the official DLV magazine, *Luftwelt*, was enthusiastically edited by Udet's old friend Walter Angermund, who did his utmost to make Germany air-minded.

Angermund also wrote that Udet was about to feature in another flying film, *Wunder des Fliegens* – Miracle of Flight. The film's story was simple; young Heinz Muthesius's father had died as a pilot during the war. Heinz's greatest wish was to become a pilot, but his mother thwarted any plans in that direction. By chance he gets to know Udet, who shows an interest when he discovers the boy's father was an old comrade. Udet takes the boy for a flight and to a flying display; then talks the mother into allowing Heinz to enrol in a gliding club. After a holiday with Udet in Switzerland the boy learns to glide and gains his brevet. Wanting to prove his ability he flies near the Zugspitze but, due to the weather conditions, crashes. Rescue teams are sent out, but it is Udet who finally finds him. Made by Heinz Paul, the film was really a succession of superb flying sequences, filmed by Schneeberger. It was a magnificent piece of propaganda for aviation, and also heightened Udet's reputation and popularity.

Among the various cartoons he prepared for the 1935 'calendar' book for his friends was one depicting himself and his pet dog Bulli weeping beside the 'grave' of his faithful Flamingo D-822. It had been totally written off when another pilot had been entrusted with ferrying the aircraft back from Innsbruck. He had attempted to make a *Kavalierstart* – flying or racing start – but crashed instead.

December 14 saw him in the Springe hunting preserve near Hannover, where he had been invited by Göring for a charity wild boar hunt. *Reichsjägermeister* (Master of Hunting) Göring had also invited, among others, Viktor Lütze, new head of the SA, and the director of the Berlin Zoo, Lutz Heck. Before the hunt, Göring, in his element as the jovial host, invited his many guests to an open-air breakfast near a wood-fire. Warmly clothed in their *Lodens* (woollen clothing), the guests enjoyed the hunter's black bread and the obligatory 'heart-warming' schnapps.

Apart from hunting, Udet's great passion remained flying. For more than ten years he had dreamed of flying a glider over the Zugspitze, free as a bird. Now, this winter, his dream was about to come true. He was to use one of the delightful DFS Rhönbussards, designed by Hans Jacobs, who at this time was busy on secret development of the first troop-carrying glider, the DFS 230. Udet's Rhönbussard was towed from the frozen Eibsee, and, using the powerful up-draughts along the Zugspitze slopes, he was soon soaring high above the peak, looking down at the observatory.

A dream had finally become reality for Göring too. Hitler had decided that the clandestine German air force was to become totally independent of the army, and form a third service. When Hitler signed the order on 26 February, the initial title used was the Reichsluftwaffe, but this name was soon reduced to simply Luftwaffe, by which the air service was known thereafter. At the same moment it was decided that, from March, the existence of the Luftwaffe would no longer be denied; the whole world was in the 'secret' by now. Additionally the Luftwaffe would be a useful political weapon; henceforth Germany's neighbours had to be impressed with the might of the new Germany.

Thus, from 1 March, life became easier for the air service. Training, ordering new aircraft, all could now be done openly. The DLV uniforms worn by all members of the secret Luftwaffe came in handy; epaulettes were changed, military rank badges and insignia sewn on, and the 'new' uniform was ready. It was Göring himself who made the existence of the Luftwaffe public, during an interview with Ward Price, *Daily Mail* correspondent, on 10 March.

Göring was also busy planning the occasion of his second marriage, to the actress Emmy Sonnemann, due to take place on 10 April, with Hitler himself as one of the witnesses. It was a big state occasion, and a full banquet was given that evening at the Kaiserhof, with Udet as one of the 224 guests. 21 April was not only Easter but also the seventeenth anniversary of Manfred von Richthofen's death. For the first time the anniversary was named *Tag der Reichs-luftwaffe*, and instead of the traditional army detachment, it was now an impeccable detachment of the Jagdgeschwader von Richthofen* which marched through the Unter den Linden.

It was also the day of the traditional People's Aviation Day at Tempelhof, with some 250,000 spectators watching, among other events, Udet flying his remaining Hawk, and aerobatting in his Rhönsperber DFS glider, D-Udlinger. Udet then visited his friend Willy Messerschmitt's BFW plant at Augsburg to have a look at Messerschmitt's latest brainchild, the revolutionary Bf 109 fighter, which was being prepared for its first taxying trials. For those, like Udet, who had fought in fighters during 1914–18, the Bf 109 was indeed revolutionary, with its retractable undercarriage, landing flaps, and – horror! – an enclosed cockpit. And it was a metal monoplane. Until then Udet had seen only drawings of the design, but when he climbed in to the cramped cockpit and the canopy was closed over his head, he did not look too enthusiastic. On getting out again he said to Messerschmitt, 'This will never make a fighter. A pilot needs an open cockpit. He has to feel the air rushing by. You should really install a second wing above, with struts in between'. Udet's outdated ideas were shared by many other contemporary pilots...

He next flew the prototype Henschel Hs 123 dive-bomber, at Johannisthal on 8 May, a design from which much was expected. Ten days later, but effective from 1 June, Udet was named an *Oberst* in the Luftwaffe, and given three months' unpaid leave until the end of August. He had finally enlisted, though for the 'leave' period he could fulfil all flying displays to which he was contracted already. Joining the military had not been an easy decision. Göring

* Named as such on 14 March, when the former secret fighter unit, Jagdgeschwader 132, based at Döberitz airfield west of Berlin, was retitled.

had continually asked him to do this, offering a command of a new *Jagdgeschwader* at Kitzingen, or a technical staff function where he could nullify the resistance being shown by some senior officers to the dive-bomber concept. Always before Udet had declined. He had his Hawk and his Rhönsperber, while his display flying earned him a luxurious living style. Even if the novelty wore thin in Germany, there was always a market for his skills in the rest of the world. Meanwhile his influence at the RLM meant he could fly virtually any aircraft he chose to in Germany. Yet he had some doubts. Inevitably the day would come when he'd be too old for flying displays; what then? Göring's incessant appeals to Udet's sense of honour and duty to the Fatherland finally bore fruit – he said yes.

Financially, his decision was a huge sacrifice as it meant relinquishing the handsome income from displays, publicity, and films, in exchange for the wages of a mere *Oberst*; 1,050 marks every month, supplemented by about 150 marks flying pay, and some 160 marks for 'living expenses'. A single flying display brought him at least 3,000 marks. However, he was still the idol of the masses, especially the young aviation enthusiasts of the Hitler-Jugende. Until September Udet was still a free man, and he pursued a round of displays, with intervals when he flew his D-ERNI all over Germany, visiting friends and simply indulging his prime love of flying. Then came 25 August – a sad day for Ernie. It was the occasion of the *Grossflugtag* at Hannover. Udet aerobatted in his Hawk and the gull-winged Rhönsperber with his usual consummate elegance and skill, then, a little after 5 pm, landed. He had starred at a flying display for the last time in his life.

Udet's first 'active service' posting was notified to him as commander of a new fighter unit, despite Göring's assurance to Udet that he would remain with the Reichsluftfahrtministerium (RLM). A telephone call to Göring quickly led to cancellation of the administrative order, and Udet was officially assigned to the RLM from 1 September. Here his first task was an agreeable one, as leader of a German gliding team participating in the International Gliding Camp from 4 to 18 September in Switzerland, high up on the Jungfraujoch. Apart from Udet, three other pilots were in the team; Peter Riedel, Heini Dittmar and Ludwig Hofmann, all very experienced glider men. During the meeting Udet flew to Nuremberg on the 15th, and next day gave a dive-bombing demonstration in his Hawk, D-IRIK at the 'Party Day of Liberty', attended by Hitler. He then flew straight back to Thun, the base for the gliding team.

By coincidence the following day saw the first flight, at Dessau, of the prototype of the most famous dive-bomber of all time, the Junkers Ju 87.

Promotion to *Oberstleutnant* for Udet came on 1 October, with seniority retrospective to 1 May 1935. Ten days later the Reichsluftahrtministerium was formally opened in its new location; a huge building designed by Professor Dr. Sagebeil, at the corners of the Leipziger-Wilhelm and Prinz Albrecht streets; thereby bringing together the RLM's former dispersed offices under a single roof. On 7 November Udet, as an active officer, swore the oath of allegiance to the Führer, Hitler. He was now an integral servant of the Nazi regime.

December 7 was the 'Day of National Solidarity' in Germany, and Udet, together with other Luftwaffe officers who held a Pour le Mérite during the war – Buckler, Lörzer, Bolle, Veltjens – could be seen standing in the streets of Berlin holding collecting boxes, inviting contributions for the Winterhilfswerk charity organisation. Much of their time was spent signing autographs, but cash flowed freely into the boxes. For himself Udet needed no charity. Though no longer earning large sums from flying displays, his book *Mein Fliegerleben* was bringing in handsome royalties; having sold 600,000 copies by the close of 1935.

CHAPTER ELEVEN

Paperwork and Records

'One thing I can promise you; don't expect too much office-work from me,' Udet had said when he first joined the RLM. Nevertheless he could hardly avoid becoming gradually entangled in the ultra-bureaucratic machinery of the ministry. Paperwork was not his metier, though occasionally he scribbled brief notes in his small, leather-bound notebook.

January 12: Design a Stuka insignia
January 13: 11 o'clock, medical check-up
January 15: Wild boar hunt, Plauen
January 16: 4 pm Milch
January 23: Kriegspiel at Damm.

On 2 February his notebook entry was a single word, Garmisch; he was on his way for the Olympic Winter Games there. Udet had arranged some special sailplane exhibitions during the Games. With Lufthansa pilot Peter Riedel as companion, Udet drove – flew might be a better description of Udet's method of driving any car – to Munich, where both men sampled the Franzsikaner's traditional *Münchener Weisswurst* (white sausage) next morning, before completing the road journey to Garmisch.

At the Games the German pilots – Udet, Riedel, Dittmar, Hofmann and the girl Hanna Reitsch – gave masterly displays each day in the sheer art and beauty of silent flight as they glided above the crowds. Udet showed that his skill and nerve were still supreme, performing loops which rounded out mere metres above the ice within the stadium area. Among the many visitors to the Games were Hitler, Elly Beinhorn and her husband, and Udet's first love, Lo. After their divorce they had remained friends and met each other occasionally. When Elly Beinhorn asked Lo why she had left Udet, however, Lo looked surprised, then said, '*I* left *him*? You should ask him again, Elly!'

Further elevation for Udet came on 10 February when it was

159

announced officially that he had been appointed Inspector of Fighter and Dive-Bomber Pilots. He was now Chief of *Fl In 3* – one of four Inspectorates of the Luftkommandoamt (LA); the others being Bombers, Reconnaissance pilots and Photography, and the third for rolling stocks for the Luftwaffe. The LA – the Luftwaffe's General Staff – was one of nine large sections of the RLM. As Chief of Fl In 3, Udet had to decide which design would be the next Luftwaffe fighter to follow the Heinkel 51. There had been complaints about the He 51; it was not an easy aircraft to fly, especially for pilots trained on the docile Arado 65F. It was planned to have the Arado Ar 68, but this offered only marginal improvements over the Heinkel. Another possibility was the Focke-Wulf 159. Udet, typically, decided to test the contenders himself and ordered a mock combat trial at Rechlin, flying the Arado 68 himself and easily out-manoeuvring the clumsier Heinkel. The Ar 68 was therefore ordered in quantity.

The Arado 68's life was nevertheless short, and by 1936 the latest choice for a new fighter virtually lay between the Messerschmitt Bf 109 and Heinkel's He 112; both monoplanes. Final selection rested with Udet, as Inspector of Fighters, and with his old comrade Robert Ritter von Greim, Udet tested both types in straight flying tests and mock dogfights. The final tests took place at Travemünde from 26 February to 2 March. Hermann Wurster, the latest chief test pilot of the BFW firm, was to fly the Bf 109, while the Heinkel was to be piloted by Gerhard Nitschke. First, both men demonstrated their aircraft's aerobatic capabilities, which quickly showed that the Bf 109 could roll faster than the Heinkel. Further spinning and other manoeuvres were flown; then came the final trial – a high-speed dive at optimum power. No specific height was given. Wurster climbed to 7500 metres, took a deep breath, put the airscrew into coarse pitch, then simply dropped the 109's nose. The angular monoplane screamed down with its speed steadily building and the engine revving ever faster. As it neared its peak speed the supercharger blew apart – then it was time to pull up. Wurster blacked out, quickly recovered, and brought the 109 in for a perfect landing. The Heinkel He 112's fate was sealed; it could not emulate, let alone better, the 109's performance. Willy Messerschmitt was ordered to set up series production of the Bf 109.

A month later, on 2 April, a less eventful occasion was the arrival at Tempelhof of Colonel the Master of Sempill, who had flown from Croydon, England in G-ADPJ, a BAC 'Drone' light aircraft, pow-

et with Erich Baier

et in conversation with
ns Grade at the
mpia Flugtag, 1936. In
background is one of
et's two Curtiss Hawks.

et (in top hat), flanked
Bruno Lörzer and Arthur
umann, at the reinterment
the body of Manfred von
chthofen on 21 April 1933
rzer and Laumann are
earing the 'new' DLV
iform.

(*Right*) *High & Low*. Udet demonstrating his superb skill at altitude among the Alps, and at zero height through a hangar.

(*Left*) Udet with Thea Rasche and Gerhard Fieseler.

(*Left*) Udet's Curtiss F-11 Hawk, D-IRIS in German markings.

(*Bottom Left*) Udet with Rhönbussard, D-UDET, 1936.

(*Right*) Udet at the Olympic Winter Games in Garmisch 1936, talking to the popular German film-star, Leni Riefenstahl. In 1945 the woman was arrested by Allied authorities for being '. . . a friend of Hitler's . . .'

(*Far right*) Among his more 'experimental' feats, Udet successfully flew this Focke Wulf 'Stieglitz' under the giant airship *Hindenburg* 1937; hooking on and releasing from the dirigible

Ernst Udet in his element
touching the grass on
Tempelhof aerodrome wit
wing-tip 'skid' at slow sp

HIERARCHY. A meeting
Nazi leaders on 15 June
1938. From left: General-
oberst von Brauchitsch;
Adolf Hitler; Hermann
Göring, Ernst Udet (then
Generalmajor); and Admi
Raeder.

(*Below left*) Udet with
Flugkapitän Hanna Reitsc
1937. Reitsch, seated her
a Focke Wulf FW 61
'helicopter', became
Germany's leading woman
pilot, and flew a myriad o
dangerous experimental
tests in many German nev
aircraft designs. (*Below*)
Siebel Fh 104s, D-ILFR,
painted all-red, which Ude
acquired as his personal
transport in December 19

ered by a 23 hp-engine. Udet, along with Milch and Freiherr von Neurath, the German Foreign Minister, were among Sempill's reception committee. During May Udet flew several trials in the stop-gap Henschel Hs 123 prototype, but the final contenders for the eventual dive-bomber design for the Luftwaffe were the Junkers Ju 87, Arado, Heinkel 118 and the Blohm und Voss Ha 137; all four scheduled for final trials in the first week of June. Of these the Blohm und Voss was a single-seater with potential as an army close-support aircraft, and as such was personally favoured by the Chief of the Technical Development Section, Wolfram von Richthofen. Accordingly, on 9 June, von Richthofen made a confidential order to stop all further development of the Junkers Ju 87.

In the meantime several events took place. On many occasions Göring had offered Udet the opportunity to take over the Technical Bureau from Oberst Wimmer; one of the highest positions within the RLM, with immense responsibilities. Udet had steadfastly declined, saying, 'I have no knowledge of production, and know nothing about large aircraft. It's not for me.' Göring's reply was that what was needed most was inventiveness, imagination. For the rest he could have as many people as he wished. Udet still declined. Then, on 3 June, while attending a meeting of Wimmer's bureau in his capacity as Inspector of Fighters and Dive-bombers, a signal was received announcing the death of Generalleutnant Wever, Chief of the Luftwaffe's General Staff. Wever, who learned to fly when over fifty years of age, had crashed on take-off from Dresden in a Heinkel He 70.

Göring's response to this news was to replace Wever by General Albert Kesselring, an army officer who had only joined the Luftwaffe three years before. He also took the opportunity to replace Wimmer, whom Göring personally disliked. Telling Udet that Hitler himself wanted him as the new chief in Wimmer's place, he thus virtually bullied Udet into accepting the appointment, and was officially named as such on 10 June. Udet was now an *Amtschef* (Department Head), one of six at the RLM, and his *Amt* consisted of three major sections; Research, Development and Supply. Thus Udet, the fun-loving bon-viveur, display pilot, film actor and practical joker, who hated office-work and detested bureaucratic intrigue, was now sitting in Room 201 on the third floor of the RLM building – the man responsible ultimately for ensuring that the Luftwaffe got the right aircraft at the right time! Göring had manoeuvred the wrong man into the 'right' place!

Udet was fortunate to retain the services of Wimmer's right-hand man Hauptmann Max Pendele, an old fox in RLM business who knew his way round the RLM. Udet's first act in his new job was to immediately cancel Wolfram von Richthofen's order for stopping Junkers Ju 87 development. Von Richthofen took the hint and a few weeks later accepted a posting as chief of staff of the Condor Legion, the German volunteer corps fighting in Spain's civil war on the side of Franco. Udet next rang Ernst Heinkel, telling him that he (Udet) had not made his mind up yet about the eventual Luftwaffe dive-bomber design, and therefore for Heinkel to prepare his He 118 for Udet to test personally at Marienehe on 27 July.

Udet's responsibilities were now immense, necessitating his travelling all over Germany; visiting factories, airfields, and the testing centres at Rechlin and Travemünde. At the latter he watched trials with his old Hawk fitted with the *Jericho-Trompete* – a siren devised by Udet for fitting to dive-bombers to make their screaming dive even more terrifying to those below. All came within his aegis – bombers, dive-bombers, reconnaissance machines, night fighters, even the heavy long-range 'Ural bombers' then under construction such as the Dornier Do 19 and Junkers Ju 89. While on one visit to Rechlin he personally tested the 'Stösser' modified to serve as a dive-bombing trainer. New techniques and devices were constantly under review, including dive-brakes on gliders and a proposal from Fritz Thiede for mounting upwards-firing weapons on fighters. Still pursuing his idea for troop-carrying large gliders, Udet asked Professor Georgii, head of DFS, and his chief engineer Hans Jacobs to produce a ten-seat glider quickly; the first three prototypes were ready in January 1937.

Udet continued to fly many trials and tests personally, as on 3 July, when he piloted the third prototype Bf 109 during a mock combat 'interception' of four Heinkel He 51's – and 'shot' all four down with comparative ease. On 27 July he went to Marienehe to fulfil his promise to Ernst Heinkel to test his He 118. On arrival he was told that Heinkel himself could not be present as he was entertaining the American trans-Atlantic hero Charles Lindbergh, but had left an urgent message for Udet to be very careful to remember to put the He 118's propeller into coarse pitch before starting a dive. Intended flaps-cum-divebrakes had yet to be fitted to the machine.

Once seated in the cockpit Udet impatiently listened to Nitschke explaining the He 118's controls, then cut him short by saying, 'Just tell me where the throttle is!' He then took off, climbed to 4,000 metres, and started a vertical dive – completely forgetting to go into coarse pitch first. The engine ran away, the propeller and reduction gear flew off causing the machine to pitch violently, and then the tail broke away. Udet heaved himself out of the seat to take to his parachute – only to find one shoe jammed. Finally wrenching his foot free, Udet tumbled out, hit the earth on some stubble – and lapsed into unconsciousness; while the remains of the aircraft plunged to utter destruction.

When some Heinkel staff reached Udet he revived for a few moments, cursed the He 118 as a 'Shit-crate', then fainted again. He was rushed to the Rostock hospital but his injuries were light, some cuts and a sprained leg. His recovery was soon expedited when Ernst Heinkel and his old companion 'Robi' von Greim arrived carrying bottles of *Sekt*, and did not leave until about midnight!

His experience sealed the fate of the Heinkel He 118, and he decreed that the Junkers Ju 87 would become the Luftwaffe's standard dive-bomber. He also put off Heinkel's renewed pleas for his He 112 fighter, and told the designer that the RLM had decided to have each manufacturer concentrate on specialised types of aircraft in future; Heinkel for bombers and Messerschmitt for fighters. Heinkel's stubborn response, that he would produce a fighter capable of 700 km/hr within a year, merely left Udet unmoved.

Berlin was the host for the XI Olympic Games on 1 August, and Hitler used the opportunity to show the world how strong, prosperous and peace-loving the modern Germany had become; no expense was spared for the preparations and the necessary building construction, sport fields etc cost some 64-million marks alone. The Olympic Committee had consented to the inclusion of gliding demonstrations in order to incorporate the sport at the next Games and these were held at Staaken airfield on 4 August. Udet personally gave an exhibition of gliding aerobatics for the many guests at Göring's elaborate *Fest* held on the lawn of his palace on the Leipziger Platz. Among the host of international visitors to the Games was an old acquaintance of Udet's, Major Al Williams from the USA, who was immediately invited to Udet's apartment. Williams afterwards said of Udet that he had changed somewhat since their previous meetings in America in 1931 and 1933. He was now ' . . . a sober, serious individual'.

As a national figure Udet inevitably had to attend a succession of official and social events and occasions, where he even entertained large audiences with his plate-juggling and quick cartoons. Sometimes however, when his host or hostess was especially straight-laced or pompous, Udet would often make some crude remark causing even the most charming host to wince. His own charm and infectious grin usually smoothed over the moment, but more often now, even in the middle of the merry-making, Udet's mood could change abruptly. On such occasions he was heard to say to some close friend, 'It makes me sick to play the clown for people'. The moods seldom lasted, however, and he would quickly become his old self again. His personal aircraft at this time usually bore highly personal registrations; D-ERNI for his Klemm, D-UDET for his Rhönbussard, and D-UDLINGER for the Rhönsperber. Another Rhönsperber had even been registered as D-ERNST UDET.

August 23 was a special day for the little town of Prien in Bavaria. A large congregation of officials and their families was gathered at the little airfield, each dressed in their best uniforms, suits or prettiest dirndl dresses. The twin daughters of Major Braun, commander of Luftgaureserve 14 and proud holder of flying licence No. 5, waited impatiently, clasping posy bouquets and trying to memorise their welcome-poem. All were waiting to meet and honour the pilot who made the 1,500th landing at the five-years' old airfield. About 11 o'clock tension grew; the 1499th landing, a student on his way to Reichenhall who wanted to land at Prien on the way home. Then, from the direction of Munich came the sound of an aircraft, which quickly came into view. A high-winged Focke-Wulf Stösser fighter-trainer, carrying the now-visible black swastika and the registration D-IGOE. It was soon on finals, its splayed undercarriage feeling for the earth – Prien's 1,500th landing! With evidence of a sure hand at its controls, the Stösser side-slipped, rounded out, touched down – then hit a soft patch and flipped onto its back, shattering the propeller, and leaving its pilot hanging upside down on his shoulder straps. Udet had arrived from Schleissheim. . .

The crowd ran pell-mell towards the crash, the Prien Mayor still clutching the bottle of schnapps with which he had intended toasting the unknown pilot. A smiling Udet was extricated from his undignified position, then heartily welcomed the unexpected schnapps – and proceeded to help empty the bottle. He stayed as a guest of the Brauns that night, and during the evening went over to join a gathering of glider pilots at the Strandhotel nearby who entertained Udet and his hosts well into the small hours. Next day another aircraft arrived from Schleissheim to fetch Udet, but not before he had drawn a caricature in Braun's guest-book, depicting himself hanging from the overturned Stösser, with the caption, 'Nothing is spared me'.

A pleasant interlude, but then back to work . . . jotting notes in his note-book to remind him of the diverse duties of the Chief of the Technical Bureau;

Aug 31: Signals by groups of searchlights
Sep 1: Go 145? Diesel airship engines.
Sep 3: Refuse Paris Salon. Forbid exhibition to C-Amt. (When the 15th Paris Aviation Salon opened on 13 September, Germany and Italy refrained from taking part.)
Sep 5: Fast relief valve for Ju 52
Sep 8: Mock-up Heinkel
Sep 15: 109 smoke-bombs? Gronau?
Sep 17: Ask Göring what kind of picture Claus has to paint
Oct 10: More powerful helicopter
Oct 14: Convert fuel in litres
Oct 28: Fixed MG camera?
Nov 7: Why BMW VI?
Nov 27: Blind-flying
Nov 28: Thea Rasche trip to America? Thiele from Lufthansa to Heinkel

Udet became very interested in development of the helicopter. The ability to hover in flight seemed too good to be true, a dream become a reality. One German helicopter pioneer Walter Rieseler had obtained the RLM's support for building his R1 helicopter, powered by a 60 hp Hirth HM5 engine, and on September 3 Udet visited Rieseler to try it out. During his second flight the engine stopped and the machine crashed, though without injury to Udet.

On 16 November Udet was at Karinhall for a conference with Göring, who kept this meeting secret from Milch. Göring was frankly alarmed at Milch's growing influence, and was well aware that many people were referring to the Luftwaffe as 'Milch's Air Force'. Having been appointed on 18 October by Hitler as commissioner for the second Four Years' Plan, Göring could no longer devote all his time to the air service; in any case, now that the Nazis were in complete power he wanted a more leisurely form of life. Accordingly, he had decided to adopt the Roman stratagem – divide and rule. He would 'divide' Udet and Milch, and play them against each other. When Milch later found out about this meeting, Göring did not even give him a copy of the notes made.

Udet also had a meeting with his old author-friend Zuckmayer, who had fled to Austria when the Nazis came to power. He returned to Germany in secret, and wanted to have dinner with Udet at Horcher's Restaurant, one of their former haunts. Udet had said, 'No, not at Horcher's. That's the meeting place for all the big-wigs now', and suggested instead a small, unobtrusive restaurant. Udet arrived wearing discreet civilian clothes and advised his friend to leave Germany for good. 'Don't come back to Germany again. Here human dignity no longer reigns.' When Zuckmayer asked Udet's own plans, Ernie replied, 'I'm addicted to aviation. I can no longer get away, but one day the devil will claim us all.'

Though Germany declined to participate in the Paris Aviation Salon of 13 to 29 November, Udet accepted an invitation from the Cercle Militaire, and travelled to Paris on 22 November, accompanied by Major Werner Junck. Their orders were to proceed wearing full uniforms, but Udet objected to this. After all, there was Montmartre; one could hardly go there in gala uniforms. . . On arrival, however, they were assigned a virtual chaperon, Capitaine Paul Stehlin of the French Armée de l'Air, who was supposed to accompany them everywhere they went. Udet solved this problem by coolly drinking Stehlin under the table – then went to see a performance of the latest Charlie Chaplin film *Modern Times*, a film forbidden in Germany! One evening they went to a bar where one could, secretly, enlist to fight against Franco in Spain. Junck, an ex-airline pilot in South America who spoke Spanish fluently, jokingly proposed that he should 'enlist'.

The last day of 1936 saw Udet in Switzerland for what might be termed a sentimental journey. He was to ferry a 1918 aircraft from Dübendorf to Berlin. Six months previously on 20 June, the Aviation Museum* had been opened in Berlin by the city mayor. Originally organised at Stuttgart in 1929, then opened at Böblingen in June 1931, the authorities had finally decided that its proper location should be the capital, Berlin. In December 1936 the Museum had asked the Swiss Air Force if it could let them have one of the Fokker D VIIs still being used by the Swiss for training purposes, and the Swiss had offered one for no cost. One Fokker CH-46, a licence-

* Officially the *Deutsche Luftfahrt-Sammlung* – German Aviation Collection.

built machine during the war by the Albatroswerke, Johannisthal, had a swastika painted on its rudder and registration D-EIRA along its fuselage flanks.

When Hitler came to power, and started to re-arm Germany, he had not expected to be involved in any war until 1941. Then, in 1936, he intervened in Spain's Civil War. Reaction was sharp, with England protesting vehemently. Göring now thought that war might come much sooner than 1941, and feared both England and Russia. Accordingly, from 4 January 1937 the German aviation industry was 'mobilised'; the Luftwaffe had to be strengthened whatever the cost. Udet therefore visited every major aircraft manufacturer, and on 11 January conferred with Göring, Milch and Kesselring and announced a planned increase in output. The planned production of 758 Bf 109's by 1 April 1938 was now increased to 1,400. A week later he was host to a visiting party of Royal Air Force senior officers headed by Air Vice-Marshal Courtney; while on 18 February he received a delegation from Switzerland. Could they buy some Bf 109's? They certainly could – Germany desperately needed foreign currency.

The 25th anniversary of the *Deutsche Versuchsanstalt für Luftfahrt* (DVL) – Aviation Research Institute – was celebrated at Adlershof on 20 April. Sitting in the front row of hierarchy was Udet, wearing the white striping of a *General* on his uniform trousers – that same day he had been promoted to *Generalmajor*. Udet was not a vain person but he had always enjoyed being the centre of attraction. He was never very fond of uniforms, yet being a *General* rather tickled his vanity. That evening a celebration party was thrown in the house of a friend, von Blumenthal, with many of Udet's personal friends attending. As more and more bottles were emptied the party grew more boisterous, until eventually his circle of friends were treated to the unique spectacle of a *General*, a tablecloth around his waist, dancing the can-can on top of a table! *General* or not, Udet privately refused to take himself too seriously in high military rank; and his feelings were partly summed at the end of the huge martial parade at the *Fahnenweihe* – 'Blessing of the Flags' – at Schleissheim on 1 April when he turned to a friend and remarked, '*Scheisse!*' . . . flashy sabre-rattling was not to Udet's liking.

During one visit to Darmstadt Udet, accompanied by most leading German aircraft designers, asked Hanna Reitsch to demonstrate the DFS dive-brakes, and Fräulein Reitsch's vertical dives impressed the assembly greatly. Udet then conferred the coveted title *Flug-kapitän* upon Reitsch, the highest attainable pilot's licence, and the first occasion this was granted to a woman pilot in Germany. Later Reitsch and Udet personally tested the huge DFS 230 glider before a distinguished assembly of high-ranking Luftwaffe officers, includ-ing Milch, Kesselring and von Greim; lifting ten fully armed soldiers and landing them in a mock-war situation. Later, after the demon-strations had been completed, Udet surprised the DFS personnel present by taking them to a small store-room, saying that this had been his cell when serving with Fliegerbatallion 2 during the war. He explained, 'I was punished for dipping the commander's dog into a barrel of petrol. This pest had a nasty habit of biting soldiers' legs when they were on parade, at attention.' Professor Georgii laughingly said that in future the room would be known as the 'Udet-bar'. . .

In May Udet addressed the personnel at Oranienburg, near Ber-lin, on the occasion of the opening of Heinkel's new factory there. Only days before, on 29 April, Göring had issued a directive halting all further development of the Dornier Do 19 and Junkers Ju 89 'Ural-bombers' – though he did not bother telling Milch of this – and on 2 June Heinkel was instructed by the Technical Ministry to proceed with his 'Projekt 1041' which Heinkel had developed to the requirements of the 'Bomber A' programme drawn up a year earlier. This project eventually produced the Heinkel He 177. 2 June also saw a re-organisation of the RLM. Kesselring was replaced by General Stumpff as Chief of Air Staff, while von Greim succeeded to command of the personnel department. Milch was now no longer Göring's personal representative, and the General Staff was placed directly under Göring. Udet, however, still had direct access to Göring at any time, usually without any necessity to consult Milch first.

Göring and the leading German industrialists formed an audience for Udet on 16 June, when he made a long speech, outlining the build-up of the aviation industry, its rapid expansion, and how it was now necessary to slow down the pace. Shortage of basic materials was becoming crucial, while all existing production capacity was at present filled. The main emphasis in his speech was laid upon slowing down actual output, and the need to concentrate on certain standard aircraft developments, such as the Heinkel He 111, Dornier Do 17 and Messerschmitt Bf 109. He stressed the need for simplification of construction and modification, combined with increased efficiency and a reduction in overall costs. Unknown to Udet this decision to restrict quantitative production was to sow the seeds of his own self-destruction four years later. . .

A pleasant interlude in his duties allowed Udet to fly to England on 26 June to become one of the near-200,000 spectators attending the annual RAF Display at Hendon the following day, and Udet was the guest of the Master of Sempill for the week-end. His report on what he had seen at Hendon was made personally to Göring on 13 July, and at the same conference Udet discussed arrangements for the German participation in the International Flying Meeting due to be held at Dübendorf from 23 July to 1 August. This annual meeting, inaugurated in 1922, was rapidly becoming one of the world's most important aviation gatherings, and Milch had approached Hitler for permission for Germans to take part. Hitler not only consented, but ordered that Germans would do so in the grand style. Fifteen engineers and forty mechanics would accompany the flying team, while no less than twenty trucks were needed to convey all material and spares to Dübendorf.

Udet intended piloting D-ISLU, a Bf 109B-2, stripped of armament but fitted with one of the latest Daimler-Benz DB 600Aa engines, in the closed-circuit race for military aircraft; one of six Bf 109's participating. He flew the all-red painted Bf 109 to Dübendorf on 22 July, and three days later took off for the race. Partway through the race, however, engine failure forced Udet to land. Next day a further attempt was bedevilled with engine problems, and Udet's force-landing became a crash, wrecking the Bf 109 but causing no injury to its pilot. If Udet gained no honours, at least the Luftwaffe's prestige abroad was greatly enhanced. The other five Bf 109's had stirred intense interest, but it was the Dornier Do 17 – the 'Flying Pencil' as it was usually dubbed – which excited most foreign government representatives. In this design Germany possessed a bomber that was faster than any fighter in service in the world!

Much of September and October were taken up with a succession of military and social events. On the final day of the German Army's annual manoeuvres on 26 September, the Italian dictator Mussolini, accompanied by Hitler and their respective entourages attended; then went on to inspect the Luftwaffe's latest airfield at Wüstrow, in Mecklenburg. At the latter Udet demonstrated the Fieseler Storch before the many VIP's. On 4 October he was piloting a Heinkel He

111, V-16 – Milch's personal aircraft D-ASAR – to Paris to take up the invitation extended by the French government. For the next five days Udet was given the red carpet treatment, visiting French factories, squadrons and other aeronautical activities. The day following Udet and Milch's return from France, both men flew south to Hitler's mountain retreat at Obersalzberg to report in person on the French 'tour'. Milch particularly emphasised the French government's desire for improved relations with Germany, but Hitler hardly responded.

Only a week later Udet piloted Milch's Heinkel again, conveying Milch, Stumpff, and their staffs to Croydon airport on 17 October. The RAF was to be their host for an extensive programme of visits and inspections spread over the following week. The week's itinerary included detailed looks at various RAF stations, and their squadrons, covering each major facet of RAF operations and training; and even a tour of some of Britain's 'shadow factories'. The final venue was RAF Hornchurch, where the visitors were shown 54 and 65 Squadron's Gloster Gladiator biplane fighters – at no time throughout the week were they shown the Hawker Hurricane or Supermarine Spitfire – and given complete access to the technical data on these out-moded aircraft. On 25 October the German delegation flew home to Germany, where Udet and Milch hurried to Hitler to report on their visit to England. Both men warned Hitler not to underestimate the RAF, upon which the Führer calmly told them not to worry, he had no intentions of ever attacking England!

Shortly after his return Udet was visited by Ernst Heinkel, who informed him that his latest fighter project – Projekt 1035 – was ready; the 700 km/hr fighter he had promised Udet a year before. Udet was impressed and immediately ordered three prototypes and ten pre-production examples, allocating the number 100 – thus naming the He 100. During November another Heinkel design, the He 119-V4 D-AUTE piloted by Gerhard Nitschke, attempted to better the existing speed record over a closed circuit carrying a 1000 kg payload; but crashed during an emergency landing at Travemünde, seriously injuring Nitschke.

The Spanish Civil War had now been raging for a year and the Luftwaffe had already culled its first lessons in the operational employment of modern aircraft. One such lesson was the inaccuracy of traditional bombing techniques when compared with the pinpoint accuracy obtained by Ju 87's in Spain. The role of the Luftwaffe was seen as primarily tactical support for the army, where accurate bombing was essential. Thus Udet found it relatively easy to convince the staff that all new bombers under development should have a dive-bombing capability built in, and in December included this requirement for the Junkers Ju 88 *Schnellbomber* – high-speed bomber – thereby necessitating various modifications to the design and, incidentally, delaying progress to some degree. Medium-angle dives were even required of Heinkel's heavy He 177 long-range bombers, resulting in a number of problems for such a large aircraft.

Towards the end of the year Udet's old manager and friend Angermund was taken into the Luftwaffe again. Originally assigned to von Greim's department, he was transferred, at von Greim's suggestion, to Udet's bureau, to help him with the vast paper-work which Udet so detested. Udet was often given to issuing large orders for aircraft or equipment simply by a personal telephone call; remonstrating with any subordinate who queried his unbureaucratic ploy by saying, 'Isn't my word good enough then?' Angermund became chief of several departments under Udet's command; photographic, radio, the aircraft pool at the service of the RLM, production, and – appropriately – the editorship of *Flugwelt*. The existing easy-going structure and methods of procedure within the Technical Department worked well to Udet's way of doing things, but lower executive pressure was attempting to push through yet another restructuring plan, which Udet learned about from Werner Junck shortly before Christmas.

Udet, typically, refused to worry about such matters, particularly on the eve of the festive season, and reserved a table for himself and his girl-friend Inge at the Esplanade Hotel in Berlin to celebrate the New Year. He tugged at the tail of the piglet which was carried through the hall by a chimney sweep, who showered newly-minted pfennig coins around him – a traditional gesture of good luck. Later Udet retired to his home, taking with him a number of close friends, where they drained several bottles of champagne.

CHAPTER TWELVE

Bluff, Counter-bluff and War

'Me. Fowler?' Udet noted in his personal diary on 13 January 1938. It referred to the possibility of having the TA's latest aircraft requirement fitted with Fowler flaps. This requirement was for a successor to Messerschmitt's Bf 110 *Zerstörer*; a high-performance strategic fighter, heavily armed, with long endurance. The Bf 110 had been built broadly to this concept, but its successor was also to have a dive-bombing capability. In the event the design chosen to fulfil the new requirement was Messerschmitt's Me 210.

Three days after Udet wrote this cryptic note Göring ordered a change in the overall structure of the RLM. He created a total of seven departments only, all under his centralised control. Milch, former head of all departments, was placed in charge of one, thus placing him on an equal footing with the other six departmental heads, including Udet. Göring alone now co-ordinated the Luftwaffe's activities and effort, and no longer needed to fear 'competition' from Milch in the constant internal struggle for power and status within the Nazi regime. Milch − energetic, highly capable and very ambitious − resented this 'demotion', one consequence of which was the start of deteriorating relationship with − among others − Udet.

Further changes in the military hierarchy were instigated by Hitler himself on 4 February. Dismissing the War Minister, von Blomberg, and the Army Commander-in-Chief, von Fritsch, Hitler took over direct command of the whole Wehrmacht − a position which Göring had secretly coveted. As a sop to Göring, he was promoted to Generalfeldmarschall and Hitler personally presented him with a diamond-studded baton. Keitel became Chief of the Supreme Command, von Brauchitsch commander of the army, and von Ribbentrop succeeded to the post of Foreign Minister. In contrast to most of his highest-ranking officers, Hitler still did not believe that England would declare war on Germany as a result of his various moves to 're-unite all Germans' into one *Reich*, including Austrians and those resident in Czechoslovakia. Certainly he had no taste for a war with England, and therefore convinced himself that it would never happen. Most of the generals, however, thought differently, and on 18 February General Stumpff ordered the commander of the Luftwaffe's 2nd Group, General Felmy, to prepare precautionary measures for any such conflict in the near future.

Such high-flown political and military 'manoeuvring' had little if any impact on Udet, except the knowledge that he no longer needed to take orders from Milch, but could continue to have direct access to the Luftwaffe fount, Göring. He therefore continued his constant experimentation with latest developments in aviation. These varied widely, but included a particular favourite of Udet's, the Focke-Achgelis Fa 61 helicopter which had received unenthusiastic foreign press comment. Piqued by this lack of praise, Udet arranged for Hanna Reitsch to demonstrate the revolutionary design as one of the turns in a revue held in Berlin's Deutschlandhalle. Another highly unconventional design was the Ha 141 prototype, an asymmetrical reconnaissance aircraft which Udet personally test-flew at Hamburg at the end of February. Delighted with its handling qualities, Udet ordered three prototypes.

Hitler's determination to include Austria within the greater *Reich* culminated on 12 March when German troops marched across the Austrian border and occupied the country. On the 24th Göring, accompanied by Udet, journeyed to Austria. Relations between the two men had become very friendly, and the pair often went hunting on Göring's hunting preserve Rominten Heath, where Göring had a wooden hunting lodge, together with other acquaintances such as Lörzer, Körner, Bodenschatz and leading German industrialists. At Wiener Neustadt Udet, on behalf of the RLM, took over the works of Wiener Neustädter Flughafenbetriebs GmbH; later it was to be amalgamated into the Wiener-Neustädter Flugzeugwerke and become a major licensee for production of Messerschmitt Bf 109's. Back in Berlin, being no longer subject to Milch, Udet started to re-organise his own Technical Bureau on 28 March. Hitherto the structure had been simple; comprising four major sections on a horizontal plan of responsibility. The new organisation transformed this 'tree' into a vertical structure of no less than 14 sections; three for research and the remainder individually devoted to airframes, engines, bombs, armament, and other specific 'ironmongery'. In the event this new organisational structure was to get out of hand, far beyond Udet's control, and become unstable, unwieldy, and mediocre in actual productive capacity. Udet's aversion to desk-work, and his many absences from his post, pursuing some purely flying venture, made the eventual result almost inevitable – a breeding ground for bureaucratic intrigue and inefficiency.

For the moment, however, none of this was apparent to Udet, who continued to be reassured by Göring, parroting Hitler's assurances, that there would never be a war with England. Udet continued to take a deep personal interest in the latest aviation developments, and on 5 June visited Heinkel at Warnemünde to see the new He 100 single-seater which the designer declared was ready for an attempt on the 100 kilometre closed-circuit speed record. The second prototype He 100, registered as D-IOUS and painted bright yellow on its under surfaces, was to have been flown by a young unknown pilot, Flugkapitän Harting, but Udet, on an impulse, asked if he might fly it instead. Heinkel, with an eye to the enormous prestige of Udet's name being associated with any Heinkel speed record, agreed readily. Making one flat-out run around the marked circuit, Udet landed back again, with the engine cooling, red danger lights in the cockpit glowing; having covered the circuit at an average speed of 634 km/hr – a new record. Officially it was claimed that the record had been broken by a Heinkel He 112U (U for Udet) which was simply a special version of the He 112; an aircraft Germany wished the world to believe was already in Luftwaffe service alongside the Messerschmitt Bf 109 – yet one more move in the creation of the myth of Luftwaffe might.

One unforeseen result of Udet's impromptu record flight was a direct order from Hitler, forbidding him to fly again; Udet was indispensable to the Luftwaffe and was not to endanger his life in such manner. Only by threatening to resign his RLM job on the spot did Udet get Hitler to relent, though he still forbade Udet to indulge in any aerobatic flying whatsoever. In his increasingly diminishing private life Udet was not altogether happy. The situation and events in Germany disturbed him, to the extent that when a gliding friend Peter Riedel came to see Udet to say farewell before emigrating to America, Udet plainly said, 'I envy you, Peter, going to America to live.'

Another blow to his well-being was learning that his book *Mein Fliegerleben* had been banned from the Luftwaffe's libraries' list by Alfred Mahncke, the general in command of the flying training inspectorate, as being ' . . . lacking in seriousness and too unmilitary'. It took a personal order by Göring to rescind this decision.

June and July 1938 were busy months for Udet, almost constantly

on the move with a round of inspections and visits; to the inauguration of the Junkers' ground crew training school at Dessau, on
15 June, followed by the official opening of the factory just set up
at Tempelhof for production of the Junkers Ju 87B 'Stuka', and
several events of possibly lesser importance. The escalating expansion of the Luftwaffe – and corresponding broadening of Udet's
responsibilities – meant that Udet virtually had no private life.
Nevertheless, flashes of the old Udet, the joker with an impish sense
of humour, showed through the impressive uniformed exterior on
occasion, even on serious occasions. It was not uncommon for Udet,
while leading the sober entourage of factory officials and hangers-
on through an official inspection, to suddenly break away from the
prescribed itinerary to greet an acquaintance or even some surprised
labourer and engage him in jovial conversation.

A meeting with industrialists at Göring's Karinhall on 8 July,
was followed two days later by the annual fly-in at Wyk auf Föhr,
where Udet was delighted to renew acquaintance with the American
Al Williams, who had brought with him his famous Gulfhawk
biplane, NR1050. Ever eager to try his hand with any aircraft which
he had never flown before, Udet finally persuaded Williams to allow
him a flight in the Gulfhawk; a privilege Williams gave to few men.
After watching Udet's brief performance in his Gulfhawk, Williams
wrote later, 'It was during this flight that I glimpsed for the first
time the artistic side of Ernst Udet, as he eased and rolled the
Gulfhawk gracefully through an entire aero ballet.'

In exchange for this privilege Udet arranged for Williams to tour
round some of the more important Luftwaffe centres, including
Kassel where Messerschmitt Bf 109's were being built under licence.
Highly conscious of Williams' influence among American aviation
personalities and journalism, Udet then allowed the American to fly
a Bf 109 for himself. Afterwards, when asked to jot down his personal
impressions of the Messerschmitt he'd just flown, Williams was
lavish in his praise, saying, ' . . . the fastest series-fighter, the most
manoeuvrable, the only one I would exchange for my Gulfhawk. I
have seen the English Hurricane and Spitfire but would choose the
109 every time.'

The German propaganda machine was quick to exploit such a
comparison with the RAF's latest fighters – though no mention was
made of the fact that Williams had flown a B 109D, the very latest
version, not yet in Luftwaffe service. . .

The official engagements continued apace, including receiving a variety of foreign VIP's, such as the Italian governor of Libya, Italo Balbo, and the head of the French Armée de l'Air, Général Joseph Vuillemin. The latter arrived at Staaken in the latest French bomber type, an Amiot 340, at the personal invitation of Göring. The visit was an unspoken contest of bluff and double-bluff. Vuillemin's Amiot, painted in French unit markings to give the appearance of an in-service machine, was in fact the sole prototype in being. Udet, secretly well aware of this fact, arranged for the French Chief of Air Staff to visit all the 'showplaces' of the Luftwaffe, ending with a visit on 20 August to Heinkel's works at Oranienburg. Udet had pre-arranged with Heinkel to have a Heinkel He 100 standing by for take-off from Marienehe, to fly to Oranienburg at a specific stage of the French tour. Thus, after a very thorough inspection of the works, plus demonstrations by the latest Heinkel He 111 bomber, the French delegation was visibly impressed when the He 100 suddenly streaked across the airfield at full boost, then landed smoothly and taxied across to them.

Udet and Milch, who had carefully rehearsed their answers to the expected barrage of questions, were almost nonchalant, with Milch saying, 'Oh, this is our new fighter, with which Udet has beaten the world speed record.' Then, turning to Udet almost casually, Milch asked, 'Tell me, how far is the series-production advanced now?'

Barely able to conceal a grin, Udet replied, 'The second production line is just beginning, and the third will commence in two weeks' time.' In fact the He 100 the French had just seen was the fifth prototype, and only five examples were in existence at that moment. . .

While the Luftwaffe did its utmost to convince the world of its might, Hitler was still intending to carry out his plan – instigated in May – to invade Czechoslovakia on 1 October. The Sudetenland, where more than half the inhabitants were German-speaking, was to be part of the greater *Reich*. However, the chances of England and France leaving Hitler a free hand to do this were apparently growing slimmer as each day passed. In spite of all Hitler's previous assurances, a war with England *was* possible.

On 23 August Göring summoned Milch and other leading Luftwaffe officers to Karinhall, to examine the Luftwaffe's potential in any eventual war with England – and the assembly was soon shocked to realise that the Luftwaffe was anything but an ideal force to attack England! Such a conflict would be a strategic attack against an island, not simply tactical support for an army in a pure land campaign. The nearest point of Germany was at least 300 kilometres away from the nearest part of England; beyond the range of any German war plane carrying a worthwhile war load. Tactical radius of the Dornier Do 17, fully-loaded, was at most 680km, better than either the Heinkel He 111 or Junkers Ju 87; only a handful of Ju 88 prototypes were in being, while the Heinkel He 177 bomber was still merely a wooden mock-up.

Göring became highly alarmed about the possibility of any war with England, and on 9 September wrote to Udet, instructing him to see to it that the 'heavy fighter' (the Messerschmitt Me 210) was developed so that it could 'cover England'. In the event it was to be another year before the Me 210 even flew. Even less advanced was another fighter project – at this stage merely an RLM requirement – that had yet to even receive its project number. Its required specification called for power by two *TL-Strahltriebwerke* – the first German jet engines – which were still in the preliminary design development stage at BMW Munich in deepest secrecy. Ultimately this project would produce the Messerschmitt Me 262 jet fighter, but this was in several years' time. As the crucial day approached for Hitler's move into Czechoslovakia, England and France hastily mobilised in September, but Göring's – and many others' – anxieties proved premature. The infamous Munich Agreement was signed and ratified at the very last moment – Germany was free to occupy the Sudetenland without bloodshed.

With this stay of execution, Göring intensified his efforts to bring the Luftwaffe up to real strength. One very vital problem to be solved quickly was the choice of the type of bomber for main operational use. Koppenberg, head of the Junkers firm, who had befriended Udet, kept pushing his Junkers Ju 88. Udet and his staff were in favour of the Ju 88, but Milch objected and advised production of refined versions of the Do 17. However, Udet convinced Göring that the Junkers should be the Luftwaffe's standard bomber, backed by Koppenberger who promised a monthly production of 250 machines, licence-built at various factories. Thus on 15 October Göring gave Koppenberger an order to take all necessary measures for the highest possible production of the Ju 88, including 'outside' firms. This order was a relief to Udet; now the industry itself, not his bureau, would be responsible for delivering the promised bombers in quantity, and on time. He was confident in Koppenberger's abilities. The man was an excellent organiser, very experienced in production problems, ambitious, even ruthless – the antithesis of Udet himself. The overall effect of such a decision was to put all the Luftwaffe's bomber 'eggs' in one basket; all its hopes centred on a single *Schnellbomber* type whose over-rated (then) range still made it unsuitable for any war against England.

Another aftermath of the 'Munich Scare' was announced by Göring at yet another conference, on 26 October, held to discuss all necessary steps to be taken for a war against England; when he told all present that Hitler had ordered him to multiply his Luftwaffe by five! One staff officer, Jeschonneck, suggested that for any attack on England a fleet of at least 500 Heinkel He 177's would be needed; to the consternation of Udet who knew too well what this would mean in terms of necessary amounts of raw materials and fuel which, at present, were already in short supply. Nevertheless, a month later, on 29 November, Udet was once more in conference with Göring, and brought with him his complete German aircraft production schedule until April 1942, drawn up in response to the order from Hitler to increase Luftwaffe strength five-fold. This programme provided for some 31,300 aircraft, including 7,700 bombers (Junkers Ju 88 and Heinkel He 177), and 3,500 fighters. It was a totally unrealistic programme, with neither the raw materials or trained labour force available for such an ambitious goal. In order to speed production Udet had ordered that mass-production techniques were to be introduced into the industry.

Four weeks before this significant conference Udet had been promoted again, this time to *Generalleutnant*, with seniority from 1 November. On the same date Milch was also promoted, to *Generaloberst*, while Stumpff, Chief of the Air Staff, became a *General der Flieger*. Udet's promotion formed the subject of one of the cartoons for his 1939 'calendar' gifts to close friends; showing himself climbing a ladder through the clouds and reaching for a star above him. Most people naturally thought the 'star' was that worn on a general's epaulette, but only his beloved Inge knew the real significance because Udet had written on the back of the original drawing, 'Inge, you are the star that I lack'.

In December he acquired a new personal aircraft, D-ILFR, a Siebel Fh 104s twin-engined light transport, painted all-red for Udet's exclusive use, and he flew it for the first time on 10 December. Udet then 'modified' the internal layout to his own taste by installing a well-stocked wooden bar. The aircraft was later re-registered as RJ+AP.

The year closed with two minor but pleasant items for Udet. On 22 December the film *Pour le Mérite* was premiered at the UFA Palast, and Udet and a bevy of high-ranking Luftwaffe officers attended. Next day Udet was awarded the *Ehrenzeichen der Flieger mit Brillanten* – the Pilot's Badge with Diamonds.

The fateful year 1939 opened on a light-hearted note, as Udet's friends received their copies of his usual annual 'calendar'. In it were cartoons of Göring contemplating his 'mighty' armada, Heinkel and Messerschmitt competing for the speed record, Udet seated in the record-breaking He 100 with its engine still steaming, Lindbergh climbing into a Bf 109, Koppenberger as a magician pulling Junkers Ju 88's out of a top hat, and other cryptic cartoon 'comments'. It was to be the last but one of these sought-after 'calendars' drawn by Udet. The previous year's cartoons had included one particularly significant drawing; the 'Dream of a Department Chief', showing Udet chained to an RLM desk while dreaming of soaring in his glider D-UDLINGER over the Alps – a succinct summation of Udet's real ambitions to be free as a bird instead of being buried in bureaucracy.

His Technical Bureau was particularly interested in the possibilities of the new jet aircraft under development, and on 4 January issued directives for the development of. jet fighters; requiring a speed of 900 km/hr and an armament of two MG 17s and one MG 151/20. At this time Udet was approached by Charles Lindbergh with an extraordinary proposition, that Germany sell Daimler-Benz aero engines to the French. Udet passed the request to Milch who sought higher decision from Göring. In the end Milch said Germany would be prepared to sell such engines, provided France paid for them in foreign currency, not goods. All further negotiations were camouflaged as transactions for the sale of a Fieseler Storch aircraft. In the event circumstances prevented the completion of this sale.

The tremendous expansion of the Luftwaffe order by Hitler in 1938 necessitated yet another re-organisation of the RLM. As head of the Technical Department Udet had already attained the rank of *Generalleutnant*, the highest possible for a departmental chief. Discussing the possibilities of attaining even higher rank with friends at the Personnel Department, Udet received the suggestion that his department draw up a proposal to make him *Generalluftzeugmeister*, analogous with the wartime position of the then Chief of Armaments Procurement. When Göring signed the effective order for

Luftwaffe re-organisation on 30 January, it included just such an appointment, and next day Udet was officially appointed as such, the title being usually abbreviated to GL.

The GL 'Department' was a massive conglomeration of bureaux, departments, divisions and sub-divisions, covering virtually every aspect of Luftwaffe activity and support, employing many hundreds of highly technical personnel apart from even more hundreds of plain administrative people. At the apex of all this was Udet; like-able, optimistic, trusting 'Ernie', a man always loth to take any ruthless decision, deeply interested in aircraft, a superb pilot – yet lacking both interest and real understanding of the myriad of prob-lems posed by logistics of supply and procurement.

Udet's terms of reference as GL made him ultimately responsible for – in war and in peacetime – research, development, experimen-tation and supply of *every* piece of Luftwaffe equipment, and for the supply and equipment of *all* Luftwaffe units. In addition he held responsibility for the build-up of the aviation industry, its financing and economic control, including manufacturing facilities, raw materials and labour. He also oversaw the export of aircraft, engines and equipment, and had to issue all necessary technical orders to the Luftwaffe. It was by any standards a formidable task and awe-some responsibility; one for which Udet was by his very nature totally unsuited. And to make matters worse he was not even totally free to make his own decisions. At the same time as Udet was elevated to GL, Erhard Milch had been reinstated as Göring's representative and appointed General-Inspector of the Luftwaffe, with wide-ranging authority, including becoming Udet's immediate superior. Udet had been adroitly manoeuvred into an impossible position by Göring. Every major decision had to be first approved by Milch, yet Udet was the inevitable target for blame for any failures. He had been set up as the perfect scapegoat. Further complications included the replacement of General Stumpff by Hans Jeschonnek as Chief of the General Staff. Though a capable staff officer, Jeschonnek had unswerving blind faith in Hitler – and thoroughly disliked Milch, a feeling deeply reciprocated.

On 15 March Hitler conveniently 'forgot' his promises at Munich and sent in troops to complete the occupation of Czechoslovakia, taking it 'under the protection' of Germany. Five days later Udet was in Prague to examine the Luftwaffe's latest 'acquisitions' of the former Czech air force. In neat rows stood 100 Avia 534's, two-seat and single-seat fighters, trainers and communications aircraft – all biplanes. Hastily – and incorrectly – each had been painted with a swastika in all six normal markings' locations. Udet also took the necessary steps to integrate the Czech aviation industry with the German. The complete aircraft inventory of the Czechoslovakian Air Force was then taken over by the Luftwaffe.

Having annexed the whole of Czechoslovakia without a jot of interference from the rest of the world, Hitler next turned to the east, intending to annex the free city of Danzig, whether Poland agreed or not. Göring, now called *Der Eiserne* ('The Iron One') by his intimate friends, remained anxious about any possible clash with England and France, and tried to dissuade Hitler from the Danzig idea. He failed – Hitler had already set his mind on the move. Accordingly Göring ordered Udet to accelerate build-up of the Luftwaffe on 25 April, and instructed him to speed up construction on all new aircraft factories. When Milch and Udet met him a week later and emphasised the serious shortages of raw materials, Göring made no response.

During March and April, while such political decisions were being postulated, the German aircraft designers were forging ahead with their latest ideas. On 19 March a Junkers Ju 88V-5, D-ATYU, broke the record over 1,000 km with a payload of 2,000 kg with a speed of 517 km/hr; on 30 March the Heinkel He V8, D-IDGH broke the absolute world speed record with a run of 746 km/hr; and four weeks later Messerschmitt's Me 209 V1, D-INJR, bettered this last by accomplishing a speed of 755 km/hr. Heinkel immediately indicated that he would do better still, but at that point Udet stepped in, forbidding all further attempts on the speed record. The Luftwaffe's standard fighter was to be the Bf 109, and he felt it appropriate that the world record should remain with Messerschmitt. On 20 June, however, an RLM test pilot, Erich Warsitz, loaned specially to Heinkel by Udet, flew the initial flight of the Heinkel He 176 – the world's first rocket-powered aircraft – built as a private venture and without official RLM sanction initially. Next day Udet, Milch and other high-ranking officers of the Luftwaffe assembled at the airfield to witness Warsitz's second flight in this revolutionary aircraft. The anti-climax came when, after a decidedly hazardous take-off and brief circuit, Warsitz came in to land and ended with a dangerous ground loop. As Udet remarked to his test pilot afterwards, 'In this aircraft every success-flight is really an unsuccessful crash!' Though not impressed with the practical performance of the new design, Udet nevertheless continued to encourage further development of the basic aircraft.

Udet's chief concern at this period was the shortage of raw materials needed so vitally for the expected expansion programme for the Luftwaffe. He approached Göring, but the Iron One had no desire to upset his *Führer*, and refused to talk to Hitler on this subject. Desperately Udet and Milch went to see Rudolf Hess to gain his support, and when this failed Udet wrote an official letter to Milch, as self-protection saying that it was impossible to fulfil the planned programme for this reason. In an attempt to persuade Hitler to release sufficient raw materials to the Luftwaffe, Milch, with the help of Udet's letter, got Göring to arrange a large display at the Rechlin experimental airfield of the latest Luftwaffe equipment for demonstration before Hitler and his staff. The date was set for 3 July, when Hitler, accompanied by Göring, Keitel, Jodl, Milch, Jeschonnek and Udet, watched demonstrations of every facet of Luftwaffe equipment; though Göring had already forbidden Milch and Udet to mention that many of the new weapons were only in an early experimental stage and a long way from being considered as fully operational.

The Rechlin demonstrations did nothing to convince Hitler to allot more raw material to the Luftwaffe; while Göring's ploy of not pointing out the purely experimental projects led Hitler to greatly over-rate the Luftwaffe's capacity, with inevitable dire results in the not-too-distant future; in particular for Udet, the perfect scapegoat for Göring's and Milch's failings. Hitler's only reactions to the Rechlin display were to issue an order via Göring to restrict the freedom of aviation industrialists in the use of private aircraft, and to summon Warsitz to a personal interview to answer questions about the Heinkel He 176 which Warsitz had briefly demonstrated. The RLM, however, was much more interested in the rocket fighter being developed by Alexander Lippitsch in the Messerschmitt works. After all, Heinkel had been ordered by Udet to forget fighters and concentrate on bombers – an order conveniently omitted from Ernst Heinkel's biography in later years, when he accused Udet of 'blocking' development of the He 176.

Udet had other problems, notifying Göring on 22 June that the promised Ju 88 production programme would suffer a three months' delay due to 'technical difficulties' – Koppenberger was apparently not the 'magician' pulling Ju 88's out of a hat, as in an old Udet cartoon. On the other hand his second 'iron' in the fighter 'fire', the

Focke-Wulf Fw 190 V1, D-OPZE, had made its first flight at Bremen on 1 June, and was now at Rechlin undergoing rigorous testing.

Udet's warning to Göring of the Junkers' delay resulted in the Iron One making a personal inspection of the works and then, on 5 August, summoning Milch, Udet and Jeschonnek to his yacht *Karin II*, where he ordered them to step-up significantly the production of aircraft, especially bombers. This order completely changed the programme already drawn up by Milch and Udet!

On 21 August both men were again in conference with Göring, this time on the Berghof above Berchtesgaden, accompanied by the commanders of the Luftwaffe's four Air Fleets. Udet had been requested to bring with him the latest available figures on the strength of the Polish, British and French air services, and performance data on each service's latest aircraft. The reason for this request became apparent when Göring revealed Hitler's plan to attack Poland on 26 August – five days hence. A non-aggression pact with Russia (signed in Moscow on 23 August) left Hitler free to carry out his plan without risk.

At 4.30 am on 27 August Udet was woken by his telephone ringing; it was Ernst Heinkel from Marienehe, telling him that the world's first jet-propulsion aircraft had made its first flight and successful landing, the He 178, powered by a Heinkel HeS-3 engine. Nevertheless Udet had bigger things to think about; preparations for the attack on Poland were in full swing even though Göring, for his own reasons, was still attempting to avert war. That day he travelled to Göring's special train inside which last-ditch 'negotiations' were being held in the hope of preventing an outbreak of war over Poland. The talks came to nothing; war was inevitable now. Udet made an appointment to receive Heinkel on 1 September, to discuss possible RLM support for the new jet aircraft. Heinkel, his wife and Udet were breakfasting that morning when the radio suddenly announced that German troops had invaded Poland. Udet became pale, almost white, and hastily fixed himself a cognac. . .

Two days later the war that Göring – and Udet – feared became reality; England and France declared war on Germany. Hitler's gamble that these countries would not intervene had not come off; perhaps the most gruesome gamble in the history of mankind. He had bluffed – and his bluff had been called this time. And on 4 September the RAF made its first bombing sortie when 15 Blenheims drawn from 107,110 and 139 Squadrons attempted to bomb German shipping at Wilhelmshaven and Brunsbüttel. Five of the

Blenheims failed to return, and a few days later a part of one Blenheim's engine was serving as a paperweight on Udet's desk at the RLM, neatly engraved with the date 4 September 1939. On 5 September, as the Ju 87's bombed Warsaw and the Polish Army started its retreat behind the river Weichsel, the prototype Me 210, D-AABF, made its first flight. On it Udet had pinned much hope as the successor to both the Bf 110 and the Ju 87 – though the day would come when he would have cause to curse the design.

With the outbreak of war Udet was allotted another personal liaison aircraft, a Messerschmitt Bf 110, registered as VF+HP. He immediately had its interior 'modified' to his private tastes, including the installation of a rear-view mirror enabling him to see the rear cockpit's occupant. It was Udet's habit when flying to take an occasional sip of cognac, and he had no objection to any passenger doing the same. However, if the rear man did so, his drinking created a sudden noise on the intercomm microphone; the mirror was to allow Udet to ensure the noise was due to drinking, not some mechanical failure, or worse.

At this time he was approached by Reinhard Heydrich, master of the Gestapo, with a personal request. Heydrich, an SS-member since 1931, had originally asked to join the Luftwaffe reserve and Milch – especially in view of his Jewish descent – could hardly refuse, and made him a Major in the reserve. Now Heydrich wanted a Bf 109, and later a Bf 110, to use. Udet too had little choice in the matter, but at least succeeded in arranging a barter. Heydrich got his fighters; Udet got a police number for his car's licence plate, together with a blue (police) light. No more worries about exceeding speed limits or jumping traffic lights!

Warsaw surrendered on 27 September and the Polish war was over. Among many other things this brief campaign had proved the Junkers Ju 87 to be a formidable weapon, but had also high-lighted its vulnerability to enemy fighters and quick-firing anti-aircraft guns of even light calibre. Udet saw to it that a higher-powered and cleaned-up version of the design was put in hand, the Ju 87 D 'Dora'. On 4 October he gave orders for the previous airliner dispersal area at Tempelhof to be put at the disposal of the Weser Flugzeugbau for series production of the Stuka. Two days later Hitler, in a speech at the Reichstag, offered peace to England and France, but on 12 October he summoned Göring, Milch and Udet to say that England had declined his offer. 'The war will continue. You must see to it that enough bombs are produced. Milch, you will be personally responsible for this.' Until then Hitler had always refused to increase production of bombs, which were in short supply within the Luftwaffe. . .

The invasion of Poland had postponed discussions between Heinkel and Udet about the Heinkel fighter projects. In October Udet visited the Heinkel works, and on the 18th sent the designer a wire, assuring him of full support and continuing 'fanatical' belief in the success of the He 280. He also gave consent to proceed with its development, and indicated that he (Udet) alone at the RLM should be kept informed of progress. On 1 November Udet and Milch went to Marienehe to watch another demonstration of the He 178 by Warsitz. On its first take-off, just after getting airborne, the aircraft's engine cut dead, leaving Warsitz to make a hasty landing and ground-loop. After two hours of repair maintenance, Warsitz took off again and landed successfully. It did not impress Milch; while Udet, though always wide awake to the potential of the new turbo engines, candidly preferred a twin-engined design rather than single-engine jets.

November – a month of the year which Udet had always detested – brought an unsuccessful attempt on Hitler's life on the 8th; while eleven days later the long-awaited Heinkel He 177 finally made its first flight. Since the order for construction of a wooden mock-up on 2 June 1937, Udet had repeatedly stressed the need to make this bomber with series production in mind. Now, two and a half years later, the prototype was making its first flight. After being airborne for a mere twelve minutes, the ungainly bomber was landed – the engines were already overheating – and there were indications of elevator flutter, propeller shaft vibration and inadequate tail surfaces; though the handling qualities appeared satisfactory. It was the first in a dispiriting sage of technical problems with the He 177, which were never fully resolved.

As the first wartime Christmas approached, Udet continued his near-impossible task of coping with escalating demands for an increase in virtually every type of armament, engine and aircraft. Germany was now involved in a major war, yet Udet had never reckoned on such a situation – even Hitler and Göring had never imagined it would come to this.

Privately, to Inge, Udet confided his true feelings, saying 'I have a feeling that we'll never win the war. We've already lost it!' But there was now no way out for Udet – he was too deeply enmeshed.

CHAPTER THIRTEEN

The 'Happy Time' – 1940

On 5 November 1939 Hitler decided to launch a large-scale assault on France, taking in Belgium and the Netherlands, despite their neutrality. The original date set for the attack was 12 November, but then postponed until the 13th. However, on 10 November a Messerschmitt Bf 108, carrying two Luftwaffe officers, Majors Hellmuth Reinberger and Erich Hoenmanns, lost its way and crash-landed in neutral Belgium. Aboard the Bf 108 were part of the intended assault's battle plans. The incident created a huge panic within Luftwaffe ranks, even at the highest level, as Hitler's reaction to the news was awaited. Thus, when Udet landed at Braunschweig airfield near Darmstadt on 11 January 1940, for a brief visit to the DFS experimental establishment, he was in a state of high tension, worrying about the outcome of the 'Belgian incident'. His purpose in visiting the DFS was to witness a demonstration of a Junkers 52/3M towing a DFS 230A-1 glider by a short, rigid bar in place of the more usual towing rope arrangement. Udet's testy comments to Professor Georgii when the demonstration was slightly delayed were untypical of his more usual affability, and he left Darmstadt immediately after the demonstration and hurried back to Berlin.

Even without the worry over the 'Belgian incident', Udet was preoccupied with a host of pressing matters; not least the increasing shortage of aluminium and other non-ferrous metals for aircraft production. Increased aircraft production was top priority, and Udet was responsible to Hitler, via Milch, for meeting all requirements outlined in the programme. Part of the policy Udet now adopted to achieve this aim was to divert a large proportion of the skilled engineering labour force at various experimental research establishments to more mundane production centres; a move which merely brought Udet a mini-flood of complaints from the research centres' chiefs. Udet also continued to emphasise to manufacturers the necessity of concentrating on those aircraft designs already in front-line service, and to produce these in ever greater quantities. In view of the serious shortage of aluminium, Göring even suggested to Udet the possibility of building warplanes from wood. Udet's response was to say, 'No, we can't do that. The whole world would laugh at us!' Unknown to Udet, on 1 March the British Air Ministry placed an order for 50 all-wooden construction De Havilland 98 Mosquito fighter-bombers. . .

Udet's department, the 'GL Amt', had by now blossomed into a vast organisation, comprising some 4,000 employees. By his background and nature Udet was really totally unfitted to head such a complicated set-up, however hard he might try. Even the American correspondent, William Shirer, after interviewing Udet on 8 January 1940, had realised this, saying of Udet, 'I could not help thinking that a man like Udet would never be entrusted with such a task in America. He would be considered "Lacking in business experience." '

Every single day Udet was required to solve problems of the most divergent nature – labour shortages, lack of raw materials, technical snags, acting as 'referee' in the many squabbles between leading industrialists – these and many other items were all put on Udet's desk for solution. He now spent a lot of time in his office, having a bathroom and a locker for fresh uniforms installed in order to be immediately available for any function or vital trip. It was always a personal relief for Udet to get away from his desk and pay a visit to some establishment away from Berlin.

That Udet was unsuited for his job did not go unnoticed by the ever-ambitious Erhard Milch. Until then there had been no open conflicts between Udet and Milch, indeed, there were occasions when they got along well with each other. But Milch's resentment of Udet's direct access to Göring, and the meetings to which he was not invited, helped Milch to begin an insidious 'campaign' of denigrating Udet at every opportunity.

When, in early March, Göring went in his special command train 'Asia' to inspect trooops along the French and Belgian borders, he took Udet and Milch with him. On the way back to Germany Göring happened to speak in praise of Udet's work for the Luftwaffe. This was too much for Milch to bear in silence, and, acidly, he remarked that it had not been Udet who had built up the Luftwaffe, and that the aircraft production programme, for which Udet was responsible, was not going well at all.

Milch was not the only critic of the GL's department. Willy Messerschmitt sent a letter to the head of Udet's technical bureau, complaining rather bitterly of the utter lack of foresight and planning emanating from the GL in general, with the inevitable chaos and confusion, hence delays, in trying to meet production quotas of aircraft etc. Only six days later more complaints poured in, one of these noting that the Luftwaffe's standard Bf 109 fighter had suffered 255 landing accidents in 1939.

As originally envisaged when he was created as the GL, Udet was now eligible for further promotion, and on 1 April, 1940 he became a *General der Flieger*. When celebrating his promotion in the Hotel Bristol, he was heard to remark, 'I'm a general in command now. The Luftwaffe has to accept the aircraft *I* give to it.' Naively, Udet had forgotten that Milch and Göring still held the real authority. . .

On 9 April Germany invaded Denmark and Norway, while from the beginning of May Hitler daily postponed *Fall Gelb* – the plan for the major offensive in the West – although every Luftwaffe 'brass-hat' knew that the assault was imminent. After days of conferences at Göring's 'Karinhall', their fears were crystallised on 10 May when German troops commenced their *Blitzkrieg* drive into France and the Low Countries; the Allies' 'Phoney War' was over. For the first time in military history gliders were used to land troops, against the Belgian fort at Eben Emael which capitulated next day. The DFS 230's – Udet's brainchild – had proved their worth superbly. Elsewhere the advancing infantry were preceded by the Stuka dive-bombers, fitted with Udet's 'Jericho trumpet' howling sirens, spreading terror wherever they struck. During the early days of the *Blitzkrieg* in the West, Udet stayed at the RLM, though he occasionally joined other Luftwaffe leaders at Göring's command train stationed at Wildpark-Werder, near Potsdam where the huge underground central command post of the Luftwaffe was situated.

Udet's presence at the RLM was necessary, *Blitzkrieg* or not; aircraft production was still the primary worry and the flow of problems showed no signs of diminishing. He sent an urgent telegram to Messerschmitt emphasising the need for promised quotas for the month being fulfilled; visited the Fokker works at Amsterdam's Schiphol aerodrome to judge its potential for additional production; all the time staying near to Göring's mobile command train to ensure that Milch did not gain any personal advantage in the unspoken duel for power and status that was growing between Udet and Milch. When France finally surrendered, Udet was elated with relief, saying openly at the RLM, 'The war is over. We don't need all these plans any longer.' The nightmare of responsibility had been halted just in time – or so Udet thought. Maybe when things became less hectic he'd be able to really control his *Amt*. . .

The need for aircraft production was still vital; nevertheless, on 1 June Udet ordered Heinkel to postpone series production of the Heinkel He 177 for three months, after which only three machines were to be built each month. Ten days later he issued instructions to Messerschmitt for 500 Bf 109's and 300 Bf 110's to be equipped to drop bombs, for future use as *Jagdbomber*, or '*Jabos*' as these were to be known colloquially. Then, on 14 June Paris surrendered as an 'open city' and two days later Udet landed at Le Bourget in a Storch; the first high-ranking Luftwaffe officer to do so. His purpose was to see something of the French aviation industry. The final armistice terms for a defeated France were staged in the same railway coach used to accept Germany's surrender in 1918, stationed deliberately by Hitler's order on the same spot as that which witnessed Germany's shame some 22 years before, in the Compiègne woods. There, on 21 June, Udet was among the array of high-ranking German officers who watched France humbly accept Hitler's terms for 'peace'. Among other things, France's surrender released large supplies of bauxite from French stocks, thus greatly increasing Udet's supply of aluminium for his aircraft production programme.

For the Luftwaffe leaders there now came a pleasant period – the 'Happy Time' – when they could to a great extent relax and enjoy the spoils of victory. France was conquered, and soon England would accept peace terms; there was now time for hunting, parties at Horchers, to enjoy life. But five days after the ceremony at Compiègne Udet was summoned by Göring to a conference at Wassenaar, Holland, along with all other prominent Luftwaffe officers. Though Poland, Denmark, Norway, Holland, Belgium and France had been overpowered, the Luftwaffe had been thwarted and lost air superiority against RAF fighters over the Dunkirk zone. And now this 'insolent' RAF was making night-bombing attacks on Germany! Also present at the conference was Hauptmann Wolfgang Falck, the only fighter-commander with practical night-fighting experience. Göring gave Falck instructions to form the first night-fighter *Geschwader*, and Udet and Falck had long discussions on aircraft and equipment needed and desired to combat the RAF's night assaults. In particular Udet was interested in the early radar equipment becoming available; the *Würzburg-A Geräte* sets and the *Seeburg-Tisch*. Trials with these were quickly made, with Udet participating personally.

German occupation of the conquered European countries opened great possibilities for personal indulgence by the soldiers and airmen of the occupying formations; particularly the luxury goods they were long deprived of back home in Germany. Due to the enforced currency exchange rate, such goods were cheap to 'buy' and Udet, Milch and other hierarchy were not slow to take advantage. Each loaded a Junkers Ju 52 with their personal 'booty' – drinks, fine food and artifacts – and flew them to Tempelhof, where they became private hoards at Horchers for individual exclusive use. On a visit to Paris on 2 July Udet, Milch and Bodenschatz, among other Luftwaffe generals, 'painted the town red'; while Udet's diary listed some of the items he wanted to take back home – face-powder from Caron in the Rue de la Paix, L'Eau d'Espagne perfume, silk, black stockings, gramophone records, tooth-paste, shaving soap, lipstick . . . The German party was in the best of moods, with Udet and Milch strolling arm-in-arm along the Champs Elysées, Udet with a bright red kerchief around his neck.

Apparently Hitler was pleased with the work of the GL, and on 13 July he awarded Udet the Knight's Cross of the Iron Cross; one of nearly 300 such awards made by Hitler since the start of the war. Further honour came when Hitler returned to Berlin and, on 19 July, at the Kroll Opera House, proclaimed the victory achieved to the German people and Reichstag; at the same time offering peace terms to England. He used the occasion to announce promotions among the highest-ranking officers. Göring was proclaimed *Reichsmarschall des Grossdeutschen Reiches* – a new rank specially created for him – while Milch, Sperrle and Kesselring were made field marshals. Udet was promoted to *Generaloberst*, the highest rank of general in Germany, entitling him to wear three stars on his epaulettes. If Hitler really respected Udet and his 'achievements', it was a feeling not reciprocated by Udet. To his closest friends Udet often gave vent to his personal dislike and contempt for the 'little corporal'. . .

Hitler's magnanimous offer of peace to England was firmly rejected by Lord Halifax within 72 hours. England must therefore be conquered like all the other countries; just one small island to subdue. On 31 July Göring called his staff together to consider the Luftwaffe's future role in the directives issued by Hitler, on 16 July and 1 August, for an invasion of British soil. The second of these, Directive 17, ordered the Luftwaffe to 'overpower the RAF as soon as possible'. It continued, 'As soon as mastery of the air was gained, attacks were to be directed against harbours and supplies. Aerial attacks against shipping were to be suspended, and the Luftwaffe was always to be prepared to support *Seelöwe* – 'Sea-Lion' – the code name for the invasion of England. Hitler personally would decide upon eventual 'retaliation attacks'.

At the conference, held at Christiansen's villa at Wassenaar, Göring appeared in his new uniform, designed by himself, and proceeded to give a bombastic speech, outlining how 'his' Luftwaffe was to 'crush' England. He then issued various orders and directives, several of these having little relation to realities. . . And when the Chief of Fighter Pilots, Theo Osterkamp, mentioned the quality and estimated quantity of RAF opposition, Göring replied scathingly, 'If their (RAF) aircraft were as numerous and as good as you say, and I were in Churchill's place, I'd have the chief of my air force shot for incapability!'

When, as Director of the Four-Years Plan, Göring had been responsible for distribution of Germany's resources, the Luftwaffe had always enjoyed high priority rating. Now, however, the High Command (OKW) allocated resources, and Hitler ordered a new overall production programme; the outcome of which was a fresh order of priorities; tanks, U-boats, weapons and ammunition, new weapons – and only then, the Luftwaffe. Udet was furious with this down-grading and immediately went to see Göring, explaining forcefully the dire effects Hitler's decision would have on the Luftwaffe's procurement programme. Yet Göring had neither the courage or the inclination to do anything contrary to Hitler's directives.

The grand opening to the Luftwaffe's assault on the RAF – *Adlertag* – Eagle Day – came on 13 August, at which time Göring's 'Asia' command train was at Laboissière, some 19 kilometres from Beauvais. The following two weeks of desperate fighting over southern England shattered Göring's dream of an easy victory, while the mounting Luftwaffe losses led many air commanders to suggest to Göring that production of replacement aircraft must be stepped up quickly. The Iron One would not hear of any such suggestion; the effects of such an order might weaken morale in Germany! By the end of August it was apparent that the RAF was far from crushed, while RAF bombers were raiding German targets almost nightly, including the capital, Berlin. Thus, on 3 September, Göring gathered his commanders again and announced a change in tactics; from now on the target was to be London – and he would personally supervise the campaign. Accordingly, his command train was moved to Cap Gris Nez.

Two days before Göring's arrival at the Channel coast, the second prototype Messerschmitt Me 210, WL-ABEO, was flight-tested by Flugkapitän Fritz Wendel at Augsburg, on 5 September. On reaching a high speed, however, severe vibration in the tail area broke off the starboard tailplane and Wendel was forced to take to his parachute. Udet, who had high hopes for the Me 210, was immediately on the telephone to Willy Messerschmitt, asking for precise reasons for the crash. The designer assured him that in every other respect the aircraft was fine; only the tail section had to be sorted out. He added that his factory had yet to receive a single DB 601 engine, and that the raw material necessary to commence series-production of the Me 210 could not be obtained in the time previously forecast.

While Udet was exchanging words with Messerschmitt, a thousand kilometres away in London some Air Ministry staff were studying a potted biography of Ernst Udet compiled by a Wing Commander Coope, who had known Udet personally, and issued to Air Ministry Intelligence on 12 September. It closed with Coope's summary of Udet's character:

> Udet is an extremely amusing man with a good deal of the comedian in his make-up. He is an excellent trick shot and an extremely clever caricaturist. He is fond of women, good food and drink, and has, like Milch and others, his private set of monogrammed wine glasses in Horchers, the best restaurant in Berlin. He has explained his attitude to his present job as: that he hoped to be allowed to help German air expansion as a test pilot, but since he has been found worthy of bearing a general's responsibilities, he is willing to carry them shoulder-high. . .

The 'amusing man' paid a visit to the fighter pilots fighting the 'Battle of Britain'. As a former fighter pilot he liked the company of men of the calibre of Werner Mölders and Adolf Galland; these young men he understood. When they complained that the Spitfire was better in many ways than their own Messerschmitt Bf 109E's, Udet assured them that a much better version would be introduced into the Luftwaffe in early 1941; the Bf 109F with a DB 601E engine and a single, improved fuselage-mounted cannon instead of the E-versions wing guns.

On 13 September Udet was summoned by Hitler to the German Chancellory, where he joined a large company of Luftwaffe, Army

(*Left*) Erhard Milch and Ernst Udet at Dübendorf, July 1937. Only four years later Milch was to be the chief instigator of Udet's fall from grace within the Luftwaffe hierarchy. (*Right*) Udet with the famous World War I naval pilot Friedrich Christiansen on 10 July 1940.

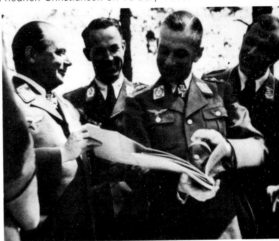

(*Left*) A jovial Göring receiving Udet at Karinhall on 21 July 1940. The occasion was a reception for Italy's Foreign Minister Count Ciano. (*Right*) Udet shares a joke with the Luftwaffe Chief of Staff, Generaloberst Hans Jeschonnek, July 1940. Jeschonnek was later (like Udet) blamed by Hitler and Göring for the 'failure' of the Luftwaffe in 1943 and (again like Udet) committed suicide on 19 August 1943. (*Below*) Channel Front. Udet visiting the forward fighter units along the northern coast of France, 4 September 1940, joking with Adolf Galland and Werner Mölders, Germany's leading air aces then.

Udet with Inge Bleyle — 'Ingelein' — the last person to speak to Udet before his death.

(*Left*) A small selection of the private mementoes decorating Udet's private rooms, Berlin, 1941. (*Right*) Udet's funeral procession, 21 November 1941. Nearest camera (left) leading a file of the casket guard is Adolf Galland; while immediately following the coffin (in white greatcoat) is Göring

and Navy chiefs for a conference about the planned invasion of England. Hitler was, surprisingly, full of praise for the Luftwaffe, saying that in his opinion only the 'bad weather' had prevented the Luftwaffe gaining complete air mastery! Then, just four days later, Hitler calmly cancelled his immediate plans for such an invasion, postponing the attempt until 1941. The Service chiefs were already busy planning Operation Barbarossa – the invasion of Russia. Hitler was utterly convinced that a *Blitzkrieg* of no more than three to five months would be needed to subdue Russia; he could then turn to England again without the constant threat to his back. Privately, however, he had told Göring that even if England was occupied, the war must go on. Canada and the USA would inevitably become bitter enemies to Germany, while the Reich would have many millions of British to feed and control.

It was the end of the Battle of Britain. Göring's fantasy of an all-conquering Luftwaffe had finally been shattered. In the past both Hitler and Göring had repeatedly assured Luftwaffe leaders that there would never be a war with England. Now the Luftwaffe's serious shortcomings for just such a war were overtly apparent. The Bf 109 had insufficient fighting range; the Bf 110 was highly vulnerable against modern fighters – the Junkers Ju 87 even more so. And there were no long-range bombers. Ground control for the *Geschwader* was inadequate, as was the sparse radar equipment available. Only the quality of the air crews, and their sublime courage, reflected well on the Luftwaffe. Ultimate responsibility lay with Göring, who had made several serious tactical blunders, apart from his failure to ensure the Luftwaffe's equipment was up-to-date and in sufficient quantity. Being Göring, he immediately sought a scapegoat to blame – and had to look no further than Udet, upon whom he now heaped reproach upon reproach. And for Udet there was no escape.

Udet had never over-estimated his personal limitations, and had long ago realised that being the head of the Technical Department, even more so the GL, was really no suitable job for him. Nevertheless he had always tried hard to keep on top of each job, although always hoping inwardly that the hectic pace of development would slow down and give him an opportunity to 'catch up'. Now, all the reproaches, outspoken or veiled, merely bewildered him. He was confused, increasingly depressed by the lack of loyalty from some whom he had counted as friends. And ever-hovering above him, a grey, menacing shadow, the figure of Milch; ready to pounce on the slightest excuse. And yet decisions continued to be needed, orders to be given. When his test pilot Warsitz reported enthusiastically on the Heinkel He 280, Udet's response was, 'The war will be over in a year, we don't need new fighters.' Udet then went on to say, 'Don't you understand? No matter what we do, we cannot win the war.'

Udet also continued to be interested in new devices, such as the air-sea rescue buoys, marked with a large red cross and anchored in the Channel along the French coast. Equipped with four bunks, blankets, food and water, distress signals, even games of draughts; these further brainchildren of Udet were put in place in October. One of his major worries continued to be the Junkers Ju 88. Almost 2,000 had by now been delivered to the Luftwaffe, yet the squadrons were apparently fiercely critical. Milch went on an inspection tour of the Ju 88 units, and on 13 October reported unfavourably on the design to Göring, saying, 'The crews do not fear the enemy, but the Ju 88' – a normal Milch wild exaggeration. Immediately Udet decided to look for himself.

On the 15th he flew to Amsterdam in his Bf 110, accompanied by the Rechlin test-pilot Carl Francke who flew a Ju 88. Udet personally demonstrated the Junkers at various units, making vertical dives and even stressing the aircraft to a 9G loading. Then the true reason for the apparent criticism was revealed. Though the Ju 88 had its teething troubles, the real kernel of the criticism concerned the various Ju 88 unit-commanders, all of whom were bombardiers, not pilots. Under the Luftwaffe system then the bombardier was in command of the aircraft; the pilot was simply regarded as a 'driver'. With the Ju 88, however, the pilot *had* to be in command for its dive-bomber role. Hence the bombardier-commanders were worried about relinquishing their command posts! Milch, with his usual blustering manner, threatening punishments and courts-martial, had failed to see the real reason behind the reported criticism; and with the Ju 88 being regarded as 'Udet's child' he had seized yet another chance to denigrate Udet in Göring's eyes.

The increasing pressure of such criticism from all quarters affected Udet's health, which began to deteriorate. His ears buzzed constantly, due to a wartime injury, and even a few glasses of alcohol had a shattering effect upon him. He even looked ill, with a puffy face. His doctor, Brühl, gave him injections, but Udet did not improve noticeably. His general mood of depression deepened, aided by the approach of November – a month he personally loathed instinctively. To some friends who visited him at this time, he remarked gloomily, 'I put a noose around my neck when I put on uniform again.' Göring was given to calling him at all hours, even midnight, requesting some item of information. Udet would then have to drive to his empty office at the RLM and try to find the answer. In order to combat his moods of depression he started taking large doses of Pervitin, and from a carefree optimist he became distrustful and a constant grumbler. He continued to smoke and drink, while his diet was hardly helpful. Now, apart from his ear trouble, he suffered from bleeding gums and often spat blood.

Meanwhile his adjutant, Oberstleutnant Pendele, was looking for a new house for Udet. On his promotion to *Generaloberst* Udet had been firmly told by Göring that he must move to a more fitting residence; the little flat in Pommerschestrasse was no longer suitable. Pendele found a villa on the Stallupöner Alle in the Grünewald, the forest south-east of Berlin bordering the Havel. Udet didn't care much for the villa. The front entrance had a covered annex, leading Udet to comment, 'That's the lid of the coffin'. It was refurbished and the cellar converted to an air-raid shelter. Udet left it to Inge and Angermund, with his servants, the Peters, to move the furniture and all his souvenirs. Then, on 19 October, he moved into the 'fitting' residence. It was a remote house, and Udet was quick to hide two guns – just in case. One he hid in the hollowed-out wood base-plate of his photo-enlarger, and the other in the hollowed leg of his trophy cabinet.

Udet only stayed in the new house two days. During the night of 21/22 October his doctor sent him to the Franzikaus hospital after a bad bout of blood-spitting. Here he was examined by Milch's doctor, who notified Göring that Udet would need five or six weeks of absolute rest. Göring immediately wired Udet, asking him to follow the doctor's advice, then adding that he had instructed Milch to 'look after things' in Udet's absence – hardly a comforting thought for Udet. He also gave strict orders that Udet was not to be bothered with work problems; all official business was to be kept away from him. After much persuasion Udet reluctantly consented to enter the Buhlerhöhe Sanatorium south of Baden-Baden, in the Black Forest, on 29 October. Officially he was not supposed to smoke or take alcohol while there – though visitors noted the cartons of cigarettes and bottles filling his car's rear seats. Just ten days later Udet was back at the RLM, though by no means recovered. His chief fear was that Milch might take over his department.

As soon as he returned to his desk Udet was plunged again into the mountain of problems and decisions; one of these being how to get heavy equipment, such as tanks, across the Channel when Operation Sea-Lion was revitalised in the spring of 1941. On 4 October Messerschmitt had proposed that tanks could be fitted with 'wings' and a 'fuselage tail with control surfaces', then towed behind four Junkers Ju 52's in each case. Udet did not accept this outlandish suggestion and instead instructed Messerschmitt and Junkers to present a project for a large glider to his office by 1 November. Messerschmitt's project was code-named *Warschau-Süd* ('Warsaw-South'), while Junkers was titled *Warschau-Ost* ('Warsaw-East'). On his return from the sanatorium Udet issued an order for 200 machines of each project. He had also given thought to how such huge gliders would be taken up and across the Channel. While visiting Heinkel at Marienehe he suggested that a 'Siamese Twin' Heinkel He 111 combination be constructed, resulting in the *Heinkel-Zwilling* – 'twins'. Another contender in the large glider field was the Gotha Go 242, already built by 21 September, and which Udet ordered into series-production. To co-ordinate all such glider projects Udet appointed Dipl Ingenieur Jacobs as his technical adviser.

At the close of the year Udet once more prepared his famous calendar for his friends. The cartoons included one of the British lion being hit by arrows, Göring setting fire to London with a magnifying glass, Kesselring and Sperrle at the Channel, long rows of RAF aircraft, Milch sprouting wings as he photographed London, Coventry and Malta, Göring looking proudly at the huge Hermann Göring-Werke, and himself lying in a hospital bed with an ice-bag on his head and studying a production programme. It was to be the last Udet calendar. . .

CHAPTER FOURTEEN

Destiny

'Anything new or interesting to fly up there?' It was Udet calling the Rechlin Experimental Establishment from his RLM office. 'Yes, *Herr Generaloberst*, a captured English Beaufighter'. Less than an hour later Udet was landing his Siebel at Rechlin. The Beaufighter's engines were still warm after a run-up by Carl Francke, and Udet climbed in through the floor hatchway and installed himself in the pilot's seat. As Francke, standing behind him, began explaining the dials and instruments, Udet interrupted, 'Do you want to fly with me?' The hatch was closed, Udet gunned the engines, then began take-off from where he was parked. Getting airborne, Udet asked how to raise flaps and undercarriage, then began a series of aerobatics to see how manoeuvrable the aircraft might be – his first time in such a machine. The flight went by too quickly – soon he was winging back to Berlin; back to the ever-increasing worries and problems of his task as GL.

Due to the past directives of Göring and Udet the German aircraft industry was still running slowly; throughout the month of January a mere 79 Bf 109's had come out of the Messerschmitt factory and its various licensees. Most Germans still believed that the war would soon be over; particularly after the hoped-for invasion of England in the spring. Therefore priority was being given to the various heavy glider projects connected with the invasion. Messerschmitt had proposed on 4 January that his works should produce a large tug aircraft to convey the gliders being built by himself and the Junkers concern. However, Heinkel was already well ahead with the He 111Z '*Zwilling*' design. Yet another Messerschmitt project under way was the Me 261 long-range bomber; three examples of which had been ordered on Hitler's express wish as prestige bombers, intended to bomb the USA, if only with propaganda leaflets. The first Me 261 had already made its first flight at the end of 1940. The Me 321, 'Gigant' glider offered possibilities, and discussions were now held as to how best to fit captured French engines, thus eliminating any need for tug aircraft. At the end of January yet another new design saw the light of day when the prototype Junkers Ju 288 first flew – the intended successor to the Ju 88 under the RLM's 'Bomber B' programme issued in July 1939.

On 7 February, Göring, as chairman of the ministers' council for defence of the Reich, introduced two new classifications to the priorities' table; S and the even higher SS categories. The latter was immediately applied to the Luftwaffe for production of 'vital' aircraft. The planning of future aircraft construction programmes was getting more complicated for Udet, who also continued to be plagued by a series of 'emergency' problems requiring his action and solution; as on 15 February when Kesselring sent him a telegram to the effect that he refused to take the new Bf 109F into service because its tail assembly was considered weak.

Apart from the main problem of simply producing sufficient numbers of standard aircraft for the fighting units, Udet had to keep a constant check on the progress of various one-off projects under way. Having inspected Messerschmitt's Me 321 'Gigant' on 20 February, Udet also visited the Junkers works at Merseburg to run his eye over their large-capacity glider, the Ju 322 'Mammut', built for the 'Warschau-Ost' project. One glance told Udet that the huge wooden monster would be lucky if it even managed to fly; the vertical tail surfaces were too small. Another visit was to the Focke-Wulf Bremen factory to inspect production of the Bf 109's successor, the Fw 190.

The designer of the Fw 190, Udet's long-time friend Kurt Tank, had also, at Udet's request, converted the splendid pre-war, four-engined Fw 200 airliner into an improvised maritime reconnaissance bomber. Despite its many shortcomings, the Fw 200C had started operations against Allied shipping in the Atlantic from bases in occupied Denmark, later France, and was posing a real threat to Britain's sea supply lines.

Part of Udet's responsibility was checking on the many factories throughout occupied Europe which were now forced to work for the Germans. One of these, Fokkers at Amsterdam, was visited on 12 March, and Udet took the opportunity to pay a social visit to his old comrade Bruno Lörzer in the latter's headquarters in the Amstel Hotel. A pleasant evening of reminiscing followed, until Udet began to vent his feelings about Milch and of being the general scapegoat for others. 'Bruno, I'm the wrong man for this job. In the end they'll get me, when they need a scapegoat. Milch is always right behind me, always smiling, and saying, "I told you it wouldn't work". But don't worry, I haven't given up yet. I'm just tired of the game.'

Aircraft production was not Udet's only major worry; the production of aircraft engines was far too slow. When, for the third consecutive month, the BMW works delivered too few of its BMW 801A radial engines, Udet summoned the BMW staff to a conference at the RLM. Here he pointed out the effect of such low production quantities upon the latest aircraft types, such as the Fw 190 and the Dornier Do 217. He next berated them, gently, on the unnecessary internal jealousies and bureaucratic intrigues which eventually contributed to such poor production figures, and announced that a technical expert, Director Werner, would in future co-ordinate BMW production. Werner, at Udet's instructions, had investigated the BMW set-up and prepared a sixty-page report in great detail on the works' failings, and this was then read out to the assembled BMW audience, while Udet left the conference on an urgent visit to Göring. When ushered in to the Iron One's presence, Udet told him that, for the moment at least, the aircraft industry was incapable of supplying the necessary quantities of aircraft for any major offensive. Göring discussed this with Hitler – who complacently told him that the Russian campaign would only last six weeks, after which all forces could be used against England!

More and more people were becoming aware that all was not well in the GL *Amt* and its control of the aircraft industry. In 1940 it had been ordered to slow down, now aircraft were sorely lacking and the promised new types were simply not forthcoming. The present emergency made it clear that Göring really had chosen the wrong man for the job, however much he was liked on a personal plane. Instead of ruling the RLM and the industry with an iron hand, Udet relied upon his subordinates too much, and by his nature was too concerned with sparing everybody's feelings. Too many departments wanted their say, yet too few were prepared to accept real responsibility. Udet simply lacked the ruthless quality so necessary for his appointment.

On 4 April Udet received an urgent signal from Kesselring in Brussels, detailing no less than twenty-five shortcomings of the Bf 109, and requesting that these defects be corrected as soon as possible. Special technical working parties from the industry were despatched to provide the necessary maintenance. It was merely one of the numerous problems brought to the GL daily, creating even more worry for Udet. Even such minor items as Rudolf Hess, against strict orders from Hitler, taking the controls of a Bf 108 and aero-batting over Rangsdorf. The airfield commander rang Udet, who then dictated a letter ordering that no more aircraft were to be put at Hess's disposal. Small wonder that Udet seized upon any oppor-tunity to abandon his desk and go to witness some pure flying test or experiment, as on 5 April when he flew to the Marienehe Heinkel base to watch test flights of the twin-jet He 280. He was no longer the old Udet.

When Milch was not around, Udet freely confessed to a feeling of persecution by Milch; always at his shoulder, seeking every slight-est mistake and saying, 'I told you so.' For Milch's part he made no secret of the fact that he considered himself well qualified to take over Udet's job, with definite ideas on how he would do it and the people he would select to assist him.

Fighters and fighter pilots were always Udet's preference. To give one example, he ensured that Jagdgeschwader 26 got the very latest explosive ammunition, the unit commanded by Adolf Galland. After one RLM conference, Udet invited both Galland and Werner Mölders back to his villa, where the finest food and ample amounts of cognac were available. Naturally, after dinner, they had to have a shooting contest. At first the two young pilots proved to be the best marksmen, but as several bottles of champagne were steadily emptied, Udet emerged as the best shot. On another occasion Johannes 'Macki' Steinhoff of 4/JG 52 had been summoned to Schönefeld to discuss night-fighter problems with Udet. After the talk, Udet volunteered to fly Steinhoff back to Staaken in his Storch. After a hair-raising display of extremely slow and narrow turns right in front of the hangar, Udet set course for Staaken, then offered Steinhoff cigars and cognac as they settled down for their journey.

Regular conferences with Göring were by now almost a weekly routine, yet while Milch never failed to inform Hitler of Udet's failures, the relationship between Udet and Göring was relatively relaxed, with Göring never directly attacking or accusing Udet. Now Udet had a new worry, Jeschonnek, who was claiming that the figures supplied by his department of the number of aircraft produced were higher than those actually delivered. Outside all these political and bureaucratic squabbles Udet was nevertheless still highly regarded by the ordinary German people. One manifes-tation of this feeling came on 26 April – Udet's 45th birthday – when he was awarded the honorary title of 'Doctor Engineer' by the Munich Technical High School, the actual award being made to Udet the day before in Berlin.

On 10 May Udet received a personal call from Hitler, who told him Rudolf Hess had flown off in a Bf 110, apparently intending to fly to Britain. Hitler then asked Udet whether in fact the Bf 110 could fly to Scotland, as intended, and what sort of weather conditions he would meet en route. Two days later Udet flew to Salzburg where he, Milch, Göring and Willy Messerschmitt had been summoned by Hitler. Udet, sensibly, took with him the letter he had dictated a few weeks before to the effect that he would no longer put any aircraft at Hess's disposal. This cleared Udet of any suspicion of complicity.

The planned attack on Russia – Operation Barbarossa – was now imminent. The Luftwaffe had hoped to have 1,000 of the new Me 210's for this offensive, and for that purpose Udet had previously ordered phasing out of the Bf 110 and the setting up of series-production of the Me 210. Yet, instead of the promised 1,000, ordered straight off the drawing board, only one aircraft plus a few trial machines had been actually delivered to date. Even after eighteen months of trials and test-flying the Me 210 continued to suffer from vicious flying characteristics; while the various complaints and formal protests to Messerschmitt by Udet had no effect.

With the Russian offensive only a month away, Milch seized the opportunity to report to Göring on 22 May, when he detailed the sorry state of the GL Department, Udet's complete inability to control the aircraft industry, and in particular pointed out the long delays in procuring such aircraft as the He 177 and Me 210. Inevitably Göring summoned Udet the next day and, for the first time directly attacked Udet over the shortcomings of his GL. This tirade bewildered Udet. How could a WW1 pilot, and one from the old Richthofen Geschwader at that, do such a thing to him? Now it was not just Milch and Jeschonnek who were against him, but Göring too; the same Göring who had pleaded and pleaded with him to join the Luftwaffe in his carefree display-pilot days!

Though Göring made no further outbursts, his deputy Milch erupted on 11 June. He had asked for some statistics from Udet, but when these arrived Milch refused to believe them, and duly reported to Göring that Udet's office was full of self-deceit. A violent row between Udet and Milch ensured.

Meanwhile, Hitler, confident of a quick victory in the east, went so far as to order on 20 June – just two days before the attack on

Russia – a slowing down on pure armaments production. Immediately after defeating Russia Hitler wanted to turn his full might against England, for which he needed aircraft primarily. Milch saw his chance and coaxed Göring into signing a document which gave Milch immense powers to step up aircraft production to four times its present level. It gave him authority over virtually every item in Germany. He could take any measures he deemed necessary, he could commandeer factories, labour, staff, nullify existing contracts, even dismiss directors. It was a sweet victory for the ambitious and ruthless Milch. It was a bad blow for Udet. Göring had dropped him cold. He was now defenceless against Milch. When he went to fetch Inge at her apartment in the Karolinger Platz, he remarked, 'I'm only a ghost wearing a uniform from now on.'

Early in the morning of 22 June three *Luftflotten* totalling 2,000 aircraft attacked Russia, while below them an army of three million men, 750,000 horses, 600,000 vehicles, 7,000 guns and 4,000 tanks were on the move eastwards. The following day Milch started a series of marathon conferences to get his *Göringprogram* – the multiplying of aircraft production by four – on its feet. Udet was not even present at these conferences. His misery at his recent treatment now turned to anger. From now on he would spare none of these 'gentlemen'. He wrote angry letters to Messerschmitt, detailing the many failings of his factory's products. When General Rüdel, chief of the anti-aircraft artillery, differed in opinion with Udet, he saw to it that Rüdel was relieved of his post! On 8 July he told Göring of his latest aircraft production programme, *Elch*, a provisional plan until Milch's *Göringprogram* was under way – but didn't bother to tell Milch of it. When Milch furiously telegrammed him to return, Udet didn't reply but simply complained to Göring of Milch's bullying methods. His complaint earned Milch a severe reprimand from Göring for failing to co-operate with Udet.

If such acts satisfied Udet's desire to hit back, they did little to uplift his personal despair and depression at his predicament. To a visiting friend Walter Gollwitzer he said, 'I tell you frankly my wings have been clipped, my job here is like a prison. Former comrades-in-arms persuaded me to take over the Technical Department, but now I realise that my former squadron buddy (Göring) didn't want to help me get on, but used me to strengthen his own position. I'm going to pieces here. I can't believe in victory.'

To his closest friends he had already spoken of suicide as the only way out left to him. He had mentioned this to Inge once, while holding a gun in his hand, but Inge had taken the gun away from him then. Strangely enough, on 30 July the London *Daily Telegraph* and *Daily Sketch* printed a report of Udet's 'suicide', based on information received from a 'diplomatic source' in America. This report was also printed in USA newspapers that day, but next day Goebbels arranged for foreign correspondents to interview the 'dead' Udet in his RLM office, where Udet treated the whole matter as a joke.

However, unknown to Udet, Göring's private intelligence staff had already tapped Udet's office telephones, and was well informed about Udet's phone calls. . .

The web of Nazi intrigue and suspicion extended even further. One night as Udet was about to enter his villa two Gestapo men came out of the darkness abruptly; they wished to search his house, and had been sent by Heydrich. They found some letters from one of Udet's friends in Sweden which made it apparent that Udet had been planning a hunting vacation in Sweden. Heydrich concluded that Udet intended fleeing to neutral Sweden, and had him closely shadowed thereafter, even having Udet forbidden from flying his own aircraft. Udet invited Heydrich for a few days hunting near Rechlin, and every effort was made to soften the matter, but the embargo on Udet piloting himself remained in force.

The effect on Udet was great. As he remarked to Hanna Reitsch shortly after, 'I can say this to you because you'll understand; others will just think I'm mad. This is the end. I'd abandon my uniform, rank, title, everything, but I must be able to fly again. I can no longer bear this.'

Henceforth Udet was permitted to use a Heinkel He 111, GA+SV for his travel needs, but had to have a pilot with him at all times.

It was a totally depressed Udet who accompanied Milch on a visit to the Messerschmitt works on 7 August, and Udet kept himself well in the background. His bright star was now rapidly sinking. He was unable to sleep at nights – the wailing of air-raid sirens keeping him awake virtually every night as the RAF pounded Berlin. When his friend Siebel visited him in his villa he found a very apathetic Udet, too weak to fight back any longer, and spitting blood again. Udet was at the end of his tether – and this did not go unnoticed. He drank heavily now, despite Inge's protestations, saying, 'Ingelein, when somebody has worries, he drinks, and I have worries. . .' Inge had her worries too – about him – she could do nothing to help him but confided in old friends like Schneeberger, the cameraman, who had accompanied Udet on his filming expeditions.

At the end of August Udet finally made up his mind; he would see Göring and tender his resignation. Only then would he be free of all his worries. On the 24th, with Inge, he drove to Karinhall, and while Inge waited outside Göring's office, the two men talked for more than three hours.

Yet even this ultimate, if humiliating step was to be denied to Udet; 'I can't let you go,' said Göring, 'People might be suspicious.' Instead he suggested that Udet take a long vacation to overcome his depression. Next day Udet reported himself as ill and, with Inge, drove to Lake Müritz and the 'home' of Dr Hermann; a totally broken, sick man.

The first visitor, of all people, was Erhard Milch, whose sole purpose in coming was to bully and cajole Udet into signing some new aircraft production plans Milch had drawn up – as if he still needed Udet's signature with the wide powers granted to him by Göring! In Udet's absence at the RLM Milch was busy getting rid of many of Udet's trusted subordinates and staff chiefs, replacing them with his own men. When Udet returned early from his sick leave he fiercely opposed these changes at first, but then became utterly apathetic to everything Milch did. Back in the RLM Udet felt a stranger, dealing with the new men appointed by Milch, and again started talking about committing suicide to end his misery. Even an occasional hunting trip no longer held any joy for him. Finally, on 4 October, Milch played his trump cards.

A conference was held at the RLM, with all Milch's new men present. The victory over Udet was now overtly complete. From then on Milch dragged Udet along on his numerous visits to aircraft factories and other industrial centres, more as a mascot than a very senior member of the RLM. Udet remained mainly silent, trying to smile at the appropriate moment, but utterly in the background to Milch's bombastic utterances.

The latest aircraft production plan was announced by Milch on 21 October at an RLM conference attended by some 200 leading German industrialists. Whereas previously four Bf 109's were to have been produced to each single Fw 190, this was now reversed and three Fw 190's were to be built for every Bf 109. When the Messerschmitt representatives protested vehemently about this decision, Milch blandly told them that the plan had been signed by Udet, not himself. On 7 November Udet spent more than seven hours in conference with Göring. Hitler had finally blamed Göring for the Luftwaffe's failure to gain mastery over the RAF; now in his usual manner Göring passed the buck – heaping reproach after reproach upon Udet's head.

This upset Udet so much that he didn't bother going to the RLM next day, and in the evening made a brief visit to his beloved mother in Munich. He stayed only for a few minutes, but as he left he muttered enigmatically, 'Yes, I believe there is reason to be concerned about me.'

Five days after his fateful conference with Göring, Udet's fate was sealed by Milch. A special conference was held at the RLM on 12 November by more than 50 RLM officers and technical staff, Milch, Udet and Willy Messerschmitt with his financial director, Fritz Seiler, and Rakan Kokothaki. Previous to the meeting Seiler had told Milch that the decision to switch production emphasis from Bf 109's to Fw 190's would result in a loss of 600 aircraft for operational issue. Furthermore, Seiler claimed that the decision had been made by comparison reports of the two types of aircraft which had been falsified by Udet's staff. Milch failed to let Udet know about Seiler's accusations before the meeting.

Milch opened the meeting by describing Seiler's claims, then with a theatrical gesture asked Seiler to prove his contentions. Seiler handed a sheaf of photostats to Milch, saying, 'These are the proof that Generaloberst Udet was wrongly informed.'

Taken completely by surprise, Udet told Seiler that this was hardly a friendly way of doing things, whereupon Seiler coolly retorted that Udet had not informed Messerschmitt of the impending change in the fighter procurement programme, so that all this was a game of chess, and that he had simply made the second move. Udet sensed that far from a game of chess, all this was a trap set up for him personally. This feeling was amply confirmed only minutes later when Seiler handed some documents to Milch proving that the planned switch in production would result in a loss of some 600 fighters in one works alone. He had even marked this on a graph in red. Udet knew nothing of these documents, but instead of passing them to Udet, Milch in a frosty tone formally asked 'my friend Udlinger', 'Why has the Department of the GL not provided me with such a drawing?' The trap had closed; Udet had been made to look ridiculous in front of his own staff. He made no answer.

It was on this fateful day that Ernst Udet finally decided to end it all. He was now a completely changed man, bewildering his closest friends with his deeply sombre mood. When he visited Göring again, Emmy – Göring's wife – noticed that Udet had hardly touched his food. Later she had a plate of snacks made and took them to Udet, who was standing outside, staring at the lake. When Emmy insisted that he eat something Udet politely excused himself, saying that he couldn't swallow a thing.

'Do you have a few minutes?' he asked.

Alone with Emmy inside the house, Udet first extracted a promise from her that she would not tell her husband anything for at least two weeks, then blurted out, '*Gnädige Frau*, I cannot go on any longer . . . everything seems pointless to me!' And he made similar remarks to various other friends during the next few days.

All the time at the back of his mind was his firm resolution to take his life and end it all. He had made up his mind; the coming week-end would be his last. He could no longer bear his fate. In his mood of black despair he thought back over his life. He had feared no man during the first war, indeed, had brought down 62 opponents. He knew no fear when performing daring aerobatics, and his courage and ability had been internationally acclaimed. Now – he wasn't even needed, and a puffed up man like Milch could make him look ridiculous. And what of the present? He *knew* Germany could never win this war. What would life be when Germany was defeated; another 'Versailles'? Or even worse? And where could he go anyway? To England? It was out of the question for Udet to desert to the enemy. To a neutral country? The Gestapo would only follow him. . . .

And his health was failing; the whistling in his ears, the blood-spitting, sleeplessness, the fear when night approached and the lonely despair of darkness. Physically too he was on the way down – he would never be young again; only bleak old age awaited him even if he survived. The years left to him in which he could fly an aircraft or love a woman were numbered. . . .

On Sunday, 16 November, at about 11 am the telephone rang. It was Erich Baier, his old friend and mehcanic. He had joined the Engineer Corps of the RLM and was due to take the official oath next day. He had only just arrived from Hamburg, and thought he should at least phone his old employer.

'Baier,' Udet shouted, 'Of course you must come. Get a cab, or I'll send someone to fetch you.'

When Baier arrived and greeted Udet as '*Herr Generaloberst*', Udet quickly replied, 'Never mind the *General* thing, I am Udet.

Well, of all men, you should come and see me today of all days', leaving Baier slightly puzzled as to what might be special about today. Udet called Inge, went to meet her at the Heerstrasse, then all three returned to the villa.

Puffing on good cigars with a glass of good cognac in their hands, the two old friends spent the rest of the evening happily reminiscing over the old days in Africa, Greenland, America – forgotten for now were Udet's problems with Milch, the RLM and the others. Baier could see how deeply the talk about the old times affected Udet, and when the time came for Baier to leave, Udet could barely conceal his emotion.

After Baier had left, Udet broke down, sobbing piteously like a small boy, and Inge tried her best to comfort him.

'What is it, Ernie? You are acting very strangely today.'

'Inge,' he replied, 'I have to tell you, today is definitely the last time we'll be together. Tomorrow you'll be a widow.'

Inge refused to believe him; he had said such wild things before. Later she told Udet that their good friends, the Winters, had called and asked if they would like to come over. Udet finally agreed to go, and when he arrived at the Winters began amusing their children. At last he seemed to be at peace with himself, composed, though Inge noticed he was drinking cognac steadily throughout the evening.

When she mentioned this quietly to Udet, he replied, 'I've always liked to drink before a difficult flight.'

Later still he drove Inge to her apartment, and when she entered her door he remained sitting in his car, staring after her for a long while.

Udet then drove around Berlin until 3 am, as if he was saying goodbye to all his old haunts where he had spent so many happy times, particularly Horchers, where his account was at present some 32,000 marks in the 'red'! When he finally returned to his villa he found his aide, Raven von Barnekow, sitting in his car. 'Udlinger, you're not going to. . .' but he didn't finish the sentence and drove away fast. His valet, Peters, was still waiting for him. Peters asked Udet when he would like his breakfast in the morning, and whether he would be going to the RLM tomorrow.

Udet exploded, 'No, I'm not going to the RLM, and don't bother me with your breakfast!'

Udet went to the bar and poured himself a glass of cognac, then telephoned Inge, asking her to come over.

'I told you I couldn't come.'

'Is there someone with you?'

'Please, Ernie, don't call me again tonight. I'll be with you for breakfast.'

Slowly Udet went upstairs, undressed and donned his red bath-robe, then went downstairs again and took a gun out of the gun rack; his Mexican 12mm Colt. He had decided days ago to commit suicide by shooting himself – but doing it was harder than he had imagined. He went upstairs again. By his bed lay the last book he had been reading, *Die Farbige Front*, but he would never finish it. It was morning already when he took a red pencil and began writing, 'Ingelein, why have you left me?. . . . Iron One, you are responsible for my death. . .'

He continued writing in an unsure hand, claiming that Göring had delivered him to Milch. The bottle of cognac was now empty, and at 8.45 am he again called Inge.

'Thank Heavens, Ernie. Did you sleep well?'

Udet's reply was an icy 'No'.

'I'll come and have breakfast with you,' said Inge, worried by the tone of Udet's voice.

'No, don't come. It's too late,' he replied, meanwhile bringing the gun up behind his right ear. 'Ingelein, nobody was dearer to me than you,' he said.

'Ernie, wait, please wait, I'll be with you at once. . .'

But as she called frantically into the mouthpiece, Udet pulled the trigger. It was the 17th of November – the month Udet had always dreaded. . .

Combat Record of Ernst Udet
1914–1918

The following tabulation is the official accreditation of combat victories for Udet during World War One. Study of the main text will reveal one or two apparent anomalies e.g. the Nieuport Scout claimed by Udet personally (in his subsequent biographies) on 13 August 1917; and the apparent error in chronology of his officially-listed victories Nos 7 and 8 – the latter due simply to delay in documentation at that particular time.

Date	Time	Aircraft	Location

Kampfeinsitzer-Kommando Habsheim

Date	Time	Aircraft	Location
18/3/16	5.10 pm	Farman F.40	Mülhausen

Jagdstaffel 15

Date	Time	Aircraft	Location
12/10/16	3.30 pm	Breguet-Michelin	Rüstenhart
24/12/16	11 am	Caudron G IV	Oberaspach
20/2/17	Noon	Nieuport Scout	Aspach
24/4/17	7.30 pm	Nieuport Scout	Chavignon
5/5/17	7.30 pm	Spad S VII	Bois d'Viller

Jagdstaffel 37

Date	Time	Aircraft	Location
14/8/17	8.30 pm	Bristol F2b	Lens
15/8/17	10.25 am	Sopwith 1½ Strutter	Pont-à-Vendin
21/8/17	8.45 am	De Havilland 4	Ascq (S of Lille)
17/9/17	7.30 am	De Havilland 5	Izel
24/9/17	12.20 pm	Two-seater (FE2b?)	Loos
28/9/17	6 pm	Sopwith F1 Camel	W of Wingles
28/9/17	6 pm	Sopwith F1 Camel	W of Wingles
18/10/17	10.35 am	Sopwith F1 Camel	Deulemont
28/11/17	1.40 pm	De Havilland 5	Passchendaele area
5/12/17	2.30 pm	SE5a	Passchendaele area
6/1/18	4.15 pm	Nieuport Scout	Bixschoote

28/1/18	4.55 pm	Sopwith F1 Camel	Bixschoote
29/1/18	Noon	Bristol F2b	Zillebecke
18/2/18	10.50 am	Sopwith F1 Camel	Zandvoorde

Jagdstaffel 11

27/3/18	11.50 am	RE8	Albert
28/3/18	9.10 am	Sopwith F1 Camel	Albert-Bapaume area
6/4/18	2.15 pm	Sopwith F1 Camel	Hamel

Jagdstaffel 4

31/5/18	1 pm	Breguet	Soissons area
2/6/18	11.50 am	Breguet	NW of Neuilly
5/6/18	Noon	Spad S VII	S of Buczany
6/6/18	11.40 am	Spad S VII	S of Faverolles
7/6/18	7 pm	Spad S VII	E of Villers Cotterets
13/6/18	5.45 pm	Spad S VII	NE of Faverolles
14/6/18	8 pm	Spad S VII	N of St Pierre-Aigle
23/6/18	12.10 pm	Breguet	La Ferté Milon
23/6/18	8.15 pm	Breguet	Crouy area
24/6/18	10 am	Breguet	SE of Montigny
25/6/18	6.45 pm	Spad S VII	N of Longpont
25/6/18	6.45 pm	Spad S VII	Chavigny Ferme
30/6/18	8 pm	Spad S VII	Faverolles
1/7/18	11.45 am	Breguet	Pierrefont area
1/7/18	8.55 pm	Spad S VII	E of Faverolles
2/7/18	8.15 am	Nieuport Scout	Bézu St Germain
3/7/18	8.25 am	Spad S VII	E of Laversine
1/8/18	9.30 am	Nieuport Scout	NE of Cramaille
1/8/18	12.15 pm	Breguet	N of Muret Crouttes
1/8/18	8.30 pm	Spad S VII	N of Beugneux
4/8/18	8.5 pm	Spad S VII	S of Braisne
8/8/18	5.30 pm	SE5a	Fontaine le Cappy
8/8/18	6.30 pm	SE5a	SE of Barleux
8/8/18	8.40 pm	Sopwith F1 Camel	SE of Foucaucourt
9/8/18	4.25 pm	Sopwith F1 Camel	S of Vauvillers
9/8/18	9.20 pm	Sopwith F1 Camel	SE of Herleville
10/8/18	11.30 am	Sopwith F1 Camel	S of Marcourt
10/8/18	7.45 pm	Sopwith F1 Camel	S of Fay
11/8/18	10 am	De Havilland 9A	Chaulnes
12/8/18	11.30 am	SE5a	Péronne area
14/8/18	7 pm	Bristol F2b	S of Vermandovillers

15/8/18	5.15 pm	Sopwith F1 Camel	Herleville
16/8/18	10.40 am	Spad S VII	S of Foucaucourt
21/8/18	6.30 pm	SE5a	S of Hébuterne
21/8/18	7.15 pm	Sopwith 5F1 Dolphin	S of Courcelles
22/8/18	8.30 am	Sopwith F1 Camel	N of Braie
22/8/18	12.30 pm	SE5a	W of Méricourt
26/9/18	5.10 pm	De Havilland 9	Monteningen area
26/9/18	5.20 pm	De Havilland 9	S of Metz

Bibliography

Allen, H R: *Who won the Battle of Britain?*, London 1974

Anders, K und Eichelbaum: *Wörterbuch des Flugwesens*, Leipzig 1937

Angot, E und de Lavergne R: *Le General Vuillemin*, Paris 1965

Bäumker, Adolf: *Zur Geschichte der Führung der deutschen Luftfahrt-technik*, Bad Godesberg, 1971

Balchen, Bernt: *Come North with Me*, New York 1958

Beinhorn, Elly: *. . . so waren diese Flieger*, Herford 1966

Bender, R J: *Air Organisations of the Third Reich*, Mountain View, 1967

Bender, R J: *The Luftwaffe*, Mountain View, 1972

Bodenschatz, K: *Jagd in Flanderns Himmel*, Munich 1935

Bongartz, H: *Luftmacht Deutschland*, Essen 1939

Bordeaux, H: *La vie heroique de Guynemer*, Paris 1918

Brandner, F: *Ein Leben zwischen Fronten*, Munich 1974

Buckler, J: *Malaula!*, Berlin 1939

Conradis, H: *Forschen und Fliegen*, Göttingen 1959

Dietrich, R: *Im Flug über ein halbes Jahrhundert*, Gütersloh 1942

Fanck, A: *Stürme über dem Mont Blanc*, Basle, 1931

Fanck, A: *SOS Eisberg*, Munich 1933

Farago, L: *The Game of the Foxes*, New York 1971

Galland, A: *Die Ersten und die Letzten*, Darmstadt 1953

Georgii, W: *Forschen und Fliegen*, Tübingen 1954

Gilles, J A: *Flugmotoren 1910–1918*, Frankfurt 1971

Göring, E: *An der Seite meines Mannes*, Göttingen 1967

Gray, P & Thetford, O: *German Aircraft of the First World War*, London 1970

Green, W: *Warplanes of the Third Reich*, London 1970

Heinkel, E: *Stürmisches Leben*, Stuttgart 1953

Herlin, H: *Udet, eines Mannes Leben*, Hamburg 1958

Hess, I: *Ein Schicksal in Briefen*, Leoni 1977

Hoeppner, E von: *Deutschlands Krieg in der Luft*, Leipzig 1921

Imrie, A: *Pictorial History of the Germany Army Air Service*, London, 1971
Irving, D: *The Rise and Fall of the Luftwaffe*, London, 1974
Ishoven, A van: *Messerschmitt*, Vienna 1976
Işhoven, A van: *Udet Flamingo*, Windsor 1973
Italiaander, R: *Wolf Hirth erzählt*, Berlin 1935
Kesselring, A: *Memoirs*, London, 1953
Kiaulehn, W: *Berlin*, Munich 1958
Knightley, P: *The First Casualty*, London 1975
Lange, B: *Das Buch der Deutschen Luftfahrttechnik*, Mainz 1970
Lewis, C: *Sagittarius Rising*, London 1936
Lindbergh, C: *The Wartime Journals of Charles Lindbergh*, New York 1970
Lochner, W: *Als die Luftfahrt noch ein Abenteur war*, Munich
Meyer, O: *Zur Geschichte des Luftverkehrs*, Augsbourg o. J.
Nebel, R: *Die Narren von Tegel*, Düsseldorf 1972
Neumann, G: *Die Deutschen Luftstreitkräfte im Weltkriege*, Berlin 1921
Osterkamp, T: *Durch Höhen und Tiefen jagt ein Herz*, Stuttgart 1952
Osterkamp, T: *Tragödie der Luftwaffe?*, Neckargemund 1971
Polte, W: *Und wir sind doch geflogen!*, Güterloh 1940
Radenbach, F: *Gottlob Espenlaub, ein Fliegerleben*, Stuttgart 1942
Reitsch, H: *Fliegen – mein Leben*, Stuttgart 1951
Rickenbacker, E: *Autobiography*, London 1968
Reickhoff, H: *Trumpf oder Bluff?*, Genf. 1945
Ries, K: *Luftwaffe, geheimer Augbau 1919–1935*, Mainz 1970
Ries, K: *Luftwaffen Story 1935–1939*, Mainz 1974
Robertson, B: *Air Aces of the 1914–18 War*, Letchworth 1959
Shirer, W: *The Rise & Fall of the Third Reich*, New York 1960
Shirer, W: *Berlin Diary*, London 1941
Speer, A: *Inside the Third Reich*, London 1970
Sorge, E: *Mit Flugzeug, Faltboot und Filmkamera in den Eisfjorden Grönlands*, Berlin 1933
Stehlin, P: *Temoignage pour l'Histoire*, Paris 1964
Steinhoff, J: *In letzter Stunde*, Munich 1974
Supf, P: *Das Buch der Deutschen Fluggeschichte, Band I*, Stuttgart 1956; *Band II*, Stuttgart 1958
Thomas, L & Jablonski, E: *Doolittle, a biography*, New York 1976
Thorwald, J: *Ernst Udet: ein Fliegerleben*, Berlin 1954
Trautloft, H: *Horridoh!*, Munich 1953

Trevor-Roper, H R: *Hitler's War Directives*, New York 1964
Udet, E: *Kreuz wider Kokarde*, Berlin 1918
Udet, E: *Hals- und Beinbruch!*, Berlin 1928
Udet, E: *Fremde Vögel uber Afrika*, Bielefeld 1932
Udet, E: *Mein Fliegerleben*, Berlin 1935
Völker, K-H: *Die Entwicklung der militärischen Luftfahrt in Deutschland 1920–1933*, Stuttgart 1962
Völker, K-H: *Die deutsche Luftwaffe 1933–1939*, Stuttgart 1967
Völker, K-H: *Dokumente und Dokumentarfotos zur Geschichte der deutschen Luftwaffe*, Stuttgart 1968
Waldhausen, H: *Ernst Udet, vom Zauber seiner Persönlichkeit*, Neckargemünd 1972
Williams, A: *Airpower*, New York 1940
Winterbotham, F W: *The Ultra Secret*, London 1974
Zuckmayer, C: *Meisterdramen*, Frankfurt 1966
Zuckmayer, C: *Als wär's ein Stuck von mir*, Göttingen 1968

Yearbooks

Die Deutsche Luftfahrt, 1936–1941, Frankfurt
Jahrbuch der deutschen Luftwaffe, 1937–1941, Leipzig
Jane's All the World's Aircraft, 1914–41, London

Sources

Much of the information for this book came from interviews and correspondence with a large circle of people. To those mentioned below and to any inadvertently omitted the author gives grateful acknowledgment and thanks:

Gerd Achgelis, Marion Adam, Gebhard Aders, Walter Angermund, Erich Baier, Bernt Balchen, Richard Bateson, Arno Bäumer, Elly Beinhorn, Josef von Berg, Walter Bönig, Peter Bowers, Chaz Bowyer, Inge Bleyle, Else Braun, Georg Brütting, Gert Buchheit, Clemens Bücker, Harry von Bülow, Charles Cain, Hans Caspari, Wulf-Dieter Graf zu Castell, Ary Ceelen, Frank Courtney, Kurt Delang, Eugen Dietschi, Oskar Dimpfel, Walter Dollfus, James Doolittle, Hans Ebert, Wolfram Eisenlohr, John Ellingworth, Wolfgang Falck, Arnold Fanck, Gerhard Fieseler, Carl Francke, Paula Freifrau von Gablenz, Adolf Galland, Walter Gollwitzer, Traute Grether, Wolfgang von Gronau, Peter Grosz, Ruth Günther, R. Gurra, Fred Haubner, Carl Heeg, Hellmut Herb, Hans von Hippel, Clara Hirth, Max Holtzem, Gerhard Hubricht, Gerhard Hümmelchen, Pit van Husen,

David Irving, Hans Jacobs, Fritz Jacobsen, Kurt Jentkiewicz, Werner Junck, Helmuth Kaden, Joseph Kammhuber, Hans Kilian, Clara Klein-Bader, Walter Kleffel, Rakan Kokothaki, Ferenc Kovacs, Adolf Krogmann, Hans-Joachim Kroschinski, Bruno Lange, Otto Lindpaintner, Alexander Lippisch, Gisela Lusser, Hans Justus Meier, Erich Meindl, Fritz Morzik, Rudolf Nebel, Gerhard Nitschke, Maria Gräfin Orssich, Theo Osterkamp, Georg Pasewald, Otto Pausinger, Rudolf Pischl, Peter Raabe, Willy Radinger,Thea Rasche, Gottfried Reidenbach, Hanna Reitsch, Peter Riedel, Karl Ries, Oskar von Römer, Leo Roth, Oskar Rumler, Wilhelm Sachsenberg, Bona Schaller, Hanfried Schliephake, Kurt Schnittke, Carl von Schönebeck, Paul Skogsted, Jacob Spalinger, Heinz Starke, Paul Stehlin, Willy Stör, Paul Strähle, John Stroud, Hans Stuck, Dix Terne, Harold Thiele, Johannes Thinesen, Luis Trenker, Walter Vetter, Woldemar Voigt, G. Voss, Wolfgang Wagner, Hubert Wähner, Hans Waldhausen, Erich Warsitz, Andreas Weise, Martin Windrow, Laszlo Winkler, Hermann Wurster, German Zettel, Carl Zuckmayer.

Special thanks for their practical help in the preparation of this book go to:
Georges van Acker, Ewald Delbaere, Jean Dillen, André Maes, Robert Rombaut.

Thanks are also due to the following institutions for their help:
Abteilung der Militärflugplätze, Dübendorf; Aero-Club Argentino, Buenos Aires; Bayerisches Haupstaatsarchiv, München; Bayerisches Kriegsarchiv, München; Bayerische Motoren Werke AG, München; Berlin Document Center, Berlin; Bibliothek für Zeitgeschichte, Stuttgart; Bundesarchiv Freiburg; Bundersarchiv Koblenz; Circulo de Aeronautica, Buenos Aires; Cross and Cockade, California; Cross and Cockade, England; Deutches Museum, München; Deutsche Staatsbibliothek, Berlin; Dornier AG, München; Imperial War Museum, London; Library of Congress, Washington; Lufthansa, Köln; Musée de l'Air, Paris; National Archives and Press Services, Washington; Royal Air Force College, Cranwell; Verein Alte Adler, Weinheim.

Index

Aalen, 18
Aboukir, 131
Achgelis, pilot, 143
Aircraft
  AEG, 33, 54
  Albatros: 132; D I and II: 39; D III:
    39, 40, 41, 44, 48, 50, 51; DVa: 52,
    54, 57, 58
  Amiot, 176
  Arado: Ar 66: 152; Ar 65 F: 160; Ar
    68: 160, 161; SC 1: 127
  Aviatik, 27, 28, 29, 54
  Beaufighter, 197
  BFW 3, 123
  Blackburn Lincoln, 134
  Blenheims, 183, 184
  Blériot, 18
  Blohm und Voss, 161
  Breguet, 14, 62, 63, 66, 68
  Breguet Michelin IV, 36, 37
  Bristol: 106; F 2b: 47, 48, 54, 69; FE
    2b: 48; FE 2d: 48
  Bücker Bü, 131
  Caudron, 33, 34, 35, 37, 38, 41
  Cierva Autogiro, 121, 132
  Curtiss: F 8c Helldiver: 127, 133,
    135; F 11c: 147; Hawk: 135–6, 139,
    142, 145, 147, 148, 149, 151, 152,
    153, 156, 157, 162
  Daimler, 100, 118
  De Havilland: DH 4: 48, 60; DH 5:
    52; DH 9: 71; DH 60: Moth: 124,
    125, 128, 129, 138; Pussmoth: 130;
    DH 98: Mosquito: 187
  Dewoitine, 127
  DFS   230   A-1:   187,   188;
    Rhönbussards: 155,   164;
    Rhönsperber: 156, 157
  Dietrich, 105
  Dornier: 'Wal': 120; Do X: 141; Do
    17: 169, 177; Do 19: 162, 168; Do
    217; 199
  Etrich Taube 20

Fafnir, 132
Fairey, 130
Farman, 27, 31, 34, 35, 36, 43
Fieseler Storch, 170, 189, 200
Flamingo see U-12
Focke-Achgelis, 173
Focke-Wulf: 106; Fw 44: 152; Fw 57:
  151; Fw 159: 160; Fw 190: 183,
  198, 204, 205; Fw Stösser: 164, 165
Fokker: 74; Dr I: 54, 58, 61; D III:
  34, 36, 37, 75; D VII: 54, 55, 61,
  62, 63, 64–5, 66, 76, 166, 167; D
  VIII: 67, 69, 70, 76; E 1-IV: 32;
  E III: 32, 33; V-40: 75; D XIII:
  89
Gloster Gladiator, 170
Gotha, 145, 196
Gulfhawk, 175
Halberstadt, 41
Hawker Hurricane, 170, 175
Heinkel: He a: 107; He 50: 151; He
  51: 159, 162; He 72: 152, 159, 162;
  He 70: 161; He 100: 174, 176, 179;
  He 111: 169, 176, 177, 203; He
  119-V4: 170; He 118: 161, 162,
  163; He 177: 168, 171, 178, 185,
  189, 201; He 176: 182; He 112:
  160, 163, 174; He 178: 183; He
  280: 185, 200; V 8: 181
Henschel: Hs 123: 151, 156, 161; Hs
  124: 151
Junkers: 106, 146; 52/3M: 186; Ju
  46: 134; F 13: 102; K-47: 152; W-
  33L: 119; Ju 322: 198; Ju 288: 198;
  Ju 87: 175, 193, 152, 158, 159, 161,
  162; Ju 88: 171, 177, 179, 181, 182,
  194; Ju 89: 162, 168
Klemm: 138; K i: 153; Ki-32 XIV:
  145; L-25: 126, 143; L-26: 128,
  129, 138, 164
Kondor, 54
LVG, 24, 25, 31, 50, 59
Messerschmitt: Bf 108: 186, 200; Bf

109: 156, 160, 162, 167, 169, 173, 175, 179, 181, 184, 188, 189, 192, 193; Bf 110: 151, 172, 184, 189, 193, 198, 199, 201, 204, 205; Me 23b: 126, 128, 129, 130, 131, 132, 138, 139; Me 209 Vi: 181; Me 210: 177, 192; Me 261: 197, Me 321: 197

Otto, 18, 19

Pfalz, 54, 67, 74, 76; 91

Raab-Katzenstein, 120, 127

RE 8, 50, 56, 58, 59

R I helicopter, 165

Robbe II, 116, 117

Rohrbach IX, 116; Roland, 132

Roland 54

Rumpler: 78, 82; D1: 54, 78; C1: 78, 83; C IV: 77

S-16a: 96; 16b: 96

Schütte-Laaz D III, 54

Schwalbe, 120

SE 5a, 51, 52, 69, 146

Siebel, 178, 197

Siemens-Schuckert, 54, 71, 72, 74

Sikorsky, 110

Sopwith: Strutter 1½: 36, 47, 48; Camel: 49, 50, 51, 52, 54, 55, 58, 59, 69

Spad, 41, 43, 44, 45, 62, 63, 64, 66, 68, 69, 70, 80

Supermarine Spitfire, 170, 175

Texaco No 13, 133

Udet: U-1: 88, 97; U-2: 88, 90, 92, 97; U-3: 90; U-4: 90, 92, 94, 95, 97; U-5: 95, 97, U-6: 92, 95, 96, 97; U-7: 97; U-8: 95, 97, 98; U-9: 96; U-10: 96, 97, 98, 101; U-11: Kondor: 97, 98, 104, 105, 108, 111; U-12: Flamingo: 97, 98, 100, 101, 102, 103, 104, 105, 106, 107, 111, 112, 116, 117, 118, 119, 120, 121, 123, 124, 125, 126, 132, 133, 134; U-13: 107, 108

Voisin, 34, 62

Wright Brothers Flyer, 121

Zeppelin, 97, 143, 60

Aisne, River, 42

Akron, 135–6

Albert, 58

Alexandria, 131

Althaus, Ernst von, 37

Altkirch, 34

Altona, 153

Amiens, 59, 68

Amsterdam, 194, 198

Amstetten, 84

Angermund, Walter, 29, 61, 86, 99, 104, 112, 114, 136, 143, 154, 171, 195

Argentina, 90ff

Arras, 50

Arusha, 128

Aspach, 40

Atcherly, Fl Lt Richard, 134, 143

Auffahrt, Harald, 106

Augsburg, 77, 84, 108, 123, 156

August-Wilhelm, Prince, 120, 138

Austria, 94, 102, 115, 166, 173

Avesnes-le-Sec, 56

Azores, 116

Babati, 129

Baden, 107

Baden-Baden, 195

Bad Reichenhal, 102

Baier, Erich, 119, 121, 125, 126, 133, 134, 137, 139, 144, 146, 149, 206, 207

Baierlein, Dr, 18

Balbo, Italo, 176

Bamberg, 18, 74, 76, 96, 100, 105

Bapaume, 58

Barlet, Maréchal de Logis, 37

Barnekow, Raven von, 145, 207

Basle, 132

Basser, Gustav, 83, 84

Baümer, Paul, 93, 94, 106, 109, 116

Baur, Hans, 106

Bayreuth, 26

Beauvais, 191

Behrend, Walter, 27, 30, 34

Beinhorn, Elly, 68, 126, 152, 159

Belfort, 27, 28, 30, 31

Belgium, 186 et passim

Belleville-sur-Meuse, 19

Bender, Ltn, 61

Berchtesgaden, 183

Bergen, Claus, 70

Bergen, Otto, 17, 52, 60, 70, 111

Berlin, 54, 55, 62, 72, 77, 84, 86, 94, 96, 98, 100, 104, 105, 109, 112, 113, 114, 116, 120, 121, 122, 124, 126, 127, 128, 133, 136, 137, 138, 139, 140, 141, 142, 143, 144, 149, 152,

153, 154, 156, 158, 160, 163, 166, 168, 171, 173, 175, 186, 187, 190, 191, 197, 201
Bermuda, 117
Berndthäusl, Herr, 18
Bernes, 69
Berthold, Rudolf, 37
Bertincourt, 35, 36
Bessel, Ehmi, 140
Bétheny, 42
Beugneux, 62, 65
Billik, Paul, 100
Bismarck, Alexander von, 101
Bixschoote, 54
Blackburn, Robert, 134
Blankensee, 153
Bleyle, Inge, 148, 171, 178, 185, 195, 202, 203, 204, 207, 208
Blindenmarkt, 84
Blomberg, F. M. von, 172
Blumenthal, von, 167
Bluthgen, Ltn, 26
Böblingen, 101, 166
Bodenschatz, Gen Karl, 57, 62, 141, 152, 173, 190
Boelcke, Hptm Oswald, 36, 37, 61
Bolle, 158
Boncourt, 43, 44
Bonn, 119, 127
Borodino, 139
Brauchitsch, Gen. von, 172
Braun, Karl, 75
Braun, Maj, 164, 165
Breiten-Laudenberg, Ltn Otto von, 57
Bremen, 86
Bremen, 136
Bremerhaven, 133, 145
Breslau, 62
Brimont, 43
Brouwers family, 49
Bruges, 48
Brühl, Dr, 194
Brunsbüttel, 183
Brussels, 199
Buckler, Offiz Julius, 50, 158
Budapest, 106
Buddecke, Hans Joachim, 37
Buenos Aires, 90, 92
Buffalo, 146, 147
Busigny, 70

Cael, Lt J., 69, 70, 80, 81
Cairo, 129, 131
Campbell-Black, 130
Canada, 193
Cap Polonio, 90
Carraciola, 122
Chamberlain, 120
Charlottenburg, 138
Chauny, 23
Chavignon, 42
Chemin des Dames, 42, 61
Chemnitz, 108
Chicago, 145, 146
Child, Lloyd, 136
Christiansen, Friedrich, 141, 191
Chur, 105
Churchill, Winston, 191
Cierva, Juan de la, 109, 121, 122
Cleveland, Ohio, 133, 134
Coeve, 28
Colmar, 26, 27, 29
Cologne, 25
Compiègne, 42, 72, 189
Conta, Ltn von, 57
Coope, Wg Cdr, 192
Copenhagen, 116
Courcelles-sur-Vesle, 67
Courtney, Air V-M, 167
Courtney, Frank T., 109
Courtrai, 32, 46
Coutemaiche, 28
Coventry, 196
Crailsheim, Rittm von, 84
Craonne, 42
Croydon, 170
Cutry, 63, 64
Cuxhaven, 116
Czechoslovakia, 172, 176, 177, 180, 181

Dachau, 146, 154
Dahlmann, Franz, 144
Daily Mail, 156
Daily Sketch, 203
Daily Telegraph, 203
Danzig, 181
Darmstadt, 25, 26, 152, 167, 186
de Broke, Lord Willoughby, 144
Delle, 28
Denmark, 116, 188, 189, 198
Dessau, 151, 158, 175
Detroyat, Michel, 117

Deulemont, 50
Dittmar, Heini, 157, 159
Dixmuiden, 50
Doldi, Adolf, 83, 84
Doret, Marcel, 120, 127
Dorme, Père, 41
Dortmund, 127
Dossenbach, Albert, 37
Douai, 46
Douglas, Wg Cdr Sholto, 130, 131
Drekmann, Ltn Heinz, 61, 65
Dresden, 80, 161
Dübendorf, 152, 166, 169
Dumont, Santos, 120
Dunkirk, 189
Duschner, Herr, 102
Dusseldorf, 108, 111, 120, 127

Ehrwald, 112, 113
Eibsee, 112, 113, 126, 137, 155
Eichenhauer, Vizefeldwebel, 40, 44
Eichler, Ernst Friedrich, 60–1, 67, 70
Einsiedel, Gräfin Margot von, 95, 98
Eisner, Kurt, 73
Ensisheim, 36
Erpf, 70
Esser, Ltn (Jasta 37), 40, 41, 52
Esser, Ltn (Jasta 11), 57
Europa, 133, 134, 145
Ewest, Julian, 114
Everbusch, Ernst, Alfred and Walter, 55, 67

Falck, Hptmann Wolfgang, 189
Falmy, 69
Fanck, Dr Arnold, 123, 126, 137, 139
Feder, Prof Gottfried, 143, 144
Feilitzsch, Freiherr von, 110
Felmy, Gen, 173
Felsing, Frau, 126, 128
Fère-en-Tardenois, 63
Ficklscherer, Tony, 78
Fieseler, Gerhard, 119, 120
Fischer, Joseph, 19
Flieger Abteilungen: 5: 46; 206: 26, 27; 204: 27; 9b: 46; 45: 32; 68: 32; (Ersatz): 24, 25
Flight, 133
Focke, Heinrich, 86
Fokker, Anthony, 32, 54, 72
Fonck, René, 67, 110, 122

France, 150, 170, 177, 183, 186, 188, 189, 198 et passim
Francke, Carl, 194, 197
Franco, Gen, 166
Frankfurt, 17, 123
Frankl, Wilhelm, 37
Freiburg, 36, 73
Frescaty, 70
Fricourt, 104
Friedrich, Herr, 124
Fritsch, Gen von, 172
Fürth, 96, 108
Fusshöler, Otto, 109

Galland, Adolf, 192, 200
Garmisch, 112, 149, 159
Garros, Roland, 32
Geneva, 127
Genoa, 128
Georgii, Prof W., 162, 168, 186
Gerlich, Ltn, 26
Ghistelles, 50
Glardon, pilot, 127
Glinkermann, Unteroff, 33, 39, 40, 41, 43, 44
Gluczewski, Ltn Heinz Graf von, 61
Gollwitzer, Walter, 202
Gontard, Edy von, 128
Gontermann, Oberltn Heinrich, 43, 44, 45, 52
Göring, Emmy, 156, 206
Göring, F. M. Hermann, 19, 46, 66, 68, 69, 70, 71, 72, 74, 94, 101, 120, 124, 136, 137, 140, 141, 142, 143, 144, 145, 146, 147, 150, 151, 152, 155, 156, 157, 161, 163, 165, 166, 167, 168, 169, 172, 173, 174, 175, 176, 177, 178, 179, 180, 181, 182, 183, 184, 185, 186, 187, 188, 189, 190, 191, 192, 193, 194, 195, 196, 197, 198, 199, 200, 201, 202, 203, 204, 205, 208
Göring, Karin, 136, 137
Gotha, 72
Götz, Willy, 17
Grashoff, Ltn Kurt, 33, 44, 46, 47, 50, 51
Grave, Ltn, 61
Graz, 102, 103, 115
Great Britain, 128, 133, 144, 150, 154, 160, 169, 176, 177, 183, 189, 190,

191, 193, 196, 201, 202, 206
Greenland, 137, 138, 139, 149
Greim, Robert Ritter von, 69, 73, 74, 76, 77, 78, 80, 81, 141, 160, 163, 168
Grete, 139
Groenhoff, pilot, 132
Gronau, Oberltn z S. a. D. von, 107
Grosz, Georg, 113
Guise, 61
Gussmann, Ltn Siegfried, 57, 58, 59
Guynemer, Georges, 41, 44, 45

Habsheim, 31, 32, 34, 35, 36, 44, 45
Haegelen, Claude Marcel, 111
Hagen, 124
Hailer, Franz, 75
Halifax, Lord, 190
Halle, 105
Hamburg, 85, 90, 123, 128, 133, 139, 144, 150, 173, 206
Hänisch, Ltn, 'Putz', 40, 42, 43, 44, 52
Hannover, 127, 157
Harbonnières, 59
Harth, Friedrich, 18
Harting, Flugkptn, 174
Hartmann, Ltn, 30, 31
Harvey, Lilian, 146
Hawks, Capt Frank, 132
Hebuterne, 146
Heiligenkreuz, 26, 29, 30
Heinecke, Otto, 90, 92
Heinersgrün, 110
Heinkel, Ernst, 120, 125, 162, 163, 168, 170, 174, 176, 179, 181, 182, 183, 185, 189, 196
Hendicourt, 52
Hermann, Dr, 204
Herrmann, Hans, 86, 87, 88, 92, 93, 98, 107, 115
Herteaux, 41
Hertz, Ltn, 61
Hess, Rudolf, 94, 182, 199, 201
Heydrich, Reinhard, 184, 203
Hindenburg, Pres von, 136, 137, 140, 141
Hippel, Joachim von, 109
Hitler, Adolf, 46, 79, 82, 85, 86, 92, 99, 103, 105, 109, 136, 137, 139, 140, 141, 143, 145, 152, 154, 155, 156, 157, 158, 161, 163, 165, 167, 169, 170, 172, 173, 174, 176, 177, 178,

180, 181, 182, 183, 184, 185, 186, 188, 189, 190, 191, 192, 193, 197, 200, 201, 202, 205
Hochmut, 100
Hoenmanns, Erich, 186
Hoeppner, Gen von, 142
Hof, 110
Hoffmann, Ernst, 115
Hoffmann, Fraulein, 126
Hofmann, Ludwig, 157, 159
Hohlwein, Prof Ludwig, 76
Höhndorf, Walter, 37
Holten, 105
Holtzem, Max, 81, 90, 91
Hühnefeld, von,.120
Hundertmark, 125
Hungary, 106

Illing, Elloys, 137
Immelmann, Max, 37, 60
Innsbruck, 101, 114, 143, 155
Isar, River, 17, 19, 82, 111
Iseghem, 46
Iser, River, 49
Italy, 103

Jacobs, Hans, 155, 162, 196
Jagdgeschwader: Nr 1 (Richthofen): 45, 46, 49, 56ff, 136, 141, 142, 156; Nr 2: 56; Nr 3: 56, 63, 69, 100; 26: 200; 52: 200; 132: 156; 6: 61, 62, 70, 17: 50
Jagdstaffeln: 1: 35; 2: 36, 56; 4: 61–72, 135; 5: 43; 10: 61; 11: 57–61, 65; 12: 56; 13: 56; 15: 36, 39, 40, 41, 42, 43, 44, 45, 52, 56; 19: 56; 20: 145; 26: 56; 27: 46, 56, 66; 36: 56; 38: 50; 37: 44, 46–53, 54–5; 90: 71
Jeanjean, Marcel, 122
Jena, 105
Jeschonneck, Hans, 178, 180, 182, 183, 200, 201
Jessen, Ltn, 61
Jodl, Gen, 182
Johannisthal, 156, 167
Johnen, Bernard, 102, 103, 118
Juba, 130
Junck, Major Werner, 166, 171
Junghaus, 128
Junkers, Prof Hugo, 90
Just, Ltn Erich, 57, 58

Justinus, Bruno, 26, 27, 28, 29, 30

Kahr, von, 94
Karlsen, Dr Paul, 148
Karlsruhe, 107, 109
Kassel, 119, 175
Keitel, F. M. Wilhelm, 172
Keitel, Hans, 18
Kenese, Waldemar, 106
Kenya, 128
Kern, Erich, 100, 110, 112, 116, 118
Kesselring, F. M. Albert, 152, 161, 167, 168, 196, 198, 199
Khartoum, 130, 131
Kiel, 72, 123
Kieselhausen, 55
Kirschstein, Ltn H., 62, 65
Kleffel, Walter, 114, 115, 127, 128, 133, 135, 143, 144, 148, 150, 154
Klemm, Hans, 100
Koblenz, 86
Koch, Minister, 120
Koepsch, Ltn Egon, 61, 70
Koerner, Paul, 136
Köhl, Hermann, 119
Kokothaki, 205
Konigsberg, 133
Kònitz, Freihers von, 75
Könnecke, 120
Konstanz, 73
Koppenberger, 177, 179, 182
Körner, 173
Kraut, Ltn, 61
Krefeld, 107
Krefft, Ltn, 57
Kreuz wider Kokarde, 67, 70, 80
Kugler, Georg, 19

Laboisssière, 191
La Bonne Maison, 41
Labrador, 119
Lachmann, Dr Gustav, 97
La Guerre Aérienne, 37, 67, 79
Landau, 109
Landsberg, 99
Landshut, 123
Langemarck, 53
Laon, 23, 40, 43, 61
La Selve, 40, 41
Laumann, Arthur, 143
Lausanne, 115, 127

Lautenschlager, Vizefeldwebel, 60
La Vie Aérienne, 79, 80, 81
Le Cateau, 56, 57, 70, 91
Léchelle, 58, 59
Leffers, Gustav, 37
Leipzig, 101, 109, 115, 119, 123, 126
Lens, 52
Lermoos, 113
Leube, 92
Libya, 176
Lichtenburg, 154
Lierval, 43
Lieth-Thomsen, Maj Hermann von der, 26, 45
Lille, 41, 46
Lindbergh, Charles, 114, 120, 162, 179
Lindpaintner, Dr, 18
Lippitsch, Dr Alexander, 152, 182
Lloyd, Harold, 146
Locarno, 103
London, 133, 192, 196, 203
Loos, 48
Lörzer, Bruno, 69, 100, 141, 142, 143, 146, 158, 173, 198
Los Angeles, 145, 146
Löwenhardt, Ltn Erich, 59, 61, 62, 65, 66, 68, 69
Lubbert, Lt Friedrich-Wilhelm, 57
Luc-sur-Mer, 19
Ludendorff, Gen, 68
Luftwelt, 46, 154
Luneau, Observer, 37
Luro, Jorge, 92
Luro, Luis, 95

Maasdorp, Lt C. R., 59
Macedonia, 50, 51
Mackenthun, Hptm Walter, 33
Mahncke, Alfred, 174
Malakai, 130, 131
Malta, 196
Mannheim, 72, 108, 117, 119
Marienehe, 162, 185, 196, 200
Marville, 72
Maushake, Ltn, 61
Mayenberger, 92
Mein Fliegerleben, 47, 148, 158, 174
Messerschmitt, Willy, 18, 87, 96, 123, 132, 151, 156, 160, 179, 187, 189, 192, 197, 201, 203, 204, 205
Metz, 27, 70, 71

Meyer, Ltn Karl, 61
Meyer, Otto, 77, 78, 81, 83, 84
Milbertshofen, 86
Milch, F. M. Erhard, 27, 46, 82, 85, 105, 120, 141, 147, 150, 151, 159, 161, 165, 166, 167, 168, 169, 170, 172, 173, 176, 178, 180, 181, 181, 184, 185, 186, 187, 188, 190, 193, 194, 195, 196, 198, 200, 201, 202, 203, 204, 205, 206, 208
Milwaukee, USA 86
Missy, 64
Modern Times, 166
Mohnicke, Ltn Eberhardt, 57
Mölders, Werner, 192, 200
Mombasa, 128, 129
Moncheaux, 46, 48
Montbéliard, 28
Montreux, 31
Mortane, Jacques, 79, 81
Mortiers, 44
Moscow, 183
Moser, Carl, 19
Mülhausen, 27, 30, 31, 32, 33, 35, 37, 39, 40, 75
Müller, Generalkonsul, 103
Müller, Rudolf, 153
Müller, Vizefeldwebel, 40, 44
Munich, 16, 18, 19, 22, 23, 59, 60, 67, 70, 73, 74, 76, 77, 81, 83, 84, 86, 87, 94, 101, 103, 105, 106, 108, 111, 112, 115, 121, 122, 123, 131, 132, 137, 138, 139, 146, 149, 159, 177, 201, 205
Munster, 114
Mussolini, Benito, 169

Nairobi, 130
Namur, 23
Naumberg, 101
Nebel, Oberltn Rudolf, 71
Nepal, 128
Netherlands, 186, 188, 189
Neubreisach, 30, 31, 32
Neuilly, 62
Neurath, Freiherr von, 161
Newsweek, 150
New York, 110, 114, 117, 126, 136, 145, 147
New York Times, 151
Niederaspach, 37
Nieuport, 50

Nile, River, 130, 131
Nitschke, Gerhard, 160, 162, 170
Nopitsch, Hptm, 100, 101
Norway, 188, 189
Nungesser, Charles, 43
Nuremberg, 79, 126, 153, 157

Obendorf, 36
Obersalzberg, 170
Oberwiesenfeld, 24
Oranienburg, 168, 176
Orguevalles, 44
Orteug, Raymond, 109
Osnabrück, 100
Ostend, 50
Osterkamp, Theo, 124, 191
Otto, Dr Nicolaus, 18
Otto, Gustav, 18, 24, 60, 67

Paris, 64, 106, 110, 114, 122, 165, 166, 189
Parschau, Otto, 37
Passchendaele, 53
Paul, Heinz, 154
Pendele, Oberst Max, 161, 162, 195
Péronne, 58, 68, 69
Peschke, 120, 121
Pétain, Gen, 42
Peters, 207
Pfälzer, Ltn, 33
Pickford, Mary, 146
Poelcappelle, 52
Pohl, Heinz, 86, 88, 90, 98
Pohl, William, 86, 90
Pohlmann, 151
Poland, 183, 184, 185, 189
Polte, pilot, 100
Poppenhausen, 152
Porsche, Ferdinand, 118
Portugal, 116
Poss, pilot, 109
Potsdam, 188
Pour le Mérite, 179
Prague, 180
Preiss, Vizefeldwebel, 29
Price, Ward, 156
Prien, 164
Princip, Gavrilo, 20
Prinz, Le Roy, 146
Puisieux, 61, 67
Puttkamer, Ltn von, 61

Raab, Antonius, 119
Ramersdorf, 86, 88, 89, 97, 107, 112
Rangsdorf, 200
Rasche, Thea, 106, 109, 115, 116, 119, 120, 125, 165
Rawson, A. H., 122, 132
Rechlin, 162, 183, 194, 197, 203
Regensburg, 104
Reinberger, Maj Hellmuth, 186
Reinhard, Willy, 61, 62, 65, 66
Reinhold, Oberltn, 36, 40, 43, 52
Reisler, Walter, 165
Reitsch, Hanna, 159, 168, 173, 203
Reznicek, Paula von, 138
Rheims, 41, 42, 43, 65
Rhine, River, 26, 29, 111
Ribbentrop, J. von, 172
Richthofen, Lothar von, 57, 59, 68, 69, 85
Richthofen, Rittm Manfred von, 37, 45, 49, 56, 58, 59, 61, 67, 85, 104, 143, 146, 156
Richthofen, Wolfram von, 59, 142, 161, 162
Rickenbacker, Eddie, 135
Riedel, Peter, 157, 159, 174
Riefenstahl, Leni, 123, 126, 139
Rist, Sepp, 126
Rodin, Yvette, 128
Roellinghoff, C. R., 120
Röhm, Ernst, 152
Rohrbach, Dr Ing Adolf, 110, 116, 117, 120
Rolff, Ltn, 70
Rome, 97, 103
Rommel, F. M. Erwin, 18
Rosenheim, 101
Roth, Leo, 20
Roth, Herr, 125
Rüdel, Gen, 202
Ruhmann, Heinz, 138
Rumpler, Edmund, 84
Russia, 53, 183, 193, 201
Rust, Bernhard, 154

St Dié, 22, 29
St Louis, 145
St Moritz, 105, 123, 142, 143
St Quentin, 59, 61
Saal, 22
Sablatnig, Dr Ing Josef, 72

Sagan, 119
Sagebeil, Prof, 154, 158
San Diego, 146
Sarajevo, 20
Scheuermann, Erich, 86, 88, 90, 93, 96, 97, 108
Schirmeck, 22
Schlege, Ernst, 73
Schleich, Edouard Ritter von, 138, 141
Schleissheim, 61, 81, 96, 103, 132, 164, 165, 167
Schneeberger, cameraman, 123, 129, 130, 131, 139, 154, 203
Schnell, air mech, 117
Scholz, Vizefeldwebel, Edgar, 57, 58
Schulz, Ferdinand, 100
Schwabing, 59, 74
Schwerin, 73
Seeckt, Gen Hans von, 82, 83, 89
Seiffert, Mrs, 33, 75
Seiler, Fritz, 205
Sempill, Master of, 160, 161, 169
Shirer, William, 187
Shriek, Franz, 139
Siebel, 263
Siedentopf, 129
Sigwart, Ltn, 36
Soissons, 42, 62, 65, 67
Somme, River, 61
Sonnemann, Emmy see Göring
SOS Eisberg, 137
South America, 166
Spain, 166, 167, 170
Sperrle, F. M., 196
Squadrons: 8 RNAS: 49; 15 RFC: 58; 40 RFC: 49; 54 RAF: 69; 107 RAF: 183; 110 RAF: 183; 139 RAF: 183; 47 Squadron RAF: 130; 54 and 65 Sqn RAF: 170; French Escadrille N 124 Lafayette: 36; BM 120: 37; Les Cicognes, 41
Steffen, Kpt Bruno, 25
Stehlin, Cpte Paul, 166
Steinhäuser, Ltn Werner, 57
Steinhoff, Johannes 'Macki', 200
Stempel, Major Friedrich, 24
Stockholm, 136
Stör, Willy, 120, 121, 132, 143
Storms over Mont Blanc, 126, 139
Strange Birds over Africa, 128, 139
Strasbourg, 22, 23

Strassmann, Antonie, 119
Stresemann, Gustav, 109
Stuck, Hans, 122, 138
Stumpff, Gen, 168, 170, 173, 180
Stuttgart, 73, 166
Suchotsky, von, 124, 139
Sweden, 116, 203
Switzerland, 28, 105, 115, 127, 152, 154, 157, 166
Szombathely, 106

Tank, Kurt, 116, 117, 152, 198
Tanzania, 128
Taylor, Lt R. E., 69
Thann, 27, 34
Thelen, Eng., 39
Thiede, Fritz, 162, 165
Thomson, Major, 84
Thun, 157
Thuy, Emil, 69
Tornquist, 92
Travemünde, 160, 162, 170
Trieste, 131
Tussmars, Nelly, 105
Tutschek, Adolph, 61

Udet, Adolf, 16, 24, 59, 60, 137
Udet, Irene, 20
Udet, Lo, 84, 88, 89, 121, 159 *See also* Zink
Udet, Paula, 16, 17, 24, 59, 114, 139, 205
Uganda, 130
Ursinus, Oskar, 83, 96
USA, 90, 127, 133, 144, 146–7, 149, 174, 193, 197, 203

Valenciennes, 46, 48, 59
Veltjens, 158
Vendlicourt, 28
Verdun, 19, 27, 72
Vienna, 84, 101, 106, 131
Villers-Cotterets, 44
Villingen, 108
Vuillemin, Joseph, 176

Wassenaar, 189, 191
Waldhausen, Hans, 27, 46, 49, 79, 80
Wanamaker, Lt Walter, 66, 135, 136

Warnemünde, 107, 111, 125, 174
Warsaw, 184
Warsitz, Erich, 181, 182, 185, 194
Weber, Oberst Edmund, 24
Weigel, pilot, 109
Weingärtner, Vizefeldwebel, 33
Weiss, Ltn Hans, 58, 110
Weller, Hermann, 25
Wendel, brothers, 40, 44
Wendel, Flugkap Fritz, 192
Wenninger, Kptn z See, 150
Wentz, Ltn, 69
Werner, Director, 199
Westerboeke, 52
Wever, Generalltn, 151, 152, 161
Weyl, Alfred R., 86, 154
White Hell of Piz Palü, The, 123
Wiener, Neustadt, 173
Wilberg, Hptm, 75, 83
Wilhelm, Crown Prince, 120, 138
Wilhelm II, Kaiser, 26, 145
Wilhelmshaven, 125, 183
Williams, Major Alford, 132, 139, 163, 175
Wilson, Pres Woodrow, 75
Wimmer, Oberst, 161, 162
Wingles, 50
Winter, Ltn, 29
Winterfeld, Ltn von, 61
Winters, family, 207
Wintgens, Kurt, 37
Wolff, Ltn Joachim, 57
Wright Brothers, 121
Wulf, Georg, 86
Wunder des Fliegers, 154
Wurster, Hermann, 160
Würzburg, 107, 133
Wüstrow, 169
Wynghene, 48, 49, 50, 51, 52, 55

Ypres, 50, 54, 55

Zander, Hptm Martin, 36
Zandvoorde, 55
Zeitz, Willy, 128, 133
Zeppelin, Count, 17, 120
Zink, Eleonore (Lo), 20, 39, 59, 60, 63, 72, 73, 82 *see also* Udet, Lo
Zinn, Major Fred, 75
Zuckmayer, Carl, 64, 140, 166